ABOUT THE AUTHORS

Born and bred in Melbourne, ALEX CASTLES
was an Emeritus Professor of Law and taught
for more than thirty years at the University
of Adelaide. A graduate of the Universities of
Melbourne and Chicago, he was a long-time
radio and television broadcaster and the
author or co-author of eight books on
Australian law and history. In 1995 he published to wide
acclaim *The Shark Arm Murders*, the true story of a macabre
unsolved murder that occurred in the Sydney underworld of
the 1930s. Alex died suddenly in December 2003 with the
manuscript for *Ned Kelly's Last Days* all but complete.

JENNIFER CASTLES started her professional life as an actress
working both in Australia and overseas. In 1997 she began
collaborating with her father on a project that would become
Ned Kelly's Last Days and since his death she has been responsible for bringing it to publication. She is now a writer and
editor and lives in Melbourne with her family.

NED KELLY'S LAST DAYS

SETTING THE RECORD STRAIGHT ON
THE DEATH OF AN OUTLAW

ALEX C. CASTLES AND JENNIFER CASTLES

WITH AN AFTERWORD BY DR JOHN WILLIAMS

A Sue Hines Book
ALLEN & UNWIN

A Sue Hines Book
Allen & Unwin
83 Alexander Street
Crows Nest NSW 2065
Australia
Phone: (61 2) 8425 0100
Fax: (61 2) 9906 2218
Email: info@allenandunwin.com
Web: www.allenandunwin.com

National Library of Australia Cataloguing-in-Publication entry:
Castles, Alex C. (Alex Cuthbert), 1933–2003.
Ned Kelly's last days: setting the record straight on the
death of an outlaw.
    Bibliography.
    Includes index.
    ISBN 1 74114 538 4.
    1. Kelly, Ned, 1855-1880. 2. Trials (Murder) – Australia.
    3. Bushrangers – Australia. 4. Australia – Social
    conditions – 1851-1901. I. Castles, Jennifer. II. Title.
364.1550994

Edited by Jo Jarrah
Text design by Phil Campbell
Typesetting by Pauline Haas
Index by Fay Donlevy
Printed in Australia by Griffin Press

10 9 8 7 6 5 4 3 2 1

For my children
Margaret, Jennifer, Susan, Kathryn and Alan
And for my grandchildren
Ellen, Alexandra and Marymaeve

... yet positive orders had been issued that these outlaws and malefactors should at any price be brought to justice

R.D. Blackmore, *Lorna Doone*

CONTENTS

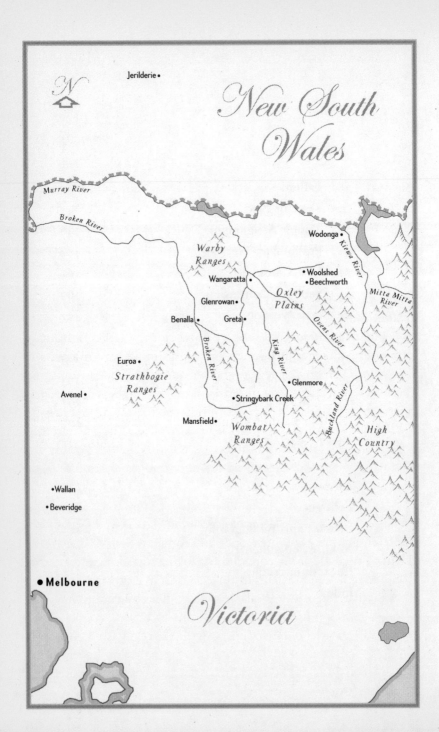

FOREWORD

Alex Castles died suddenly in the middle of a hot summer's night, sitting at his table reading a novel about Victorian London. He was surrounded by mounds of documents, folders and scraps of paper related to the various subjects he was working on – including, of course, bits and pieces on Ned Kelly. Amongst it all were several cheap classical CDs, scattered heaps of old pipe tobacco, a plunger of his rotgut coffee and the debris of a takeaway meal. It was typical Dad.

Physical comfort was not a priority for my father. His living space was chaotic and rudimentary, yet his mind was ordered and meticulous. He had a photographic memory and an amazing capacity to put seemingly unrelated facts and snippets of information together. This was a man who truly lived inside his own head.

At the same time he was a legendary talker. Effusive and theatrical, once he got onto a subject he was passionate about, it was hard to get him off it. Alex loved a good yarn – even more, he loved a good mystery.

As one of Australia's foremost legal historians, he had the skills, the knowledge, and the sheer bloody-minded tenacity to thrash out the truth behind Ned's case once and for all. When he discovered the legal loophole at the core of this book he was incandescent with excitement. Here was the historical detective at his best: using material that was readily available to the public, but assembling it in a completely original way.

Dad had an infectious enthusiasm that he passed on to his children. I remember as a little girl being transfixed by his bush-ranger stories (mostly because they were gory) and the interest has endured and flourished. After the success of his book *The Shark Arm Murders*, which sold well beyond his usual academic audience, he decided it was time to finally tackle Ned. He didn't want it to be a tome aimed at legal scholars, he wanted it to be a good read for anyone with a passing interest in Kelly. This is where I came in.

The eight years that Dad and I collaborated on *Ned Kelly's Last Days* were infuriating, exasperating, and deeply rewarding. As a professor of law, Alex was a stickler for detail and for using highly formal legal language that could not be misconstrued. As a writer and editor working at the commercial end of the market, my job was to 'shape' the work so that it was accessible to a wide audience. To say it was a volatile process is putting it mildly; I swore many, many times that I would never work with him again. I guess in this case 'be careful what you wish for' is an understatement.

Alex Castles' work was the defining factor of his life. The responsibility of completing his final book and the desire to do my father justice has presented a daunting task. It has also been an intensely moving way to honour him and to say goodbye.

JENNIFER CASTLES

KILLING NED

Like so many Victorians of a certain age, I grew up knowing the Kelly story well, if not accurately. I also grew up with the small distinction of having some tenuous links to Australia's most famous bushranger. The first concerned my grandfather, George, who died long before I was born. A native of the northeastern Victorian town of Wangaratta, he lived in the same neighbourhood as Sergeant Arthur Steele, who became known as 'The Man Who Captured Ned Kelly'. George Castles encountered Steele several times over the years and solemnly declared him to be a 'solid and respectable character', which by all accounts was high praise indeed from my reticent forbear.

The more tangible association came from my father, who was raised forty-five kilometres away in Benalla, a town situated in the very heart of Kelly country. When pressed, he would recall how on several occasions in town during his childhood he caught glimpses of Ned's ageing mother, the long-suffering Ellen Kelly, as she went about her shopping accompanied by her son James and various grandchildren.

Although I undoubtedly enjoyed a measure of schoolyard credibility with my 'Kelly connections', the truth is, members of my paternal family were very reluctant to discuss these local celebrities. Whenever he spoke of them, my father displayed a palpable enmity for the people he claimed had brought such dishonour to the district. On one occasion we were driving through Glenrowan when he began to tell me about a man he'd done odd jobs for as a teenager – a Mr O'Shea, who'd been the proprietor of the *Benalla Ensign* newspaper. O'Shea was a former schoolmate of Ned's and made no bones about the fact that he disliked him intensely. 'O'Shea reckons he was wild and violent and there was nothing anyone could do about it.'

But the decisive verdict came from my grandmother, a stern, no-nonsense countrywoman who'd been widowed young and undertook the Herculean task of raising nine children on her own. I remember as a little boy pestering her for details about the notorious clan. She would silence me in no uncertain terms with the words, 'We don't talk about the Kellys around here. They were bad people.'

My curiosity about the Kelly Outbreak steadily increased over the years but, inevitably, as I grew older I began to focus on the part of the story where my area of professional expertise lay. Having studied law at university, I made the decision very early on not to practise, instead embarking on an academic career that involved teaching, advising, commentating and writing about the subject for thirty-odd years. Australian legal history has been of particular interest, especially the landmark cases, so of course I was eager to examine the case of one of the country's most famous criminals. But I soon discovered that although there's a mountain of material on the man, his crimes and the myths surrounding him, by comparison there's only a minute amount on the legal process that convicted and ultimately killed Ned Kelly. Exploring the truth behind what happened during the one hundred and thirty-seven days that elapsed between the bushranger's capture and his death became something of a personal mission and the inspiration for this project.

Tracking the original source material has been a journey in itself. I was appalled to be told by a number of major libraries and archives that vital Kelly documents and records listed as being held by them are 'unaccounted for' or have simply 'disappeared'. Whole months and sometimes even years of newspapers from the 1870s and 1880s are no longer in existence: a devastating state of affairs for historians and researchers across the land and surely a source of deep shame in regards to the preservation of our national heritage.

Nevertheless, my own penchant (my daughter calls it 'obsession') for detail has led me to several rich sources of information that have been invaluable to this work. Among them are the unpublished memoirs of Thomas McIntyre, the sole surviving officer of the killings at Stringybark Creek, along with an interview with one of his surviving granddaughters, Mrs Irma Hookey. The personal diary of Police Commissioner Charles Standish also proved to be a goldmine for expressing views that were unique in illuminating certain attitudes prevalent in 1880.

I put to good use an original copy of the Crown brief held by the chief prosecutor at Ned's trial – one of the many treasures held in the Thomas Ramsay Collection at Melbourne's Scotch College library. This contained his personal annotations and shorthand notes as well as two important addenda that the Crown did not need to use at the trial because of the ineptitude of Ned's defence (it includes new evidence against Ned that was previously unavailable).

As for contemporary media, many former discussions of the trial have relied on the seriously condensed versions of evidence published in the *Age* and the *Argus*. Considerably more information was published in editions of the *Daily Telegraph* and the *Herald*, and I referred to these again and again. Regional newspapers also contained some wonderful morsels of intelligence that did not find their way to the city dailies.

Then there are all the random scraps of information I picked up over the years from friends, colleagues and Kellyphiles from all walks of life, as well as fascinating yields from some unlikely sources, like the four unsorted envelopes of clippings and other materials held at the Mitchell Library in Sydney.

In the end, placing that small slice of history under a microscope has yielded a wealth of material that far exceeded my initial expectations. It's a story packed with intriguing contradictions, revealing a world full of fascinating characters overshadowed in time by the glamour of Australia's most famous outlaw. Here I found men and women who typified their class, race and religion, poised at the dawn of the technology age. They included Ned's truly heroic sister, Maggie Skillion, who fought her own battles every day with poverty and prejudice, yet still managed to mount a fierce campaign on behalf of her brother when the rest of her kin melted into the background; Chief Secretary Robert Ramsay, who wielded tremendous power in the colony and viewed the destruction of Kelly as an almost biblical struggle between the forces of good and evil; and Constable Thomas McIntyre, the staunch, silent Irish policeman who was haunted by the events in the isolated bush clearing at Stringybark Creek for the rest of his life.

On a wider scale, I was fascinated to come upon abundant evidence that exploded one of the more prevalent Kelly myths. Some popular historians would have us believe that in his lifetime Ned was a revolutionary hero, a Robin Hood character loved and revered by a large portion of his countrymen. On the contrary, by 1880 it began to look like just about *everyone* wanted him dead. Across the board I found numerous instances where fierce rivals and even bitter enemies came together to guarantee that it was done. Among them were leading politicians, high government officials and legal dignitaries whose names rated only a passing mention in so many accounts of Ned's last days. Each had their own specific agenda, but all were united in their desire to see the bushranger hang. What's more, the dominant religious forces of the time, hugely influential in the daily life of the colony, spoke as one in their condemnation of Kelly. (This included the leaders of the church to which Ned's family had belonged for generations.)

And then there were the newspapers and journals that played a commanding role in public life and were crucial in swaying mass opinion. Passionately divided on so many issues, each and every one dismissed Ned and his companions as ruthless murderers after the killing of three police officers at Stringybark Creek. In a relentless propaganda war, they painted Ned Kelly as a monster, and readily suppressed news and comment that might reflect unfavourably on the bushranger's accusers.

Perhaps the most satisfying find for someone with my professional background was the unearthing of an extraordinary legal glitch. Close study of certain legal documentation from the time revealed a surprising loophole. Evidence shows that from the moment the bushranger's capture became known, those in authority were uncertain how to deal with him according to law. Many in the community had confidently expected that he would be hanged as soon as possible without an ordinary trial because of his highly publicised status as an outlaw. But due to the discovery of one of the most bizarre coincidences in Australian legal history, the prospect of immediate execution without trial was quickly dismissed. It left behind a maze of legal complications and became the prelude to a well-hidden campaign that history has largely ignored.

To my growing dismay, I discovered through various sources that during the four and a half months between capture and death, these powerful men stretched the law to its outer limits and beyond, engaging in subterfuges, outright dishonesty and monumental legal deceptions which ensured that in the end there was absolutely no chance for Kelly to escape the hangman's noose. In short, I became convinced that regardless of whether the accused was guilty of his crimes or not – among them capital offences punishable by death – it could well be argued that according to the law at the time, Ned Kelly was tried, convicted and hanged *illegally*.

Finally, as I approached the end of the case, I was oddly moved to discern another side of the man himself, gleaned through snippets about his state of mind in his last days. Although the bushranger never completely lost his fondness for boasting and lying disingenuously like a naughty boy in a bid to protect himself, there seems no doubt he experienced a significant shift in his personal ethos and outlook. During his last months in gaol, his thinking increasingly followed time-honoured patterns of so many who have found themselves in such a position. It seems Ned underwent a reawakening of religious faith as he prepared to meet his maker, stimulated not only by regular visits from members of the Roman Catholic clergy, but also by contact with at least two Protestant evangelists who saw him in his cell. It stands to reason that his very public display of indifference to the legal proceedings that led to his execution was not the product of someone seeking martyrdom, as his behaviour has frequently been interpreted, rather it was the conduct of a man prepared to acknowledge his legal guilt. At the end of his life, Ned Kelly had come to believe that the only judgement that mattered was the one he would face in an 'afterlife'.

If numerous novels, histories, films and television series about the Kelly Outbreak are anything to go by, you could well be forgiven for thinking everything that came after the siege of Glenrowan was an anticlimax, warranting little more than cursory attention. What follows is a range of evidence proving that this widely held assumption deserves some serious reconsideration. By deliberately turning the spotlight *away* from Ned Kelly, history reveals a tale with all the drama, intrigue, pathos and humanity of the main event.

This, then, is the side of the story rarely told.

ALEX C. CASTLES
November 2003

At precisely noon on Monday 28 June 1880, a thunderous volley of cannon fire echoed through the streets of Melbourne. Scores panicked as an already jittery populace jumped to dramatic conclusions, fearing pitched gun battles in their midst. The blasts were in fact a perfectly harmless salute to the forty-second anniversary of Queen Victoria's coronation, but several anxious minutes passed before the explanation circulated and the sources were revealed to be an artillery battery close to the city centre and two warships berthed a few kilometres away.

Despite the benign nature of the explosions, a near-hysterical atmosphere that had gripped the Victorian capital from an early hour continued to intensify. During the morning thousands left their homes or places of work and crammed the city streets. Businesses ground to a halt, shopkeepers waited in vain for customers, and the ornate chambers of the city's most prosperous banks were deserted. For the first time in many years, officials at the two city stock exchanges were considering early closure.

By far the most chaotic scenes took place outside the offices of the city's four daily newspapers. Hundreds besieged the buildings, spilling onto adjacent streets and blocking traffic as they strained for a glimpse of the latest updates posted on the exterior bulletin boards. Special editions were rushed out to meet the demand of city and suburban outlets, and jubilant newsboys calculated their extra profits from the grossly inflated prices they were charging. The entire colony was focused on a gunfight taking place in a tiny insignificant country hamlet located approximately two hundred and twenty kilometres northeast of the Victorian capital.

First news of the drama unfolding at Glenrowan had come to the outside world just after five o'clock on Sunday morning when a locomotive powering at full steam arrived at the town of Benalla. Whistle shrieking, it emerged ghostlike through the raw winter mist and ground to a shuddering halt. As townsfolk gathered on the station platform the driver reported that a fierce battle was taking place. Four bushrangers under the leadership of the notorious bushranger Ned Kelly had seized the Glenrowan Inn. They had cap-tured approximately forty civilian hostages, including women and children, and then embarked on a clash with police in the early hours of the morning.

On Saturday evening, gang member Joe Byrne had murdered his former friend Aaron Sherritt, who had betrayed the Kellys to the police. The *Age* newspaper described the victim as a 'private detective' but the authorities knew of him simply as a paid govern-ment informer who happened to be a long-time associate of the Kelly gang. Ned's younger brother, Dan, and Byrne staked out Sherritt's home at Woolshed and shot him dead in the doorway with his mother-in-law and very pregnant wife standing close behind. The execution was a grim warning to any others who might be tempted to collaborate with the police.

Rumours were rife that the victim had been shot while the four police constables who were supposed to be guarding him cow-ered inside his two-room hut. Months later, the truth came to light that these policemen had, in fact, not ventured outside for hours after the shooting because they were terrified that the killer was waiting to ambush them. This delay meant that news of Sherritt's death did not reach the colony's police commissioner in Melbourne until Sunday afternoon. Charles Standish was then obliged to pass the information directly to Chief Secretary Robert Ramsay, who was second-in-command of the colonial government and one of the most powerful men in Victoria. Ramsay's party, led by Premier Robert Service, had taken office just a few months earlier, at which time Ramsay was immediately placed in charge of all government dealings with the bushrangers. It was a tall order. In the previous twenty months the four members of the gang had succeeded in evading capture despite an enormous man-hunt.

In April 1878 a warrant had been issued for the arrest of Ned Kelly and his brother Dan for the attempted murder of Constable Alexander Fitzpatrick. The policeman claimed he went to the Kelly homestead on the evening of the fifteenth to arrest Dan Kelly for suspected horse stealing. Instead he was viciously attacked by family members and ultimately shot (sustaining a wrist wound) by Ned Kelly himself. The Kellys categorically denied his version of events, claiming they only turned on the officer when, in a semi-drunken state, he made a pass at Kate Kelly, who was fifteen years old at the time. When the police returned later with reinforcements the brothers were nowhere to be found, so they arrested the family matriarch, Ellen Kelly, her son-in-law Bill Skillion and family friend William 'Brickey' Williamson. All were subsequently found guilty of aiding Ned in his attempt to murder Fitzpatrick and given harsh sentences, while the rest of the so-called perpetrators fled into the bush. So began the notorious 'Kelly Outbreak'.

At first their criminal activities attracted a reasonable amount of press attention, but after they stormed a police camp in October 1878 and left behind the corpses of three officers who were murdered – allegedly – in cold blood, they were subject to a vehement outpouring of public rage and hatred. It was the first time in ten years that Victorian police officers had been shot on active service and the first occasion of multiple police deaths since the British occupation of Victoria began in the mid-1830s. Then in early 1879 the gang disappeared from public view after two successful bank raids on the towns of Euroa in the north of the colony and Jerilderie, just across the border in New South Wales. Under the previous government the hunt for the Kellys had languished despite the most costly police campaign ever mounted in Australia and the highest reward ever offered. Once Ramsay took the reins, the hunt for the gang was not only an important priority, it was a deeply personal crusade that was frustrated at every turn by their refusal to emerge from hiding. When Ramsay learned of Sherritt's killing he knew this was the long-awaited signal that the Kellys were finally out in the open again.

He immediately hurried into town. Because all government offices were closed on the Sabbath by law, temporary headquarters were set up in the Melbourne Club. In the hushed genteel atmosphere of the city's most exclusive establishment he began to orchestrate the groundwork for the hunt with Commissioner Standish. He then met with Sub-Inspector Stanhope O'Connor, who was in charge of a special squad of Aboriginal members of the Queensland police force. These special officers had come closer than anyone to tracking the gang, but a long-running feud between O'Connor and Standish had thwarted their efforts and finally resulted in their dismissal from the hunt, much to Ramsay's frustration. Their services no longer required, they were on the verge of returning home when news came through that they were to be recalled. Ramsay was enormously relieved to discover they had not yet departed the colony. He directed O'Connor and his officers to travel to the scene of the murder forthwith before the tracks of Sherritt's killer disappeared.

His next move was to override the law forbidding railway services on the Sabbath, so that a special train could take the Queensland officers north. Along the way it would collect the officer in charge of operations – Superintendent Francis Hare – from Benalla, together with a contingent of well-armed police officers.

And then sometime during that afternoon (no doubt with an eye to potentially favourable publicity) several hansom cabs were dispatched to local journalists, with hastily scrawled notes inviting them to join the special train. Whether it was Ramsay himself who gave the order or some other official, we will never know as the notes were cryptically signed 'Someone In Authority'.

As nightfall approached, Ramsay broke the habit of a lifetime and missed the evening service at his local Presbyterian church. Then, just after seven o'clock, he received an urgent telegram from Superintendent Hare: 'Do you think I had better send a pilot engine from Benalla before the special? ... They may pull up the rails [and] I have an engine ready here.'

For those of Ramsay's vintage the possibility of the train-tracks being sabotaged was a potent reminder of tactics that had been used in America's Civil War, a conflict that had engrossed local interest in the early 1860s. The proposal to send a pilot engine to scout ahead of the special train looking for danger was a frequently employed strategy that had helped prevent several military disasters in the American conflict.

Without hesitation Ramsay gave his approval. 'A good idea', he telegraphed, 'there's no knowing what desperate deed the outlaws may now be guilty of ... Have the pilot.'

An anxious night followed. Ramsay slipped home for a few hours but he was back in town early Monday morning shifting the centre of operations to his offices in the Treasury building. By start of business the premises on Spring Street were a hive of activity, and as the day wore on it began to take on more than a passing resemblance to a military headquarters in the middle of a major conflict.

Meanwhile, news continued to trickle through from the north. Soon after 5 am, a message came from Benalla that Superintendent Hare had apparently been wounded, 'shot through the left wrist' in the first police assault. The gang was now barricaded in the Glenrowan Inn. Then there was another gap until a transmission announced that the special train had narrowly escaped disaster and that, fortunately, Hare was only superficially wounded. With no direct means of communication to the besieged town other than engine crews carrying messages, the news was garbled and often conflicting – an immensely frustrating state of affairs.

Finally a message was passed on from Hare himself, who had returned to Benalla for medical treatment. He reported the pilot engine had been stopped short of the town and the crew warned that the line had been pulled up by the Kellys a mile beyond Glenrowan. (Later the story would emerge that local schoolteacher Thomas Curnow had slipped away from the Kellys to sound the alarm. With a makeshift signal consisting of a candle sputtering behind a red scarf, he flagged down the pilot, halting the train just before it reached the damaged section of the line and certain disaster.) Hare went on to say that a gunfight had erupted in the vicinity of the Glenrowan Inn and, ominously, 'everybody in Glenrowan has been taken into the bush by the Kellys' (this information was later disproved). He also implied the police were having major problems controlling the situation and desperately needed reinforcements. 'I have telegraphed for the men from Wangaratta [the next large town north of Glenrowan on the main northeastern railway line], and have arranged for police reinforcements to be sent to Glenrowan from Benalla.' Soon news came from Wangaratta that extra police were heading for the small town and a well-armed group of officers had been dispatched from nearby Beechworth.

Then followed another maddening silence for more than two hours during which Ramsay's spirits steadily plummeted. The impasse was shattered by another telegram. 'Engine and carriage just arrived from Glenrowan bring news Ned Kelly shot and taken alive on railway platform at Glenrowan. Ned Kelly armed with iron mask and helmet.' The chief secretary's office erupted, the corridors choking with excited staff and a fleet of couriers coming and going with urgent messages.

Once he received confirmation that Ned was seriously wounded, Ramsay ordered Commissioner Standish to proceed directly to Glenrowan and take charge of the prisoner. He also sent for prominent Melbourne surgeon Charles Ryan to accompany Standish. The doctor was best known for his expertise in treating gunshot wounds, an acclaim that followed him after distinguished medical service in the 1877–78 war between Russia and Turkey. Ramsay was determined that the leader of the gang be kept alive, so he needed the best medical man available.

In the midst of all this commotion a significant communications breakthrough occurred, allowing Melbourne to receive messages from close to the scene itself. A telegraph operator stationed at Beechworth had accompanied the police contingent on the train to Glenrowan with a portable morse code set. He assembled his apparatus beside the railway line, connected it to a nearby telegraph wire and, at 10.05 on Monday morning, triumphantly reported to Melbourne: 'We have telegraph communication with Glenrowan ... You can now speak if necessary.' Soon a steady stream of information was coming through from the small township.

As news trickled in from the north, tension increased with every new revelation. The killing of Aaron Sherritt was serious enough. The general feeling was that this 'assassination' was much more than an act of personal vengeance, rather, it was a calculated move – an act of 'terrorism', as newspapers called it – which was intended to warn police collaborators that their lives were in grave danger.

And there was further intelligence to horrify the chief secretary and his staff as details began to come through on the fate of the special train. Had the train crashed, the surviving passengers would have been trapped in their compartments as it was standard practice that they were all locked. Carriages had no internal passageway and each 'compartment non-corridor', or 'dog box' as they were commonly known, opened directly onto the platform. For reasons of safety and security, each compartment was locked at the outset of the journey. In this instance it would have amplified the potential carnage because it was believed the bushrangers intended to riddle the derailed carriages with gunfire, killing police and innocent civilians indiscriminately. This included the driver and guard; two women who had been invited to join the expedition by Sub-Inspector Stanhope O'Connor; and four newspaper journalists, the most notable being Thomas Carrington, the artist for the *Australasian Sketcher*.

Clearly, the gang was not averse to employing desperate measures, a fact confirmed by the information that despite Ned's capture, the other three members continued to stubbornly defend their position in the small hotel. At least forty people were still trapped inside, cowering in terror as deadly gunfire raked the building. Their captors appeared to be well armed and shielded. Not only had Ned been apprehended wearing an iron mask, his torso was also protected by crude but effective body armour. First eyewitness accounts of the bushranger described him withstanding a hail of bullets when he emerged from the bush just after dawn on Monday, and only those shots aimed at his exposed legs succeeded in eventually bringing him down. Further reports implied that at least two of the bushrangers still holding out in the Glenrowan Inn had been seen similarly clad, 'with breastplates clearly perceptible'.

The use of armour brought a chill of apprehension to the government officers, reminding them of American Civil War stories about the first deadly clash between ironclad warships which had instantaneously rendered many of the world's naval vessels obsolete. It was sufficiently alarming for Superintendent John Sadleir, who had taken command following Hare's injury, to urgently request Ramsay's permission for a high-powered artillery piece to be sent to Glenrowan so that, if necessary, it could 'blast' the bushrangers out of their hiding place. Ramsay summoned the commandant of

Victoria's artillery to his office and authorised a special train to carry a twelve-pounder gun to Glenrowan with a contingent of soldiers.

As the day wore on a new fear emerged that the remaining members of the gang might escape into the bush after dark. Ramsay met with a government astronomer who was responsible for the electric arc lighting equipment that had recently lit the first night football match in Victoria. Ramsay hoped the new technology could be used to illuminate the besieged hotel at Glenrowan that night, but the astronomer believed his equipment would cast too many shadows to perform effectively. He suggested large bonfires would serve the purpose far more satisfactorily, and the information was swiftly telegraphed to the police at Glenrowan.

Then came the news that after a brief truce the hostages had been freed. Ramsay wired that now the way was clear for the police to mount a wooden shield on a dray close to the besieged building where they could fire at the inn from relative safety. But in the end no such measures were required. Soon after 3 pm, Melbourne received word that the last three members of the Kelly gang were dead. The body of Joe Byrne had apparently been snatched from the building before a wall of flame engulfed him. The corpses of the two others – Dan Kelly and Steve Hart – were recovered later, burnt beyond recognition, their charred stumps found lying side by side.

Word soon got round that just before the bodies were incinerated, witnesses saw they were lying in curious positions. Apparently both men had ended their lives with their heads resting on pillows of sacking, suggesting they committed suicide by either shooting each other simultaneously or taking their own lives before the flames took them. The police officer who performed the task of raking around the bodies with an iron rod and forked stick also discovered the remains of a dog in the ruins. The animal was believed to have belonged to the bushrangers.

By mid-afternoon the artillerymen speeding to Glenrowan

were on their way back to Melbourne. As night closed in on the
Treasury building, congratulatory telegrams began to pile up on
Ramsay's desk. For the time being he could only give them a
passing glance but he did pause for a moment to savour one from
Henry Parkes, the premier of New South Wales: 'Great satisfaction
in prospect of destruction of the Kelly Gang'. It was sweet recom-
pense for the scathing criticism the neighbouring colony had
heaped upon the organisers of the Kelly hunt in the previous
months.

News of Ned Kelly's capture spread with lightning speed. By
midnight it was reported that all previous records for sending tele-
graphic messages to neighbouring colonies had been smashed. Tens
of thousands of words were sent to Sydney, the greatest number
since the opening of the line to the New South Wales capital in
1858. In Melbourne alone, more than one hundred thousand copies
of the 'special' newspaper editions had been sold in a city with a
population of just under two hundred and fifty thousand.

And so the battle was over. Yet despite the celebratory mood,
Ramsay continued to work at his desk late into the night. Already
rumours were circulating that the surviving bushranger would be
hung without a trial in the next twenty-four hours, but Ramsay
knew that the true legal situation was far more complicated. He
also knew he would not rest easily until he had done everything in
his power to ensure that Ned Kelly ended his life on the gallows.

For Chief Secretary Robert Ramsay, the final destruction of the Kelly gang meant a great deal more than just professional vindication. The son of a Presbyterian minister, his religious upbringing had given him a keen sense of the vast rift between good and evil. As a former student of Scotch College in Melbourne, Ramsay had voiced his personal creed in an emotional speech he delivered at a gathering of Old Collegians the previous year. He explained to his former schoolmates that his political career was far from accidental, that it was a natural outcome of his unshakeable belief that there were moral imperatives accompanying his privileged background and worldly success which obliged him to service the community in return, giving practical expression to his religious beliefs. Ramsay challenged his audience to become 'defenders of their household gods' and to act militantly in pursuing corrupting influences that were contrary to their personal creeds.

This was not just idle rhetoric, it was a fact already demonstrated in the way he conducted himself throughout his political career. In the late 1860s he began to show strong support for a number of parliamentarians who were agitating to introduce payment for members of the legislature despite vehement opposition from his conservative colleagues. In Ramsay's view, if the community was to be properly represented in the legislature, then the poor as well as

Robert Ramsay

the rich must be able to participate fully in parliamentary activities. If a fee needed to be introduced to ensure their participation, then so be it.

With his long scraggly beard, Ramsay looked like an ancient patriarch far beyond his thirty-eight years. He was already regarded by many as the future leader of the conservative political forces in Victoria. If he presented as rather dour and lacking in flamboyance, he made up for it with his keen intellect and a sense of purpose that was well nigh impossible to match among the other members of the colonial legislature. Ramsay strongly espoused the values of the Old Testament and the Ten Commandments. It was an integral part of his everyday being, his measure for distinguishing between right and wrong. This lay at the heart of his dealings with the Kelly gang.

One of his first public statements had come just two days after the reports of the police killings at Stringybark Creek reached Melbourne. He expressed his profound outrage to the Legislative

Assembly, saying he was not aware of crimes 'approaching this mag-
nitude . . . having been perpetrated in this or any other Australian
colony'. Such was his ire that he laid all partisanship aside, and
pledged full support for the opposition government that was in
power at the time in regards to their efforts to rout the gang.

When Ramsay took charge of the hunt two years later, he was
determined to succeed where the others had failed. To him, the
Kellys were long past earthly redemption and their annihilation was
not to be viewed so much as vengeance, but as a divinely inspired
and just retribution – much like the destruction of Sodom and
Gomorrah in the Old Testament. There's no doubt a part of him
would have loved to be present at the scene of their demise in
Glenrowan, but his position as coordinator made it impossible to
leave the capital, so he had to be content waiting for reports from
his representatives there.

Commissioner Standish, however, had been delayed on his
journey, stopping at Benalla for half an hour to visit the wounded
Superintendent Hare. He finally arrived at Glenrowan just before
5.30 pm to find the inn no more than a smouldering ruin. The
incinerated remains of nineteen-year-old Dan Kelly and 21-year-
old Steve Hart had been placed on sheets of bark on the station
platform. Nearby lay the body of 23-year-old Joe Byrne, dragged
from the burning hotel. His clothing intact, he seemed to have
escaped the flames entirely. Further down the platform was the
body of the hostage Martin Cherry, a railway worker who had been
shot in the hotel in the early hours of the morning and died just a
few minutes after being rescued from the burning inn. Two other
hostages had been wounded. The teenage son of Anne Jones, the
hotel's licensee, was in a critical state and not expected to live, and
the other, the son of a railwayman, was out of danger.

For much of the day Ned was lodged in a room in the station-
master's house. He was being treated by Dr John Nicholson from
Benalla, who had arrived with police reinforcements before dawn.

In the afternoon Ned had been given the last rites of the Roman Catholic church by a priest en route to New South Wales who, hearing of the siege, had left his train to see if he could be of assistance. But by the time Standish arrived, the doctor believed the bushranger was out of danger and had a good chance of survival.

Ned was becoming increasingly lucid, although he still lapsed into periods of unconsciousness. Fortified with whisky, he was carrying on reasoned conversations with members of the police force and some newspaper reporters. The police also allowed three of his sisters – Margaret (better known as Maggie), Catherine (better known as Kate) and Grace – to see him. They had ridden to Glenrowan from their hometown, the small settlement of Greta, just over ten kilometres away.

As daylight faded, concerns were raised that Glenrowan was not an appropriate place for Ned to be left overnight. There were no proper medical facilities and Dr Ryan, the specialist from Melbourne, was in Benalla where he had left the commissioner's special train to attend to Superintendent Hare. There was also a possible security risk, with dozens of Ned's relatives and friends in the vicinity prompting fears there might be an attempt to rescue him if he remained in the town. Soon after dark, then, Ned was loaded into the van of the commissioner's special, stretched out on a mattress. Accompanying him was Standish and the posse of police officers that had travelled up with him from Melbourne. Several other officers who had taken part in the siege came aboard for the ride. Their destination was Benalla.

The bodies of Byrne and Cherry were loaded on but when the police attempted to do the same with those of Dan Kelly and Steve Hart, a potentially explosive situation arose. Legally the bodies were supposed to remain in custody pending official inquiries into their deaths, but relatives had come forward demanding the right to take them away for burial. In order to avoid any unnecessary confrontation, Superintendent Sadleir authorised they be released even though Standish hotly disputed the decision. Eventually the charred remains of the youngest bushrangers were wrapped in blankets and solemnly borne away by grieving family members.

As day melted into night, the Victorian capital continued to buzz with excitement. In the crowded hotel bars on Bourke Street, where most of the city's chief entertainments were located, special edition newspapers continued to be hot property. Outside, prosperous bankers stood under gas lamps scanning the main story, side by side with streetwalkers and pickpockets plying their trade. At the so-called 'mounting yard' attached to the Theatre Royal, the prostitutes were complaining that too many 'men about town' were distracted from their customary visit because of the day's events. At the waxworks, employees worked overtime on plans to stage a display featuring the Glenrowan siege that they hoped to have ready before the end of the week. The proprietor had already set off to the scene of the battle with the aim of gathering on-site mementos. He had with him a box of equipment with which to make casts of the dead bushrangers' body parts.

Now that the immediate danger of the Kelly Outbreak had been resolved, Robert Ramsay was able to turn back at last to the circumstances threatening his own political life. Over the past decade there had been frequent changes of government in the colony. Graham Berry's left-wing Liberal party (not to be confused with the Liberal party of today) had been ousted in March and the Conservative party of Robert Service took power. But still the upheavals continued. The siege at Glenrowan had eclipsed all other news at a time when Victoria was in the grip of yet another domestic political crisis. As on a number of previous occasions, the tension centred on resolving conflicts between the two houses of the colonial legislature. The Upper House, or Legislative Council, was elected on a franchise that was limited for the most part to adult males with substantial landholding interests. In contrast, in the 1850s the Lower House, or Legislative Assembly, had gone the way

of South Australia by granting all white adult males a vote in elec-
tions for the Legislative Assembly. This was far in advance of
electoral reform in Britain, where roughly only one in eight adult
males were permitted to vote for members of the House of
Commons.

While the Kellys were planning their descent on Glenrowan,
Ramsay and his colleagues were locked in a bitter struggle in the
Legislative Assembly. For most of the previous week they were
immersed in a volatile series of marathon parliamentary sittings in a
bid to gain approval for a new means of settling disputes between
the two houses of the legislature. In the end the Robert Service
government was defeated on this issue in the early hours of Friday
morning, and the Liberal party confidently expected to be called
upon by the governor to form a new government to replace it in
the next few days. Much to everyone's surprise, on Saturday the
governor decided to call a new election for the Assembly, even
though the previous one had been held only three months earlier.
This left Service, Ramsay and the other members of their government still retaining office, pending the result of the new poll. It was
a precarious position to say the least.

News of the Kelly uprising had come to overwhelmingly
dominate the newspapers. This had worrying repercussions for
Ramsay and his colleagues as their campaign strategy for the
coming election was forced to take a back seat to the far more
exciting events at Glenrowan. The government had staked its
reputation on a vigorous crusade to stay in power but Ramsay
himself was unable to give much attention to urgent cabinet
discussions and had been forced to reschedule political rallies for
endorsing candidates.

One of their primary tactics pre-Glenrowan had been to give
the public a full and detailed explanation of the constitutional
reform that led to the government's recent defeat in the Assembly.
For this, they needed maximum coverage in the press but, as the

day's events highlighted, their timetable was in considerable jeopardy. Melbourne's only evening newspaper, the *Herald*, had already withdrawn reports of the political crisis to make way for events at Glenrowan, and the morning papers would surely follow suit. Ramsay knew they couldn't afford to lose even a day of their normally extensive coverage of political affairs. He needed to remove Ned from the public eye as quickly as possible and the best way to achieve this was to retain direct control over him. The solution was a simple one: relocate Ned to Melbourne where his enforced isolation would ensure the newspapers had little to write about.

Before Ned could be moved, though, there was a minor legal argument to overcome. Under normal circumstances, anyone suspected of committing serious criminal offences in northeastern Victoria would be taken to Beechworth to await trial. The town had a large, strongly guarded gaol, reasonable medical facilities, and the forthcoming investigation into the Kelly Outbreak would be conducted there. Furthermore, if Ned was to be tried in the correct manner he would have to be present at a preliminary court hearing at Beechworth. But Ramsay managed to dismiss all these protocols on the basis that none of them prevented the bushranger's transfer to Melbourne 'for the time being'. He knew the greatest risk he faced as chief secretary was that the move might be construed by the public as a sleight of hand, particularly with an election in the offing. But on that score, at least, Ramsay needn't have been concerned.

In the previous two years the Kelly gang had risen to a pinnacle of notoriety rarely equalled in Australia before or since. Their activities were condemned by all factions in the legislature, including those who would have been expected to support the Kellys as their own. Every one of Melbourne's daily newspapers slammed the gang. Ramsay's great political opponent, David Syme of the *Age*, came out in support of the government on the Kelly situation and entered into a secret arrangement which suppressed publication of classified plans to apprehend the outlaws. And even the short-lived *Sam Slick in Victoria*, one of the more radical publications of the period, expressed no sympathy for the bushrangers, though it was equally scathing towards the police force for its failure to rout the fugitives.

The news of Aaron Sherritt's shooting and the siege that followed created a highly charged atmosphere that made the public even more hostile towards Ned. According to newspaper reports the gang showed a remarkable indifference to human suffering and the death of innocents. Sherritt was killed in full view of his pregnant wife. Civilian men, women and children were used as human shields under terrifying circumstances. And much was made of the devastation that would have occurred had the derailment of the special train been successful. The crash itself would have wreaked havoc amongst the occupants and those who survived the wreckage would have then been helpless to defend themselves against the ensuing gunfire. These were images that the press played upon.

Such was the atmosphere of hostility towards the Kellys that no one seemed to be paying much attention to the correct and proper procedure of dealing with the surviving gang leader. It appears that Ramsay's swift, decisive actions were accepted without question, though under history's scrutiny the legality of what occurred leaves much to be desired.

3 | AN UNEASY ALLIANCE

When Ramsay sent Standish to the scene at Glenrowan, it was more about protocol than priority. Those close to the two men knew there was no love lost between these powerful bureaucrats; their animosity towards each other was amply demonstrated when one of the chief secretary's first acts upon taking control of the hunt was to fully exercise his ministerial might over the police commissioner by drastically reducing his authority – a task Ramsay relished wholeheartedly.

Victoria's police force had progressively deteriorated under Standish's command, to the point where the officers were ill fitted to carry out many of their duties. Mounted constables who had borne the brunt of the Kelly hunt were not only poorly armed but their training periods were often spent perfecting useless sword drills like members of a showpiece British cavalry regiment. Many of them had little knowledge of the far more effective use of firearms.

Standish also represented some of society's most corrupting influences, which thoroughly repelled men like Robert Ramsay. He had traded shamelessly on his aristocratic English connections to gain appointment as police commissioner in 1858, despite his meagre experience of law enforcement. He also insisted on being addressed as 'Captain', although his service in Britain's

Royal Artillery had been relatively short-lived and certainly not distinguished.

The commissioner was highly sociable, gregarious, meticulously well-groomed and, as his personal diary reveals, spent much of his time pursuing his own pleasures. A lifelong bachelor, his reputation as a dandy made him a subject of ridicule as the hunt for the Kellys staggered along unsuccessfully for almost two years, but this didn't stop him from gracing the drawing rooms of Melbourne's society matrons with characteristic aplomb. Standish was a habitual presence at their balls, charming the guests and keeping a watchful eye out for new female conquests. In the highest 'gentlemanly' circles of Melbourne, he prided himself on his reputation as a man of the world and was no stranger to the large brothel district where a variety of different sexual tastes were catered for. He had reputedly served as a discreet intermediary providing 'solace' for visiting dignitaries at Government House, including Queen Victoria's second son, the Duke of Edinburgh, and his retinue when they visited Victoria in 1861.

Gambling was also one of Standish's great passions. He had arrived in Victoria in 1852 in seeming penury after selling his English assets to meet his gambling debts. Nevertheless, after becoming police commissioner, he still managed to raise the funds to meet large gambling debts from all-night card-playing sessions and betting plunges at the racetrack. Where the money came from remains a mystery, though it's not hard to imagine a little strategic bribery may have been part of the commissioner's repertoire.

It's no surprise that Standish's moral conduct deeply offended Ramsay, ensuring they were at loggerheads from their very first meeting. But Standish was certainly no novice when it came to gathering support and over the years he built up powerful local connections that served him well. His permanent address since the early 1870s had been the exclusive Melbourne Club, where he had a carefully selected coterie of influential friends and acquaintances.

Among them was a longstanding friendship with Redmond Barry, the senior judge of the colony's Supreme Court, with whom he had spent 'jolly evenings', as his diary records. Then there was Henry Gurner, the Crown solicitor, who would play a crucial role in future dealings with the bushranger. Another local network he diligently maintained was the Masonic Order that operated in three manifestations in Victoria: English, Scottish and Irish. From 1861 he held the position of grand master of the English chapter. This conveniently provided him with a range of influential acquaintances who helped quash a lot of the public criticism levelled at him.

Standish was adept at protecting his own interests and on more than one occasion proved he was not averse to employing thinly veiled threats of blackmail. During the previous government's office under Graham Berry he'd become privy to information about a senior minister who was engaging in activities that were considered 'criminal' at the time. One of Standish's officers – Superintendent Sadleir – revealed the details years later when he recorded in his memoirs that the person concerned was a 'high official' who lived a 'notoriously unclean life' and had been detected in a 'gentleman's' home at night in 'ambiguous circumstances'. The commissioner made full use of this potentially ruinous scandal as a subtle form of persuasion when the need arose.

Unfortunately for Standish, Ramsay's staid lifestyle ensured that he was impervious to extortion tactics. The chief secretary considered his married life and the nurturing of his children to be sacrosanct. It was no secret that one of his greatest pleasures was the wholesome pastime of bushwalking. In several articles published in the *Argus* years before he took office, Ramsay had waxed lyrical about the joys of communing with nature where one could ponder the purpose of life in rugged isolation.

Within days of assuming office the chief secretary stripped Standish of any effective power and took over command of the search for the Kellys. He launched an entirely new strategy, personally directing that Superintendent Francis Hare be placed in charge. Forthwith, Hare was ultimately responsible to the government rather than the police commissioner, and Ramsay pledged all his ministerial powers to assist him.

There is something deliciously ironic about the fact that in the end it was Ned Kelly who inspired an unusual kind of alliance between these two bitter opponents, uniting them in a common goal. For like Robert Ramsay, Standish badly wanted to see Ned hang, but while Ramsay's motivation was deeply moral, Standish's motivation was far more personal and vindictive. The abysmal failure of the long and highly expensive police search for the Kellys had been a profound humiliation and emphasised to one and all how ineffectual he was as police commissioner.

Then there was the debacle of a badly engineered publicity stunt that continued to plague him. At the height of the police search, Standish organised for a carefully contrived publicity shot to be taken of him 'actively participating' in the hunt. Word soon leaked out that the whole episode was a set-up. The picture shows him outside a tent at field headquarters in full bush regalia striking the pose of a heroic lawman. In actual fact these so-called headquarters never existed. The tent and other items scattered around, including a burning campfire and a dog, part of a tree and bush in the background, had all been provided by the photographer. What had begun as an exercise to boost his flagging public image resulted in a permanent visual record of him as an object of ridicule.

He was publicly derided once again when a newspaper reporter visited him in his Benalla hotel room and noted that he had a telegraph extension specially installed there. The journalist wryly observed that in addition to being used for official business, it was linked to a nearby card room and was being used to obtain 'the latest sporting intelligence'. In Charles Standish's eyes, Ned Kelly was responsible (albeit indirectly) for most of his recent humiliations. He was also convinced his public standing would be

Faked photograph of Police Commissioner Standish

redeemed and his personal honour restored once the bushranger suffered maximum punishment.

Late on Monday the roads in Benalla streamed with locals heading for the railway station as the word passed around that Ned Kelly would arrive on the regular passenger train to Melbourne. Spectators were afforded only a glimpse though as, lying on the mattress, he was whisked away under heavy police guard to the town's lock-up. Weary, begrimed police officers alighted from the train. The bodies of Byrne and Cherry were laid on the platform.

Standish hurried off to send a telegraph to the chief secretary: 'Please inform if there is any objection to his being taken to Melbourne instead of Beechworth, former preferable for many reasons'. Like Ramsay, he knew the best way to assure Ned's swift dispatch was to have him as close to the centre of government as possible. Ramsay personally signed the telegraph form with his reply to the police commissioner. He agreed that Ned should be transferred to Melbourne 'as soon as he can be moved'. For the time being he had to trust Standish to act sensibly and discreetly.

Meanwhile, another member of the police service slipped into the town virtually unnoticed. While Standish busied himself secretly coordinating Ned's transfer, Constable Thomas McIntyre found a bed for the night in the police barracks near the cell block where the bushranger was housed. The sole police officer to survive Stringybark Creek, he was to be a major player in the days to come.

4 | WILD ANIMALS

More than twenty-four hours since his capture, it now appeared highly likely that Ned would survive his wounds. People began to speculate about how the bushranger would be dealt with and opinions were as wild as they were varied. Central to Ned's legal situation was the fact that eighteen months earlier, an extraordinary act of parliament (originally formulated and introduced into English law before the Norman conquest of 1066) declared that the members of the Kelly gang were now considered to be 'outlaws'. This was not the first time the ancient method of law enforcement had been used in Australia. In the first decades of the century it was implemented so that bushrangers could be shot on sight in Tasmania. In the 1860s it had been used in New South Wales in a bid to combat a particularly widespread outbreak of bushranging. But in Victoria, it was the first time since the establishment of its modern system of government in 1855 that anything like this had been contemplated.

Within days of the police shootings at Stringybark Creek, in response to a tremendous public outcry, the Victorian legislature revived outlawry as part of the working of its criminal law. The wheels were set in motion six days after the news of the police killings reached Melbourne, even before the body of Sergeant Kennedy had been recovered from the site. In parliament the

Proclamation

By His Excellency Sir George Ferguson Bowen Knight Grand Cross of the Most distinguished Order of Saint Michael and Saint George Governor and Commander in Chief in and over the Colony of Victoria and its Dependencies and Vice Admiral of the same &c &c

Whereas under and by virtue of the provisions of the "Felons Apprehension Act 1878" Numbered 612 the Governor with the advice of the Executive Council is empowered to proclaim the fact that any person has been adjudged and declared to be an outlaw Now therefore I the Governor of Victoria with the advice of the Executive Council do hereby proclaim that by a Declaration under the hand of His Honor Sir William Foster Stawell Chief Justice of the Supreme Court of Victoria dated the fifteenth day of November 1878 and filed of record in the said Supreme Court Edward Kelly of Greta in the said Colony was adjudged and declared to be an outlaw within the meaning and under the provisions of the said act.—

Given under my hand and the Seal of the Colony this fifteenth day of November 1878 at Melbourne Victoria in the forty second year of Her Majesty's reign.

G. F. Bowen

His Excellency's Command

Bryan O'Loghlen

God save the Queen!

Proclamation declaring Edward Kelly an outlaw

governor assented to the Felons Apprehension Act (or the outlawry act, as it was to be commonly known), confirming that Ned and his companions were now officially outlaws. By this procedure, Ned and Dan Kelly, and the two other members of the gang who had still not been officially identified, were given fourteen days to surrender themselves at Mansfield, where they would be placed on trial for the murder of Constable Scanlan. Such was the sense of urgency that the arrangements were hastily squeezed in on the one working day that remained before the running of the Melbourne Cup.

When the bushrangers failed to give themselves up, they automatically fell under the jurisdiction of the act, which stated that if any 'outlaw shall be found at large armed or there being reasonable ground to believe he is armed it shall be lawful for any of Her Majesty's subjects whether a constable or not and whether its use be preceded by a demand for surrender or not to apprehend or take such outlaw dead or alive'. Punishment of up to fifteen years imprisonment could be imposed on anyone found to have assisted the outlaws. If a suspect tried to launch a plea that he or she was forced to help them, it was deemed no defence unless the person went immediately to law enforcement officers and owned up to having had contact with the bushrangers. Special provision was also made to waive normal safeguards enabling the authorities to break into private homes if they believed the fugitives were in the vicinity, or if they were seeking to arrest persons believed to have assisted them.

As one member of the Legislative Assembly, John Gavan Duffy, confirmed without dissent, those outlawed under the act had the status of 'wild animals' and were stripped of all rights or recognition as human beings. In the Legislative Council, the Hon. Henry Cuthbert, who introduced the legislation, assumed that a declaration of outlawry under the act amounted to full and instant convictions for any hanging offences for which the bushrangers were outlawed, making them immediately liable to the imposition of the death penalty if they were captured alive. In a long article published shortly after the act was introduced, the *Age* explained that this meant any offences for which the bushrangers were outlawed amounted to findings of guilt by order of the legislature, removing any rights they previously enjoyed, such as an ordinary criminal trial.

For the people of Melbourne at this time, the act revived memories of childhood tales about fictional outlaws like Robin Hood, Hereward the Wake and Blackmore's *Lorna Doone*, which had been one of the most popular novels in Australia and England in the previous decade and was rumoured to have been Ned's favourite book. It even seeped into such seemingly unrelated activities as children's play, in particular the language of schoolyard battles. My maternal grandfather, Alexander Cuthbert, was seven years old at the time and living in suburban Melbourne. He recalled years later with surprising clarity that in a short space of time his favourite game 'Troopers Against Bushrangers' became 'Troopers Against Outlaws'.

For the police, the implementation of the act was a major boost to their authority, but they were still severely handicapped by the ongoing problem of their shoddy, well-worn and largely substandard equipment. An overwhelming concern for many officers in the field was the serious deficiency of even the most basic accoutrements of their everyday kit. Few officers were lucky enough to possess modern rifles and the rest had to make do with the long outmoded single-shot breech-loading 'pepperpots'. Most of their packsaddles were in a dreadful state and they were forced to improvise with bits of rope and strips of leather.

With the Kellys in hiding, the initial impact of their new status was negligible. The flow-on effect, however, was subtle and deadly. Whether the act directly affected the fugitives' state of mind when it was first introduced is difficult to ascertain, but on two occasions at least Ned sought to respond to his accusers. The first clear pointer came in December 1878 soon after the arrest, under the outlawry act, of a number of men who the police claimed (in most cases, if not all, incorrectly) were aiding the bushrangers. A 3500-word letter was delivered to a member of parliament signed 'Edward Kelly A Forced Outlaw' (although the missive was almost certainly penned by Joe Byrne, who was acknowledged as the gang's resident scribe due to his high level of literacy). The letter told of how the bushranger's 'peculiar' situation had made it 'impossible for me to get any justice without I make a statement to someone that will take notice of it'. His outlawry put him in a situation that 'could be no worse'.

There were strong indications the bushrangers were no longer directing their angst solely towards the police and government authorities: '… if the Public do not see justice done I will seek revenge for the name and character which has been given me and my relations while God gives me strength to pull a trigger … Circumstances have forced us to become what we are – outcasts and outlaws, and, bad as we are, we are not as bad as we are supposed to be', the letter declared. 'Beware for we are now desperate men', it concluded ominously.

The recipient was Donald Cameron, a member of the Legislative Assembly who had attacked the police in parliament, accusing them of being scandalously inept in their search for the gang. It seems that Ned interpreted Cameron's open criticism of the police as a sign that the parliamentarian was a potential ally and might take up the fugitives' cause. He was sorely mistaken. Cameron had merely seized the opportunity of a public platform to gain some political mileage against Premier Berry's government. When the letter's existence became public, he vehemently denied he had any sympathy for the Kellys. What's more, after he had shown the letter to the premier, the version that finally appeared in the newspapers was heavily edited. When published, all the charges made against the police in relation to their treatment of the Kelly

family were excluded, leaving intact other sections which acknowledged Ned's involvement in the deaths of the police officers at
Stringybark Creek.

In January 1879 further indications of the bushrangers'
growing desperation came to light. During the gang's raid on
Jerilderie, Ned left behind a document he described as his 'autobiography' with the request that arrangements be made for it to be
printed. For those of his contemporaries who saw it, including
Thomas McIntyre, who viewed the original, there was little doubt
Joe Byrne had once again penned the words. Much of the text was
merely a reiteration of the contents of the Cameron letter. But it
also showed that after three months on the run, faced with the daily
prospect of being shot on sight, the bushrangers were feeling far
more antagonistic towards the general community: '... there are
civilians who take fire-arms against me, for what reason I do not
know unless they want me to turn on them and exterminate them
with out medicine'. And this time the sense of persecution was
palpable. Their ultimate fate, the letter went on, was to be 'outlawed
and declared unfit to be allowed any human burial their property
either consumed or confiscated and them theirs and all belonging
to them exterminated off the face of the earth'. As for their feelings
towards the constabulary, one passage of particularly colourful
invective left no doubt, describing the officers of police and justice
as a 'parcel of big ugly fat-necked wombat headed big bellied
magpie legged narrow hipped splay-footed sons of Irish Bailiffs or
English landlords ... cowards – every one of them'.

The majority of Melburnians believed that the Kellys' status as
outlaws would ultimately determine their fate if they were captured
alive. As the newspapers were quick to point out, not only had the
act of parliament sanctioned the capture and killing of the outlaws,
it had also made them guilty in law of the murders of the three
police officers, removing the necessity for them to ever be brought

to trial for these offences. Soon after Ned was apprehended, inveterate betting men in Bourke Street's bars were laying odds on when he would be hanged. Some only gave him twenty-four hours, others a little longer, perhaps a week. There were those who could claim, perhaps with good cause, that this was also the thinking of the government. As one newspaper recorded, it was believed that the outlaw would be hanged as soon as the formality of positive identification in court was out of the way. Legally, this could not have been further from the truth.

5 | STRINGYBARK

If in the early days the Kelly gang had been viewed by certain sectors of society as a band of misguided youths who were victimised by an overzealous police force, the murder of three officers at Stringybark Creek in October 1878 all but destroyed any sympathy the public had for them. What happened that cool spring evening in a bush clearing has been retold countless times with countless variations. Of course, we'll never know the truth of what actually occurred. After all, only one badly frightened and disorientated policeman survived the attack and as for the bushrangers, it was several months before they attempted to put their case forward in the Cameron and Jerilderie letters, in which their prime motivation was to defend themselves.

Reliable sources are few and far between, but it's possible to draw a number of conclusions by examining the site itself in conjunction with the autopsy reports done on the victims by the local medical practitioner, Dr Samuel Reynolds. Another intriguing piece of 'evidence' comes in the form of a ballad that began to do the rounds at local pubs soon after the killings. It was called 'Stringybark Creek' and according to regional folklore it is said to have been written, at least in part, by one Joseph Byrne. There's considerable irony in the rumour, for the ballad undeniably supports McIntyre's account of the event, not Kelly's. Nevertheless, it's a piece of oral history that presents an interesting view of what happened.

On Friday 25 October two police parties set out from Benalla. Superintendent John Sadleir had organised the groups – one from the north, and one led by Sergeant Michael Kennedy from the south – to scour the countryside for the fugitives between Mansfield and Benalla. Kennedy's colleagues, Constable Thomas Lonigan, Constable Michael Scanlan and Constable Thomas McIntyre, were all instructed to 'disguise' themselves as ordinary bushmen. At this time there was a two hundred pound reward for the capture of Ned and Dan Kelly and although policemen were not technically entitled to monetary compensation, in practice they almost always collected the promised payment. Kennedy in particular was known to have significantly augmented his sergeant's income over several years, a large portion of the reward money being issued by the Stockholders' Association for the recovery of stolen animals.

It appears that Kennedy had learned from a local informer that Dan was doing some gold fossicking at a well-hidden camp in the vicinity, and this is why the police chose to base themselves in the area. They made camp close to the remains of an old hut that had reportedly been used as both a base for fossickers and a site for a still to make illegal hard liquor. The isolated bush clearing was situated in mountainous terrain, approximately twenty-three kilometres from Mansfield. Surrounded by towering trees ragged with long strips of shedding bark and dense clumps of tangled scrub, this was a place where sunlight struggled to reach the forest floor even in the middle of the day.

Dan Kelly's camp was a lot closer than the officers thought. The bushrangers were unaware that men hunting them were less than two miles away and only learned of their presence when they heard gunshots echoing in the distance. Oblivious to their human quarry so close by, McIntyre and Lonigan were shooting native birds (cockatoos or parrots) to make a stew for the evening meal while Kennedy and Scanlan were combing nearby bushland for the fugitives. By five o'clock twilight was advancing rapidly, making visibility poor. This is amply demonstrated by the fact that although they observed the two policemen for several minutes before entering the clearing, Ned believed McIntyre and Lonigan were police officer Flood and Senior Constable Strahan. (The Kellys held deeply personal grudges against both these men: Flood had fathered their sister Alice's child then deserted her, and Strahan had several months earlier unceremoniously dragged Ellen off to gaol.) Only when Ned stood over Lonigan's corpse and came face to face with McIntyre did he realise his mistake.

Of all those present, McIntyre was in the best position to witness the circumstances leading to Lonigan's death. He recalled the bushrangers had crept stealthily through a patch of long grass about sixty paces from the nearest of the two constables, and then suddenly burst into the clearing. At the cry of 'Bail up. Hold up your hands!' McIntyre had immediately surrendered, caught completely unawares as he prepared their evening meal. With a fork still in his hand, he raised his arms and thought longingly of the regulation pistol in a tent behind him.

Slightly further away from the advancing bushrangers, Lonigan dropped the pot of water he was carrying and ran for cover. His weapon was in a holster attached to his belt, secured by a flap and held in place with a brass stud, but he would barely have had time to even reach for it. His quick actions were just not quick enough. He was shot and died almost immediately. Ned claimed in the Jerilderie document that Lonigan 'ran to a battery of logs and put his hand up to take aim at me, when I shot him, as he would have shot me, as I knew well'. McIntyre, though, was adamant: Lonigan's pistol was still in his holster when he died.

It is an axiom of the law that statements made when persons are in fear of losing their life are considered trustworthy. To this end,

McIntyre hurriedly scribbled a few words in his notebook as he later fled from the bushrangers. Believing they were still after him and there was every chance they would shoot him down, he wrote, 'The Lord have mercy on my soul', and then, 'Lonigan tried to get his gun out'.

It is another quite acceptable belief that statements made soon after the events they describe are more than likely to be truthful and authentic. Shortly after McIntyre stumbled into the police barracks at Mansfield the next day he wrote a brief account of the events at Stringybark as part of his official report: 'Constable Lonigan made a motion to draw his revolver which he was carrying, immediately he did so he was shot by Edward Kelly and I believed died at once'.

Dr Samuel Reynolds, who carried out Lonigan's autopsy, confirmed that the constable had died as a result of a single bullet entering his brain after it passed through his right eye. But he also found other marks on Lonigan's body that looked like they had been inflicted before the fatal wound, directly contradicting Ned's claims that he shot him in self-defence. A wound on the officer's left thigh, as Dr Reynolds reported it, indicated that Lonigan was shot while he was upright, probably as he ran for cover. There were other wounds on the left arm that could not have been inflicted if Lonigan had taken shelter before the firing began, as the Jerilderie document claimed.

In the ballad 'Stringybark Creek' the versifier tells us Lonigan had made tracks 'to gain the wood', and then:

Reaching round for his revolver, but before he touched the stock
Ned Kelly pulled the trigger, fired, and dropped him like a rock.

While they waited for the rest of the police party to return, the bushrangers made tea, smoked and ate the food of their would-be hunters. They spoke amiably with their hostage too, especially

Ned, who was examining the policemen's weaponry and substantial stores of ammunition. He was convinced the officers were prepared for nothing less than wholesale slaughter. Despite this, Ned asserted he had no intention of killing McIntyre ('I could have shot you half an hour ago when you were sitting on that log') and proposed that if the constable could persuade his companions to surrender when they returned, no more blood would be shed that day.

When Sergeant Kennedy and Constable Scanlan returned to the camp on horseback an hour later, the clearing was well and truly shrouded in evening gloom. But the darkness was not the only factor that could account for the marked differences between McIntyre's and Ned's stories. The large cooking fire continued to burn, adding its own deceptive, flickering shadows to the scene. And the bushrangers had positioned themselves in different locations so they could surprise and surround the returning officers. When gunfire began, shots seemed to come from all directions. Blasts echoed off the surrounding rocks and no one could be certain from where they originated.

In the Cameron document Ned claimed that Scanlan was shot in self-defence, that he 'slewed his horse to gallop away, but turned to fire at me with his rifle, and was in fact in the act of firing again when I shot him'. According to McIntyre, however, after Kennedy and Scanlan had been called upon to bail up, both officers instinctively reached for their firearms. In Scanlan's case, his breech-loading American-made Spencer repeating rifle was slung on a strap across his back. Seconds later, Scanlan 'received a ball under the right arm which I feel assured has caused his death'.

Doctor Reynolds' examination confirmed that Scanlan had indeed been seriously wounded under his right arm, helping significantly to corroborate McIntyre's version of events.

Ned asserted that Scanlan fired on the bushrangers before he was shot at, but as the autopsy revealed, in addition to the fatal wound under Scanlan's right arm he had also been shot several

more times, just like Lonigan. There were at least three other bullet
wounds on his body: one on his right hip, another on his chest and
a third on his right shoulder. This raises the possibility that he was
already wounded before the fatal shot, which rendered him incapable of operating his rifle at all. And the shoulder wound was
positioned in such a way as to indicate he was turning his body
away from his attackers when he was struck and slipped from his
mount. It would have been a substantial gymnastic feat for Scanlan
to have freed his rifle from his shoulder and swung it into a firing
position as he pulled on the reins of his horse to turn away. And
again, the Stringybark ballad confirms this:

> *Then trooper Scanlan made a move his rifle to unsling,*
> *But to his heart a bullet sped and death was in the sting;*

The exact circumstances of Sergeant Kennedy's death are the
most difficult to ascertain. Immediately after his return to Mansfield
McIntyre recorded: 'Sergeant Kennedy I am unable to say anything
about, he was advised by me surrender he said it is all right I will,
but as the desperadoes continued shooting at the Sergeant and me,
I seized his horse which he had abandoned and made my escape on
it'. He believed that the bushrangers had reneged on the earlier
agreement he made with Ned to give the officers a chance to
surrender. The attack left him in no doubt he would be killed if
he stayed.

It was two days after the corpses of the other victims were
recovered that Kennedy's broken body was found. Lying at some
distance from the others, it had been disturbed by animals. The story
that one of his ears had been cut off when he was being tortured
was a complete fabrication, but it had done much to inflame public
opinion against the gang. As indeed had the misguided belief that
pages from his notebook containing a message to his wife were torn
out by his murderers, adding a special poignancy to published

accounts of his death. The bodies were stripped of all valuable pos-
sessions. Wedding rings were ripped off fingers, pockets rifled,
Kennedy's cherished watch was taken and it is believed a religious
medallion was torn from around the dead sergeant's neck. This
would cause his widow a great deal of anguish in the years to come.

McIntyre was quite clear about not having witnessed the
sergeant's death because he had already left the scene. Kennedy's
autopsy showed he had died as a result of being shot in the chest at
close range. It confirmed what had been alluded to in the Jerilderie
document, that the policeman had been subject to a 'mercy killing'
after a number of serious shotgun wounds. Significantly, one of
them was under his right arm, indicating he could well have been
shot while holding his arms above his head as he attempted to
surrender.

The Jerilderie document basically confirmed the results of the
autopsy. During an exchange of gunfire, Ned says he shot Kennedy
in the armpit and then fired again, not realising that the sergeant
had dropped his revolver and 'slewed' around to surrender.

'I did not know he had dropped his revolver, the bullet passed
through the right side of his chest and he could not live or I would
have let him go ...' With more than touch of remorse he ends:
'I put his cloak over him and left him as well as I could'.

Whether or not he meant to exonerate himself in the
Jerilderie letter, Ned's version of the police killings hardly excused
his actions. Even if he hadn't fired a single shot, the law still
provided – as it does today – that individuals acting in concert with
each other in causing death can be held equally guilty of murder.
Ned's written justifications merely served as enduring evidence that
he was legally culpable for the deaths of the three officers.

At the Benalla police barracks on the evening of Monday 28 June 1880, celebrations continued well into the early hours of the morning. Officers who had taken part in the siege gathered to share their experiences and several good-natured arguments broke out over who among them had played the most crucial role at the scene. A unique bond now existed between these men. Many of them would speak of the siege at Glenrowan as the most significant event of their careers, if not their lives.

Ned's stay at the Benalla lock-up was a brief one. Just before 9.30 pm, Ramsay signed the order for Ned to be transferred to Melbourne, thus clearing the way for Standish to implement a top-secret plan. Earlier that day he learned that the first regular train to Melbourne from Benalla would leave town before 9 am – a full hour before the local police court would be convened. If he could ensure that Ned was on that train, it would mean the prisoner was unlikely to fall into the hands of the local court system, and so would remain primarily under the central government's control. Standish hastily arranged for an extra van to be attached to the morning train. Officers who had accompanied him from Melbourne were told they would escort the bushranger back to the capital just after dawn. He also ordered the prisoner to be removed from the train at North Melbourne, one stop short of the terminus.

There, a heavily armed contingent of police would be waiting with a vehicle to convey Kelly to Melbourne Gaol.

Ramsay and Standish never formally disclosed the precise reason for moving Ned to the Victorian capital. The only comment the chief secretary made long after the event was that 'special circumstances' had justified the decision. Ramsay would have believed the bushranger's outlawry exempted him from the concessions due to a criminal under the ordinary workings of the law. It remains a matter of conjecture, though, whether he truly believed that Ned would be immediately hanged as an outlaw without an ordinary criminal trial. Certainly his actions immediately prior to the Melbourne transfer appear to negate this because he made arrangements that indicated he was preparing for the possibility that Ned would be incarcerated for some time before his fate was determined. In his capacity as minister in charge of the colony's gaols, Ramsay issued a specific set of orders to the governor of the Melbourne gaol forbidding him to allow Ned any visitors or to send or receive any letters without Ramsay's personal authorisation. It would seem the chief secretary was leaving nothing to chance.

As festivities continued in the nearby barracks, Ned did not spend an easy night. He had a number of very painful wounds and was badly bruised where bullets had pummelled his protective armour. Senior Constable John Kelly interviewed him at some length and a stream of officials came to his cell throughout the night to gawk at him like a prize exhibit at a travelling sideshow.

There was also a great deal of disturbance coming from the cell next door, where Joe Byrne's body was lodged. Instead of being placed under the control of the local coroner and his remains being held in the mortuary, his body remained in police custody and a number of visitors came to view it by candlelight. An artist spent several hours making a drawing that was published in the *Sydney Illustrated News,* among other journals. He later described the experience as 'the most miserable assignment I ever had'. The proprietor of the Melbourne Waxworks, Maximilian Kreitmayer, also spent several painstaking hours making a cast of Byrne's head and body parts for his forthcoming exhibit.

Sometime in the early hours of Tuesday, the prisoner stirred and, to the surprise of Senior Constable Kelly, asked him to fetch Thomas McIntyre, whom he had apparently recognised in the train to Benalla the night before. Ned wanted to talk.

Thomas McIntyre was born in Belfast in 1846 and raised as a Protestant. He served for a time in the Irish constabulary and then, like his three Irish-born colleagues killed near Mansfield, he ventured to Australia as a land of opportunity, a place for a new beginning and a refuge from the terrible scourge of tuberculosis that had ravaged his family. But unlike his colleagues, McIntyre had a reputation as a rather bookish fellow. He had received a good education and continued to read widely and avidly whenever he could, even when he was out on patrol in the bush. He could quote Shakespeare and selections of colonial writing at the drop of a hat, and he even dabbled in writing poetry. He was fluent at shorthand (a skill he learned during a brief stint as a journalist) and read the *Age* newspaper regularly – an anathema to most of his senior officers because of its espousal of liberal causes.

The Irishman's first job in his new country was as a school-teacher in New South Wales but he soon moved on to join the Victorian police. He was drawn to the mounted force because it provided opportunities to live an outdoor, adventurous lifestyle free of urban restraints. It also ensured a healthier environment where he believed he was less likely to contract tuberculosis – a deep-seated and ever-present fear for him. Respected, well-liked and seemingly contented with his lot, Thomas McIntyre's world was suddenly turned upside down on the evening of 26 October 1878.

The events at Stringybark Creek gave him a great deal of public attention. Some regarded him as a hero but there were others who quite openly deemed him a coward because he had fled from

Thomas McIntyre

the murder scene. It was this allegation that scarred him deeply. In
the months after Stringybark he briefly held the position of acting
police orderly at the office of Ramsay's predecessor, but it was far
too sedentary for him. Pleading to be returned to more active duty
he was seconded to the city detective force where he was given the
task of guarding the port in the unlikely event that the bushrangers
might attempt to escape overseas. There he spent day after tedious
day patrolling the waterfront, a lonely, haunted figure.

When news of Ned's capture reached McIntyre he hurried to
the police commissioner's office only to find that Standish had
already set out for Glenrowan. He rushed out, hailed a cab, and
ordered the driver to take him at full speed to Spencer Street
railway station on the other side of the city, arriving just as the
commissioner's special train was about to depart. With only minutes
to spare he found Standish and babbled his request. Unhesitatingly,

the police commissioner gave McIntyre permission to join the expedition and he was assigned a compartment with some other junior officers.

For both Kelly and McIntyre, their encounter in an isolated bush clearing twenty months earlier had enormous personal repercussions. As Ned revealed in the Cameron and Jerilderie documents, he was fully aware that the police deaths had labelled him a dangerous public enemy. Some who had supported or sympathised with the fugitives now condemned them for what they saw as the callous execution of the Stringybark victims. In the Cameron document Ned complained that the official accounts of the officers' deaths were supplemented by more and more elaborate rumours, particularly in relation to the circumstances surrounding Sergeant Kennedy's death. One particularly malicious piece of gossip was that Ned had handcuffed the officer to a tree and cut his ear off with a knife, an idea that people naturally found horrifying. The fabrication was disproved the day Kennedy's body was returned to Mansfield, but versions of the story continued to circulate, fuelling the bushranger's indignant rage.

As for McIntyre, he was racked with doubts about his role at Stringybark. The sole police survivor, it had taken him almost twenty-four hours to reach Mansfield once he escaped from his assailants. Initially he fled on horseback but gave up after a nightmare ride and proceeded on foot: 'I was torn off the horse by the timber and severely hurt', he wrote later. Still fearing pursuit he staggered on through rough country, barefoot for the most part because he took his boots off in order to avoid leaving tracks. With the few matches he had in his possession, he illuminated his small pocket compass from time to time to guide him on his way.

McIntyre arrived in Mansfield covered in bruises and deep scratches. He'd been awake for more than thirty-six hours straight but after taking a little food he immediately sat down to write a report of his ordeal. Less than two hours later he voluntarily joined

a search party to return to the scene of the police killings. By now
almost comatose, he had to be lifted onto a horse and spent a miserable night in driving rain recovering the bodies of Lonigan and
Scanlan. They couldn't find Kennedy. The expedition returned to
Mansfield in the afternoon and he prepared an official report for
the police commissioner before finally taking to his bed.

There's no doubt that McIntyre acted courageously and
showed great physical and mental endurance throughout his gruelling ordeal, and yet public perception of him remained decidedly
negative. He acknowledged later that he made a fateful error in
revealing that he had hidden in a wombat hole during his getaway.
With great bitterness he recalled, 'From then on I left home every
morning with full assurance that I would hear something about a
wombat hole before I returned at night'.

Such persistent insinuations of cowardice greatly disturbed the
proud Irishman. Even more so, he was troubled by his own uncertainty about specific aspects of the events at Stringybark. In the panic
and confusion of the attack, McIntyre had been unable to see a lot of
what was going on, particularly with daylight fading fast. The constable desperately needed to talk to Ned – the only other living
witness – about what had happened that evening. He needed to
confirm details that continued to haunt him and to clarify his own
actions to satisfy his personal honour. More than anything, Thomas
McIntyre needed to know that he had not acted like a coward. 'My
object', McIntyre later affirmed, 'was to exonerate myself'.

Yet when the moment came, McIntyre was reluctant to face
Ned. During the night in the Benalla lock-up, Senior Constable
Kelly informed McIntyre that the bushranger was asking for him,
but the constable continued to make excuses to avoid the meeting.
Only when daybreak began seeping through the barred windows
did McIntyre finally relent. Just after seven o'clock he accompanied
the senior constable to Ned's cell where he found the bushranger
'quiet in his manner ... he did not appear to be in pain'.

Ned lay in his dank, chilly cell with only the thin mattress between him and the freezing floor. Groggy and exhausted in the gloom, he couldn't work out who McIntyre was at first. Then recognition dawned and he uttered the constable's name. The flood-gates opened and McIntyre launched into a barrage of questions: 'You remember the last time we met', McIntyre babbled, 'didn't I tell you then I would rather be shot than tell you anything about the other two men if you were going to shoot them?'

After a pause Ned agreed with him and then, as if he realised how important this was to McIntyre, he turned to Senior Constable Kelly and emphasised, 'McIntyre would rather be shot than bring the other two men into it'. He went on to confirm that when he first caught sight of McIntyre the constable had been unarmed. Delegated camp cook for the day, the only weapon he held in his hand was a fork.

The two men discussed details of the encounter for about fifteen minutes, disagreeing on some points and agreeing on others. One of the issues McIntyre was determined to clarify was the bushrangers' exact intention when they entered the clearing. He was convinced the killings 'must have been an afterthought of theirs' and in one newspaper interview soon after Stringybark he had stated categorically, 'I do not believe that the murderers went to the camp with the intention of taking life'.

At no time had McIntyre ever denied the violence of his captors. Tapping his gun, Ned told him, 'Don't attempt to go away. If you do I shall track you to Mansfield and shoot you at the police station.' And as the constable escaped he heard Dan Kelly shouting, 'Shoot that bastard, shoot that bastard!' Admittedly, he could not be sure whether this was directed at him or Kennedy but the malicious intent was plain.

And yet despite all the threats and violence, the bushrangers' actions appeared to McIntyre to be impulsive and their behaviour erratic. The conduct of one of them was particularly bewildering.

As they waited for the other policemen to arrive McIntyre spent a few quiet minutes with Joe Byrne. The constable took out a cake of ordinary dark tobacco and offered it to the bushranger. Both men teased strands from it, filled their clay pipes and quietly smoked together. Calling him 'mate', Byrne then presented him with a pannikin of tea. McIntyre kept the tobacco for many years as a relic of the encounter. It also served as a reminder that he had witnessed a side to Joe Byrne that was far removed from the bloodthirsty killer depicted in the press.

That morning in the cell, McIntyre was not seeking to remove the Kelly gang from any criminal liability for their actions, he simply wanted to satisfy his own mind that they were not the cold, calculating murderers so many insisted they were. 'Why did you come near us at all?' he asked Ned. 'You could have kept out of our way when you knew we were there.'

'You would soon have found us out and if we did not shoot you, you would have shot us.'

McIntyre could scarcely believe his ears. Unwittingly, Ned had admitted their intention to murder the police officers. Though earlier in their conversation he insisted he'd offered Kennedy and Scanlan the option to surrender and that the bulk of his actions had been in self-defence, this disclosure was more than enough to nullify that claim. Not only was the constable convinced that the murders had probably been premeditated, but now he also had to take on the additional burden of knowing that if he disclosed the information in any court proceedings arising from Stringybark, it would guarantee the death penalty for Ned.

McIntyre could hear the guards approaching. He knew it was now or never: he had to pose the question that had tormented him for so long: 'Did I show any cowardice when bailed up?'

Despite the fact that McIntyre's future testimony could well seal his own doom, Ned put his mind at rest without hesitation. 'No', he replied.

The officers entered the cell, brushing McIntyre aside. Ned was lifted up on his mattress, carried outside, laid upon an open cart and covered up with a thick blanket. As McIntyre and Senior Constable Kelly walked out together, McIntyre swore his companion to secrecy about the interview and, true to his word, the newspaper reporters waiting outside didn't learn about it until much later.

Though well aware of its weaknesses, Thomas McIntyre was intensely loyal to the Victoria Police and proud to be a member of the force. He would always be grateful for the way Standish, whom he referred to as 'The Chief', had supported him after Stringybark Creek. Nevertheless, having encountered the bushranger face to face he was unable to reconcile Standish's view of Ned as a cold-blooded murderer with the memory of the much-diminished man lying in his cell. Perhaps this is why he chose to keep to himself the startling admission that the gang had entered the clearing with murderous intent. As a result, he did not file an official report on the meeting: completely uncharacteristic behaviour for someone so meticulous about paperwork. His silence also meant that although he was protecting Ned, he was also choosing not to record events that would reflect badly on the Victorian police and, most particularly, its chief commissioner. For the time being however, he wrote a personal record of it and added it to the extensive archive of documents and newspaper clippings he collected about the Kellys. (Donated to the Victorian Police Department by his descendants in the 1970s, McIntyre's scrapbook, which includes the remainder of the cake of tobacco he shared with Joe Byrne at Stringybark, has somehow been 'mislaid' amongst the records – an irreplaceable loss of vital source material.)

Years later McIntyre finally made public details of the exchange with Ned and his vow not to reveal the incriminating disclosure. To him it was a silent acknowledgment of his respect for the injured bushranger. Other officers, like Senior Constable Kelly, were happy to talk to newspaper reporters about their impressions of the prisoner but McIntyre would have none of it. Fortunately, his desire for confidentiality was not held against him. In fact Senior Constable Kelly himself openly declared his admiration for the quiet, dignified officer affectionately referred to among his colleagues as 'Mac'.

The dawn encounter in the cell clearly indicates Ned had no ill-feeling towards McIntyre, though they disagreed on a number of key details about Stringybark. He made several deliberate efforts to exonerate the constable from any claims of professional misconduct and was more than willing to absolve him from accusations of personal cowardice. Despite their vastly different circumstances, it seems these two men identified with one another to a degree, and both shared a common sense of loyalty and honour.

As the prisoner embarked on the last leg of his journey to Melbourne, McIntyre remained in Benalla on police business for the rest of the day. It would be several weeks before he came face to face with Ned Kelly again, this time in a secret court hearing where the bushranger would be on trial for his life.

Before 1851, Benalla had been a part of New South Wales and was merely a wayside stopping place on the overland track – grandiloquently titled the 'Sydney Road' – to the New South Wales capital. By the late 1870s the town had grown into a thriving rural centre with almost two thousand residents, servicing a considerable hinterland that stretched as far as the mountains of the Great Dividing Range. Then in the space of two short years it became a veritable no man's land in the midst of a drawn-out battle. For Benalla was only a short ride – just sixteen kilometres – from Greta, the heart of Kelly country.

When Ned's widowed mother moved there with her brood after the death of her husband John 'Red' Kelly in 1866, the district was already well populated with her kin. Her father, John Quinn, had secured a large landholding not far away, financed by the sale of a property closer to Melbourne that was worth a small fortune. Quinn fathered ten children, several of whom worked the family land, and a contingent of her late husband's relations was also not far away as three of Red's brothers and two of his sisters had emigrated from Ireland in 1857. All in all, more than sixty of Ellen's relatives – by blood or marriage – were scattered about the district by 1880.

With such a palpable family presence in the area it's not surprising that as the hunt stretched on, Benalla gradually came to resemble a small armed camp. The Kelly gang was believed to be hiding in the nearby ranges, so naturally the police used the town's existing police headquarters as a base for their searches. Knowing the fugitives' survival depended on the provision of food and supplies from friends and relatives, a parade of officers carried out surveillance on the homes of suspected supporters for weeks on end. At one stage there were even members of the colony's permanent military force stationed there to guard the banks. It was a drastic move, but authorities considered Benalla to be a prime target for raids like those on Euroa and Jerilderie.

The 'police camp', as it was known (even though permanent buildings had replaced the original tents many years ago), also fulfilled a more clandestine function as the centre for gathering local intelligence. Since late 1878 a goodly portion of the government's secret service funds had found its way there, enabling numerous informers to be placed on the government payroll. In January 1879 Aaron Sherritt walked away with two gold sovereigns following his induction as a 'private detective'. Town gossip was rife when other local identities were observed calling at police headquarters, sometimes in the dead of night. After these covert visits, neighbours kept close tabs on them to see if they appeared to have an increase in spending money, a sure indication they were on the government's secret payroll. They usually did.

For weeks before the siege at Glenrowan the people of Benalla had been in constant fear for their lives as rumours flew thick and fast that the Kelly gang was planning to raid the town. It all began when folk from Greta had whispered to local shopkeepers that another hold-up like Euroa was a very real possibility. Since the gang had been in hiding, visitors from the nearby hamlet were the chief source of information on the outlaws. Their spending habits were also an important indicator of the gang's fluctuating fortunes. Soon after the raids on Euroa and Jerilderie, family members were seen flush with cash, handing over sovereigns and mountains of small change to Benalla shopkeepers. Local tradespeople had no doubt it was money stolen during the Kelly raids, but if their consciences were troubled they consoled themselves with the fact that the booty would otherwise be spent in Beechworth or Wangaratta.

In the last few months, however, there had been a noticeable drop in the buying power of some of these customers. It was further confirmation that warnings of the gang's imminent reappearance must be true. Several of these 'supporters' were believed to have slyly changed sides, sneaking in to the police camp for a piece of the government payroll, now that the outlaws could no longer supply them with hard cash. This increased the general uneasiness as nervous locals feared the Kellys would come looking for those who had betrayed them.

Tension was high when news came through that the Kellys had emerged from hiding, and peaked in the early hours of Sunday morning with the departure of the special police train northward. The murder of Aaron Sherritt had stunned everybody, and with several other turncoats in their midst the townspeople were understandably afraid. There were tearful scenes at the Benalla station as local police officers heading for the scene of Sherritt's demise at Woolshed were farewelled by emotional family members. Their fears were compounded by a bad omen that appeared in the sky. Just before the train set out, a full moon emerged from behind scattered rain clouds, bathing the countryside in bright light. It was common knowledge that the gang favoured such conditions and its most successful forays had been on nights like this. Sure enough, the gang lay in wait for them up ahead at Glenrowan. But now, it seemed, the danger was over, the conflict had passed, and all that remained was a defeated man so ill that he could barely lift his head.

Shortly after 8 am on Tuesday 29 June 1880, a modest procession emerged from the Benalla police compound and turned towards the railway station. In less than an hour the regular train from Wodonga to Melbourne was due to pass through. On this morning – twenty-four hours after the Battle of Glenrowan ended – the train would be collecting a special passenger.

The little band moved along at a slow pace, the driver carefully steering around potholes in the rough unpaved roads to avoid jarring the wounded passenger. Eight uniformed constables surrounding the cart had their guns at the ready. Their black helmets and full dress uniform gave the scene a martial air and their well-polished boots struck the ground in unison as if they were on military parade.

And yet despite the precautions there was no wild excitement amongst the scattered groups of bystanders, no demonstrations of protest or support. It must have been hard to reconcile the pale, listless prisoner with the swaggering, violent bully who had plagued the district with his crimes since his early youth. (One of the more popular stories circulating told of the occasion when, in a fit of violent temper, a teenaged Ned had pummelled a close relative to unconsciousness and then attempted to drown him in a waterhole.)

Huddled together, the townsfolk gazed silently at the rough open cart drawn by a single horse. The only flurry of activity occurred when some schoolchildren rushed forward to glimpse the man who lay barely visible under a swathe of blankets. It seemed extraordinary to these youngsters that just twenty-four hours ago he had been an object of terror.

As the cart approached the station a group of passengers for the Melbourne train waited restlessly on the platform. Amidst the commotion of the prisoner's arrival, few noticed when a senior police officer in civilian clothes joined their ranks. It was Superintendent Francis Hare, the man who had headed the assault on the Glenrowan Inn. With his injured left arm in a sling, he stood solemnly with his wife by his side.

Nearby a silent and composed figure was also waiting patiently, but not for the arrival of the train. Kate Lloyd was a cousin of Ned's, the sixteen-year-old daughter of Ellen's sister, Jane. She was an

Kate Lloyd

attractive young woman with delicate features and a mass of long dark hair tumbling down her back.

It was no secret that women were drawn to the ruggedly handsome outlaw and local gossip had linked him romantically with many attractive females over the years. The fact that there were blood relatives among them did not attract criticism as it would do today. Close liaisons and even marriage between first cousins was accepted practice in the district at the time.

In the months before the Glenrowan siege, Kate Lloyd had come to be regarded as especially close to her cousin Ned, so much so that there were those who referred to her as his 'fiancée'. A fine horsewoman like so many of her clan, the police suspected that on several occasions she had succeeded in carrying news and supplies to the fugitives when they were hiding out in the nearby ranges. The wife of the licensee of the other Glenrowan hotel, where Kelly sympathisers gathered during the siege, confided to a Melbourne reporter that Kate was very fond of him. 'It will break her heart, poor girl, if he is hanged', she added sadly.

Apart from Kate, all Ned's relatives were conspicuously absent from the station that day. His brother James was nowhere to be seen. Nor had he been spotted at the Glenrowan Inn, although it was known he had recently come back to live at the family home after serving a three-year sentence for cattle stealing in New South Wales. There was also no sign of sisters Maggie and Kate, both of whom had been seen bitterly remonstrating with the police after the siege. Overnight the families had converged on Maggie's hut where a wake had commenced for the souls of Dan Kelly and Steve Hart. For the Kelly clan, it appears that observing the rites of mourning for the two youngest members of the gang superseded the need to show support for the one who had survived.

Their grieving was acute. Maggie and her sisters had been especially close to Dan and had always treated him more like a son than a brother. They had pampered and spoiled him as a child and went out of their way to indulge him during the long absences of his elder brothers in his middle teenage years. Perhaps they felt sorry for him, for he was shorter than the other Kelly boys and of slim stature. But to many who met him, including Thomas McIntyre, he was an uncontrollable youth with a vicious nature. After the police killings at Stringybark Creek, McIntyre told of the seventeen-year-old being angry and sullen when Ned refused to let him handcuff the constable. He observed that Dan was 'nervously excited', broke frequently into 'a short laugh, almost hysterical' and peppered his utterances with violent oaths and threats. 'I knew who was most likely to be my executioner', McIntyre concluded.

In contrast, Steve Hart appeared to be little more than a pale copy of Dan and his presence had barely intruded on McIntyre during the events at Stringybark. Hart was the classic camp follower who always took his lead from Dan, though he was more than two years older. Physically small and noticeably bow-legged, he was best known for his prowess as a jockey. His sole claim to individual notoriety during the previous eighteen months was that he had managed to elude the police by riding around the district disguised as a woman, or so the rumour went.

Witnesses at the station observed that Kate Lloyd was deeply distressed at the sight of her cousin. Like many others there, she was aware that this could well be the last time she would see him alive. As the train pulled into the station Ned lay stretched out on the cart, haggard but alert. First Superintendent Hare approached him and exchanged a few words with the enemy he had pursued unsuccessfully for so many months. Then the specialist from Melbourne, Dr Ryan, checked on the bushranger's medical condition as he prepared to accompany him to the Victorian capital. All the while Kate's gaze never left her cousin's face and she was visibly fighting to maintain her composure.

Her attempts at restraint so impressed a couple of the police officers that they stood aside and discreetly indicated she had permission to speak with him for a moment. Hesitantly she moved forward. When she reached his side she bent down and they exchanged a few hushed words – a scene immortalised by a sketch in the *Australian Pictorial Weekly*. Moments later, the officers closed in around him and he was lifted into the van.

As Kate watched him disappear inside she tentatively dabbed her face with her handkerchief but when the door finally slid shut, her resolve broke and she began to weep uncontrollably. The guard waved his flag, the whistle blew and the locomotive pulled out of the station, cranking its way noisily across the iron bridge that spanned Broken River. Slowly the crowd began to disperse.

Apart from Ned's immediate family there was another significant absentee that morning. Police Commissioner Standish did not come to the station even though he was primarily responsible for the prisoner's transfer. Perhaps he wished to avoid any questions from the assembled press.

The manner in which he'd achieved the move was still unclear according to the Melbourne newspapers. A reporter for the *Age* wired from Benalla that Ned was simply 'removed by Captain Standish to the Melbourne Gaol'. A special late edition of the evening *Herald* covering Ned's arrival in the Victorian capital recorded that John Castieau, the governor of the gaol, stated the bushranger had been placed in his custody under a 'remand warrant', but there were serious doubts as to whether he actually had the document in his possession. Next morning, the *Age* added another dimension to the mystery when it claimed that Ned was actually being held in Melbourne Gaol under the direct orders of the colony's Executive Council, 'until it decides the steps to be taken in this case'.

Whatever the circumstances, Standish effectively ensured that no legal proceedings in Benalla could prevent the bushranger from being kept in Melbourne. The small triumph was made doubly sweet because he managed to compromise Ramsay at the same time. By making him a co-conspirator, it could be used in the future against the chief secretary if Ned's move to Melbourne was found to be of doubtful legal validity.

It was expected that the police commissioner would be returning on the train with his prisoner but Standish had other plans. He decided to stay on in Benalla for the time being, the reasons for which he had no intention of communicating to the chief secretary.

After Ned's departure Benalla continued to be a hotbed of gossip, rumour and intrigue, the bulk of it emanating from police headquarters. Throughout the day dozens of officials were seen entering the buildings, including Commissioner Standish and a host of local dignitaries. It was a heavily charged atmosphere in which secrets were very hard to keep. Reporters harangued the visitors as large crowds gathered nearby, with several of the gang's associates among them. As soon as anyone of note appeared on the scene they were approached for news on the latest developments. Shouts of recognition greeted local identities as they slipped inside, whilst the arrival of strangers met with whispered speculation.

Standish was a master at dealing with situations like this. He'd had years of practising his poker face as he pulled off betting coups at the Flemington racecourse or nursed a winning hand of cards at the Melbourne Club. He spent much of the day parading around town in fashionable civilian clothes, like a prosperous country gentleman. The fact that he had so little to do with the battle itself (he'd spent most of it in the compartment of a railway carriage discussing the finer points of card playing) remained a well-kept secret.

Meanwhile, authorities in Melbourne were alarmed to discover Standish had not accompanied Ned on the train. In the late morning a telegram arrived in Benalla seeking his whereabouts: 'If at Benalla ask when he will return – cheques need signing'. When there was no reply another soon followed: 'Premier requires answer to telegram'. But the commissioner had no intention of responding, for the moment at least. He was quietly carrying on his own personal correspondence with Melbourne, and earlier that day dispatched a telegram to a legal contact of his with specific instructions that it was not to be seen by those government officers who were trying to contact him.

The next day there were conflicting reports in the newspapers on his activities during the day but on one matter they all agreed. At some time the chief commissioner had managed to organise a hearing in the Benalla courthouse to deal with the death of Joe Byrne. It had been arranged so discreetly that even the regular court officials who should have been present were not told about it.

Not one of Melbourne's three morning newspapers was able to state precisely when the hearing had taken place. The *Age* recorded it had been held during the afternoon, the *Daily Telegraph* claimed it was in the evening and the *Argus* simply made no mention of the time at all. At Beechworth, where almost hourly reports were being sent to the *Ovens and Murray Advertiser* from Benalla, the paper could only report that it had been held in secret, with no attempt to name the time. Many years later Thomas McIntyre stated categorically that it had taken place at 9 am. Surrounded by the contents of his large file of newspaper clippings and numerous documents on the Kellys, it is highly likely he was correct given that he had taken part in the event itself. If so, it would appear Standish had organised a deliberate diversion to keep the hearing away from prying eyes, for at the very time the proceedings began, an extraordinary event was taking place not far away ...

Word had got round that some Melbourne photographers had managed to set up a unique snapshot opportunity. Newspapermen and townsfolk rushed to the police lock-up and court officials and police officers left their posts to join the throng. It was a sensational spectacle ensuring that if McIntyre's timing was correct, Standish had deftly managed to clear everyone away from the

Benalla courthouse apart from a fellow JP, three witnesses and Superintendent Sadleir. All participants were summarily pledged to secrecy.

The crowd gaped as the body of Joe Byrne, still officially in the police commissioner's custody, was unceremoniously carried from the police lock-up and strapped to one of the doors. It was a scene reminiscent of much earlier times, a throwback to the barbaric days in Tasmania when the severed heads and bodies of bushrangers were publicly displayed as a deterrent to criminals. It appeared the body was in much the same state as when it was recovered, but Kreitmayer's overnight ministrations would certainly have altered things somewhat. At the very least, the cast made of Byrne's head would have affected its coloration and in all probability the beard would also have been trimmed. According to the Waxworks' subsequent advertising, casts of the limbs were also made which would have required the removal of clothes, interfering with evidence that might otherwise have helped to determine precisely how Byrne died. In fact, there was no guarantee that the garments on the body were the clothes Joe Byrne was wearing when he died.

Still, that morning no one was questioning the legitimacy of the corpse they saw before them, and they set to work documenting the display. One bystander described how a photographer stepped forward to remove traces of smoke from the bushranger's face for a 'cleaner' picture. Witnesses affirmed later that Byrne's trousers bore signs of bloodstains – or at least some other 'dark substance', possibly a result of his bladder and/or bowels emptying after death – although the prints do not show this. Pictures taken that day record what is surely one of the most powerful photographic images to survive from the Kelly era: Byrne's puppet-like corpse roughly strung up for display before an ogling crowd. In 1880, as indeed today, such spectacles made great press ('If it bleeds, it leads', so the saying goes . . .).

When the reporters gathered around the body they were told

Strapped to a door, the body of Joe Byrne

a coronial inquest into the cause of Joe Byrne's death would be held the following morning. This was regular procedure and was already underway in Beechworth to investigate the death of Aaron Sherritt. It was also assumed that the proceedings would be presided over by Alfred Wyatt, the local Benalla police magistrate and chief judicial functionary in the area. But despite all of the commotion in Benalla, Wyatt had mysteriously left town that morning. During the night he had been in personal contact with Standish and was later reported to have signed a warrant that could be used to support Ned's removal to Melbourne. Wyatt never explained the 'pressing business' that took precedence over his legal responsibilities relating to the siege. The Kelly case was surely the highest priority judicial business in the colony.

Wyatt was a popular local figure, more fair-minded than many in his position, but he was nevertheless a servant of the government and personally responsible for his conduct to the chief secretary, who could have had him dismissed at will and without redress. Whether this had anything to do with his disappearance from Benalla we will never know, but his absence enabled Standish to carry out a scheme that came perilously close to circumventing the law.

For the hearing Standish enlisted the aid of the pompous and overbearing local dignitary, Robert McBean. Like Standish he was a justice of the peace, an honorary office that gave both of them much of the legal authority that could be exercised by police magistrates. He was also a close friend and ally of the police commissioner. McBean was a rich, successful winemaker who formerly had substantial grazing interests in the district. He had known Standish for years as a fellow member of the Melbourne Club and they had worked closely together in organising police efforts to combat horse and cattle stealing in the area.

McBean's personal acquaintance with the Kelly family dated back many years, with a particularly notable encounter a decade earlier. In 1870, McBean was robbed by a bushranger named Harry Power. Hovering in the background was the teenage Ned Kelly, acting as Power's so-called apprentice. After Ned was arrested McBean had refused to officially identify him, and so ensured that Ned would go free despite his obvious involvement in the hold-up. This earned McBean a reputation as a man of compassion who was prepared to give the young criminal a second chance. But there were those who believed he had allowed Ned to go free in return for information from one of the bushranger's relations that eventually led to Power's capture. Those even more cynically inclined said he had agreed to a deal to ensure the return of a valuable and treasured watch that was stolen in the raid. Whatever his past associations, by 1880 McBean was recognised as a sworn enemy of the Kellys. It was said he had rushed to Glenrowan the day before, armed to the teeth, ready to assist the police if necessary. For the rest of his days he boasted with pride of being present when the gang was taken.

McBean presided over the hearing with Standish sitting on the court bench beside him. It was technically legal as Victorian law allowed justices of the peace to hold inquiries into violent and unexplained deaths, but this could only occur when those vested with coronial functions, like Wyatt, were unavailable. Beyond that, it bore little resemblance to any normal coronial proceedings. Like others who had played a key role in the siege at Glenrowan, Senior Constable Kelly was shocked later to learn he had not been called as a witness.

First witness Thomas McIntyre briefly confirmed that Byrne had been one of the bushrangers at Stringybark Creek. Then a local constable identified Byrne as someone he had known for eight years. The third witness, Louis Piazzi, was a Glenrowan resident who had been one of the gang's hostages and might actually have been able to help explain how Byrne died. And yet on this day – his one and only court appearance – he was merely required to confirm that he had seen the dead bushranger in the Glenrowan Inn and was not questioned further. Superintendent Sadleir then read out details of the reward offered for the capture of the bushrangers, linking Byrne to the money that might be available to the police for their roles in destroying the gang at Glenrowan. Clearly he was not going to shed any light on the events.

There was no medical evidence produced on Byrne's cause of death, and no suggestion his body had been subject to an autopsy as the law normally required. McBean delivered the verdict a few minutes later. Without any reference to the circumstances surrounding Byrne's death, he declared the police had shot the bushranger 'whilst in the execution of their duty'. The verdict of justified homicide was passed down, enabling police officers to claim their share of the large reward offered for the bushrangers' apprehension.

Had there been any formal speculation as to the method by which the bushrangers met their deaths (possible suicide, for example) the central role of the police would have been considerably reduced, thus jeopardising the amount of reward money they would have been eligible to receive. As it was, Superintendent Hare received the largest portion, and men like Sadleir and Senior Constable Kelly shared lesser amounts along with several other members of the attacking force. Incidentally, the schoolteacher Thomas Curnow was also rewarded financially for his heroic action at Glenrowan. Funds were drawn from the official reward money to begin with and were later topped up by the government. McIntyre also had a sum added to his pension, though it was not drawn from the reward money because he did not take part in the siege itself.

Formalities over, the way was clear for the authorities to deal with the outlaw Joe Byrne's remains however they deemed fit, and nothing – legally – could stop them.

'So quietly was the whole affair disposed of that no one was made aware of it', the *Argus* told its readers. The *Age* declared: 'The proceedings were completed so quietly, so quietly in fact that no one knew of the affair until it was over'. The *Daily Telegraph* conjectured that Byrne's body might be decomposing rapidly, which had forced the inquiry to be arranged hastily. No mention was made of the fact that the body of Martin Cherry was not subject to the same urgent inquiry, even though it had been pulled from the Glenrowan Inn at the same time. Nor did the paper point out that Byrne's body had been kept in an unheated cell all night which would have delayed decomposition or that it was common practice for bodies subject to coronial inquiries to be left unburied for forty-eight hours as the inquest on Aaron Sherritt had shown.

Given the way the brotherhood of journalists had been duped, it is not surprising that the mystery surrounding the hearing then immediately disappeared from public view. Outfoxed and out-manoeuvred by Standish, McBean and Sadleir, the reporters' failure to know about the hearing was an adverse reflection on their professional abilities and something to be glossed over as quickly as possible. And so it has remained for a more than a century.

Not only had Standish and McBean dismissed any further

investigation into Joe Byrne's death, they had also succeeded in heading off what was promising to be a major public conflagration about the role of the police at Glenrowan. Within hours of the siege, the people of Benalla were voicing their discontent at the way the police had behaved. One by one, a litany of serious allegations were levelled at them and were soon being talked of throughout the colony. Most prominent amongst them was the belief that unnecessary risks had been imposed on the hostages in the police attacks on the Glenrowan Inn. This had culminated in the death of Martin Cherry and the mortal wounding of one of the child hostages (thirteen-year-old John Jones, the son of the inn's licensee), both of whom were killed by police bullets.

There were also strong intimations that the police had shown cowardice by setting fire to the Glenrowan Inn instead of charging it much earlier, particularly as the exchange of fire between the police and the bushrangers had long ceased. The hearing ensured that none of this would appear on official court records, decreasing the possibility that Superintendent Hare and other police officers could be indicted for crimes arising from the Glenrowan siege.

This questionable behaviour continued when, the day after the Police Commissioner left Benalla, Robert McBean sat alone in a 'magisterial inquiry' to investigate the death of Martin Cherry. With magistrate Wyatt still inexplicably absent, there was no regular coronial inquest, and certainly no jury like the one at Beechworth. The only evidence came from fellow hostage Constable Hugh Bracken, who had escaped from the bushrangers while Cherry was still unharmed, before Hare and the other police had even attacked the hotel.

The rest of the evidence McBean received was quite formal, comprising details of the identification of the deceased railway platelayer and a report on his wounding by Dr Nicholson. This was followed by evidence from Superintendent Sadleir, who said that after learning Cherry had been wounded, he tried to stop the police firing at the kitchen where the platelayer was located. This time McBean went even further than he and Standish had done the day before in exonerating those who had besieged the Glenrowan Inn. Now, it was not merely the police who were wholly justified in the attack on the inn. In addition, he ruled that any others who participated actively in the siege (this may have included himself) were also to be exempted from legal responsibility.

There's no doubt that had the normal sequence of legal proceedings been followed, the coronial inquiry into the death of Joe Byrne would have been rather different. First and foremost, it would have passed entirely out of the hands of the police and McBean and been presided over by Alfred Wyatt. But even he would not necessarily have had the final say in the delivery of any decisions arising from the events at Glenrowan. As the law operated at the time, local juries were quite regularly empanelled to participate in coronial proceedings, often taking a very active part in them. They were permitted to question witnesses themselves. They could also exercise their own discretion in recommending whether an individual – police officer or civilian alike – should be charged with criminal offences arising from events like Glenrowan.

A prime example of this occurred on the day of the Glenrowan siege when William Foster, who was the local police magistrate at Beechworth acting as coroner, had launched a regular coronial investigation into the killing of Aaron Sherritt. He conscientiously visited the scene of Sherritt's death, empanelled a jury of twelve to assist him, and had a full autopsy carried out on the deceased's body. During the following proceedings police officers were questioned by members of the jury. This revealed just how ineffective the officers hiding out at the Sherritt home had been. Chief among their failings was that it had taken several hours for one of them to pluck up enough courage to ride to Beechworth and raise the alarm. One juror suggested that the proceedings could not be complete without calling Ned Kelly as a witness because he was 'implicated in the matter to some extent'. William Foster did not deem this inappropriate, but under the circumstances (presumably with Ned's injuries and his recent removal to Melbourne in mind), he ruled that it was not a sufficient reason to delay the inquest's findings that Aaron Sherritt had been murdered by Joe Byrne, aided and abetted by Dan Kelly.

Another fine example was the official inquiry held on Wednesday 30 June at the Wangaratta hospital by Justice of the Peace Alex Tobin. John Jones was rushed there for treatment after being released from the Glenrowan Inn, and subsequently died. At the inquest, the dead youth's mother and sister described in graphic detail the terror among the hostages as Superintendent Hare bombarded the inn with scant regard for the safety of those held inside. She testified that after her son was wounded she had shouted to the police outside that he had been shot, but they did not hold their fire and she and her family were only able to leave the inn some time later, when the bushrangers gave her permission. Alex Tobin refused to state that police actions at the siege had been justified. All he was prepared to hold was that John Jones had died as a result of a wound inflicted on him by shots fired from outside the inn.

The Standish/McBean hearing effectively suppressed any chance of us knowing the truth of Joe Byrne's final hours. It has always been assumed that he died as a result of a wound from a stray bullet while he was standing at the bar. This is probably correct but in the absence of a proper autopsy it was never confirmed. Nor was any mention made by the police of a small brown packet labelled 'Poison' that the *Argus*, and later the *Australasian Sketcher*, reported was found in one of his pockets when his body was dragged from the burning hotel. No official reference was made to whether the packet had been opened, which would have suggested that Joe committed suicide, as both Dan Kelly and Steve Hart may well have done. For the police, evidence like this would have detracted from their victory and endangered their chances of collecting the reward.

Many years afterwards Sadleir stated categorically that Byrne had died not long before 6 am, when a 'chance bullet struck him in the groin'. However, hostages interviewed about Byrne in the immediate aftermath of the siege claimed he died later. As the *Australasian Sketcher* reported: 'Some say he fell at daylight, others that it was about 9 o'clock in the morning'.

The day after the hearing there were wildly conflicting reports about what had happened to the body. The *Age* and the *Argus* claimed it had been handed over to his relations for burial. The *Daily Telegraph* provided a substantially different account, saying that after dark, Byrne's body was 'stripped, wrapped in canvas, placed in a roughly made coffin'. It was then 'taken in a conveyance to the cemetery, where a grave had been prepared in the paupers' portion of the ground' and where 'the only witness of the scene was a constable who merely went officially, in order to prove the burial'.

Once more, it seemed, newspaper reporters were successfully kept at bay as the bushranger's body was disposed of. Thomas McIntyre, who was still in town at the time, recorded that Byrne was privately buried in the Benalla cemetery by police on the same day as the secret court hearing at approximately 4 pm. The official record of his interment was signed later by Robert McBean, who entered the bushranger's occupation simply as 'Outlaw'.

Surrounding evidence indicates the burial was a premeditated act by the police commissioner, who was fully aware that he was in breach of the law. That afternoon he received a reply to the telegraph message he had sent to his legal contact in Melbourne about the disposal of Byrne's remains. It came from the rarely used and therefore secure Eastern Market Telegraph Office in Melbourne and stated unequivocally: 'If identity established neither Police nor Government can retain body, if no one comes forward to ask for body Police should deal with it as in all cases where they have unclaimed body'. As friends of the dead bushranger clamoured at the Benalla police station for his remains to be released to them,

Standish had the corpse spirited away and buried in an unmarked pauper's grave.

Had the corpse of Joe Byrne not been displayed so publicly and recognised by so many, this secret burial may have encouraged the belief among a number of present-day northeastern Victorians that he actually survived the siege and that another body was substituted by the police. Joe was the only gang member who had been specially targeted as a potential collaborator, and it was believed he was offered a free passage to the United States and a substantial monetary reward if he betrayed his companions. Thomas McIntyre recorded: 'There were overtures made to him offering him a reward and a free passage to America if he would betray his mates. These overtures he rejected.' Whatever his motivation for turning down the offer, Joe Byrne was no turncoat. There was a special empathy between him and the bushranger he called 'Neddie'. McIntyre went on to say that although Byrne was 'a nervous man, Kelly seems to have had great confidence in his bravery and devotion to him, and they frequently rode out at night together'.

With the disposal of Byrne's body, Standish was finally free to make his way back to Melbourne. If he was at all uneasy about his transgressions he certainly didn't show it. He caught the evening train to the Victorian capital secure in the knowledge that he had forestalled any attempts to criticise the police for their actions at Glenrowan and kept public attention centred on what he saw as the 'villainy' of Ned Kelly. He left behind him an unclothed body in an unmarked grave in a remote corner of the Benalla cemetery, and a host of baffling questions that remain unanswered to the present day.

On the afternoon of Tuesday 29 June, roughly two thousand people congregated at the Spencer Street railway station in the belief that it was here Ned Kelly would enter the city. Some spectators even hired drays along the street with the intention of standing on them for a better view. But less than a mile away, excited shouts were drawing hundreds to the North Melbourne station, where Ned was hurriedly offloaded and transferred to a horse-drawn wagon. 'Half a dozen or more women were observed weeping, some very bitterly, and sobbing out "Poor Fellow"', described the *Herald*, though the majority appeared to be hostile to the bushranger. Although the crowd at Spencer Street was deeply disappointed when Ned did not appear upon the train's arrival, there were resounding cheers when Superintendent Hare disembarked and he received a round of applause as he was driven away.

Half an hour later across town, about five hundred people watched the carriage enter the main gate of Melbourne Gaol, surrounded by a detachment of police. Some half-hearted cheering erupted as Ned was whisked inside the grim bluestone walls, but it was unclear whether this was for the bushranger or for the policemen escorting him.

Whilst Ned Kelly prepared to spend his first evening in Melbourne Gaol, the biggest public event of the day was being held a few streets away. More than three thousand people were packed into the Melbourne Town Hall to celebrate the establishment of England's first Protestant Sunday School a century earlier. It was a significant meeting, a fact confirmed by the presence of the chief justice of Victoria, Sir William Stawell, and a range of other civic and political dignitaries including one of the colony's longest serving premiers. As for the rest, it was a diverse crowd representing all classes and local-ities, from the stately tree-lined avenues of prosperous Toorak to the crowded backstreet slums of the inner city. Despite the theological differences that divided many Protestant congregations, the meeting was a symbol of attitudes and activities that could actually bring them together – a united, powerful and strongly influential force.

By 1880 Protestants outnumbered Roman Catholics almost two to one in Victoria, and they owned the vast majority of the colony's almost four thousand churches. From their richly endowed religious establishments on upper Collins Street to the humble wattle and daub huts they used for their services in some of the most isolated parts of the colony, there were emanations of political and social influences that were enormously significant in the ordering of the colony's affairs.

In the previous decade, militant Protestant churchmen had been successful torchbearers for change in the colony. Railway officials were severely castigated for their actions when they dared to permit a special train for use on a Sunday workers' picnic. It was also decided the 'Continental Sunday', as they vilified it, was not to be allowed in Victoria, and they demanded the closure of all places of public entertainment and hotel bars on the Sabbath. Even the use of children's playgrounds was on their list of unacceptable Sunday activities. But the Protestant conscience had gone well beyond merely guarding the sanctity of the Sabbath, and by the 1880s it encompassed attitudes on a much broader spectrum of public issues. For example, the consumption of alcohol was regarded as a great social evil. Young church members were vigorously canvassed to sign the pledge to abstain, at least until they were twenty-one, and they were warned they could risk eternal damnation if they succumbed to its influences.

Long before his capture at Glenrowan, Ned and members of his family had been classified as ones who had 'fallen'. One local newspaper stated that a root cause of the bushrangers' infamy lay in their addiction to the 'demon drink'. According to the *Benalla Standard*, the Kelly brothers had no capacity to distinguish between right and wrong and had led a 'depraved and vicious life' which could at least in part be traced to the 'intemperate' drinking 'customs' which had led them to 'lawlessness and contempt for all constituted authority'.

James Moorhouse, the Church of England Bishop of Melbourne, was a great believer in the notion that idleness and crime were major sins and deserved the opprobrium of the community. An accomplished, energetic and popular orator, he was never one to hold back in his vigorous condemnation of what he considered to be sinful. His only apparent vice was that he smoked his beloved pipes in public – a habit the more puritanical members of the church frowned upon.

That Tuesday night in June 1880, Moorhouse mounted the podium at the Town Hall meeting to a burst of enthusiastic applause. Although he never mentioned the bushranger by name, it was clear his speech, frequently punctuated by spontaneous cheers and clapping from the audience, was a decisive condemnation of Ned. He declared the rising generation of criminals in the colony lacked even the semblance of a moral conscience and the time had come for far greater indignation to be directed at crime and criminals: 'Sentiment there was, but too often it was enlisted on the side of the criminal,' he boomed theatrically and was met with thunderous approval from all sections of the crowd.

It was a rallying cry that was not lost on his listeners. In the following weeks it would be one of their chief topics of conversation at the hundreds of tea meetings that characterised their community life. Organised by churches across Victoria, these gatherings were the social highlights of the week for many of the faithful. They were modest occasions where volunteers served sandwiches and cakes, accompanied by heavily watered non-alcoholic beverages and, of course, oceans of tea. In their own way they played a substantial role in marshalling opinion on a variety of issues. Amidst the clattering of cups and saucers the conversation would be laced with pressing moral questions and, particularly after Moorhouse's tirade, intense speculation about the bushranger. Some Protestants considered that their deity preached forgiveness for all souls, and they frowned upon the imposition of the death penalty. At the same time they had to acknowledge that, according to the scriptures, the laws of a state that decreed capital punishment should be obeyed under all circumstances. But those reared in the shadow of the Old Testament favoured by many of their preachers believed in an eye for an eye and a life for a life.

For the one-third of the colony's population who were Roman Catholics (the bulk of them of Irish ancestry), the divisions between themselves and the Protestant majority were bitter and longstanding. In its simplest form this was demonstrated in the fact that they were not permitted to belong to such institutions as the Melbourne Club and the Stock Exchange. Preference was also given to Protestants as the top officers in the Victoria Police, while many in the ranks were Roman Catholics. Most of all, the exclusion of state aid for church-run schools had created a deep-seated source of rancour that spilt over into local political life.

The split between these two religious communities, however, had been overcome in some quarters. In the past Roman Catholics and Protestants had joined together on a number of moral issues such as opposition to the excessive use of alcohol. And on a wider scale, their commonality could be seen in the fact that many small landholders of opposing religious denominations worked side by side to create a livelihood for themselves and their families. Together they seized the opportunity to possess land as a tangible sign of the personal security that had been denied to their ancestors in Britain. They shared collectively and harmoniously the good and the bad that followed them from one season to the next, regardless of faith.

In much the same way, within days of the killings at Stringybark Creek religious differences were thrust aside as Protestants and Roman Catholics united in their condemnation of the Kelly gang. The fact that Ned and Dan (the only two bush-rangers positively identified at the time of the killings) were known to be Roman Catholics carried no weight whatsoever. The outrage crossed all religious divides, and was poignantly symbolised at the Mansfield funeral of Sergeant Michael Kennedy, a devout Catholic. That day the town turned out en masse to watch silently as his coffin was solemnly borne to the local cemetery. In an unprecedented sign of solidarity, it was led by a Roman Catholic priest and the local Anglican minister, with Bishop Moorhouse between them and the local Presbyterian clergyman not far behind. The bishop's wife personally made the wreath that Kennedy's widow laid upon his coffin.

The next day the leading Roman Catholic newspaper in the colony, the *Advocate*, made it abundantly clear this was not to be an isolated phenomenon. Allying with its Protestant contemporaries, the paper declared that the killings at Stringybark Creek had been 'willful' and 'unprovoked' and that the officers had been 'mercilessly shot down'. 'Not a city or town in the colony would not have fur-nished volunteers to capture the miscreants. If general assistance of that kind had been required.' In some of the first reports of the police deaths it was claimed that two of the dead officers were likely to have been related to Roman Catholic priests in the colony. A week later the *Advocate* admitted the statement was incorrect but that the priest most commonly believed to be related to one of the victims had praised all of them as 'right brave fellows' and had openly declared he 'would have been proud to be one of their relatives'.

As the Protestant audience from the celebration at the Town Hall spilled out into the frosty winter night, a far more exclusive event was taking place at a fashionable restaurant just half a block away down Collins Street. Instead of the raspberry vinegar (cordial) available at the Town Hall, an array of fine alcoholic beverages was being laid out for the diners. Selected members of the Robert Service government had come together for a special meeting at Gunsler's restaurant (later the site of the Hotel Australia and now an up-market shopping plaza).

Premier Service was already lauding Robert Ramsay as the man who had caught Ned Kelly, a claim he would repeat over and over in his election speeches as proof of the superiority of his party. After the previous government's resounding failure, they had succeeded in routing the gang in less than three months. Even the *Age*, the Service government's most persistent critic, joined Melbourne's other newspapers in praising the chief secretary, with reflected glory for his fellow party members.

Along with his colleagues' heartiest congratulations Ramsay was also being commended for his worthy actions that day in relation to an unsung hero of the siege. For it was Ramsay who recognised that the lame schoolteacher, Thomas Curnow, had displayed selfless bravery at Glenrowan and he had taken it upon himself to launch a mini-crusade ensuring the courageous act of this modest man was brought to public attention. Curnow was one of the gang's first hostages when they took over the inn. He was horrified by Ned's callousness when he boasted about the helpless victims who would be trapped on the railway tracks that had recently been sabotaged. Taking advantage of Ned's jovial mood, Curnow talked the bushranger into allowing him to return home with his family.

It was then that Curnow improvised the signal which was seen by the crew of the pilot engine preceding the special train and they braked just in time to avert a catastrophe. Curnow was one of the few genuine heroes of Glenrowan. Ramsay knew that Curnow's life could be in grave danger if he remained at his post with disgruntled Kelly supporters all around. As minister of education (as well as chief secretary) he ordered the teacher and his family's immediate removal to Melbourne where he planned to commend him personally.

For the moment, Ramsay had to turn his attention to matters of a more party political nature as he joined his colleagues in the sumptuous atmosphere of Gunsler's. A few hours earlier the governor had formally proclaimed a new election would be held in fifteen days. Planning their campaign was a top priority but, as at the Town Hall meeting, the topic of the bushranger's capture dominated the conversation. In an age when loyalties to political groupings were still fluid, cabinet solidarity could never be guaranteed. Nevertheless, there was a firm consensus among Service and his colleagues that the bushranger deserved to end his life on the gallows.

One prominent member of the Service government with impeccable Roman Catholic and Irish connections was John Gavan Duffy, the minister for agriculture. His father, Charles Gavan Duffy, had been one of the leaders of an open revolt against British rule in Ireland in 1848 and only just escaped a conviction for treason. Later he became premier of Victoria for a time. His son typified the way the political leaders of the Irish-Catholic community in Victoria had forsworn the Kellys once they learned of the killings at Stringybark Creek, and he lent his full support to the legislation that outlawed the gang. He was joined in this by several other prominent Irish-Catholics, among them Peter Lalor, the much revered leader of the armed revolt against British colonial policies at the Eureka Stockade in 1854. Another was John O'Shannassy, a former Victorian premier who bore the title 'Sir' because he was a baronet as well as a papal knight. The majority of the local Roman Catholic hierarchy joined them in not showing even the slightest hint of support or sympathy for the condemned man.

Besides, the Kellys had ceased to be identified with a traditional creed. At Benalla there were those who maintained Ned's immediate clan could no longer be said to have any relationship with Roman Catholicism at all. A primitive Methodist clergyman performed his mother's second marriage and his grandfather, John Quinn, was buried without any church rites at all. As for the members of the Kelly gang, they had not been noted for attending religious services. Locally it was assumed they had no interest whatsoever in churchgoing and the responsibilities it engendered.

While they were waiting for the return of his fellow officers at Stringybark Creek, Thomas McIntyre asked Ned to show mercy to Kennedy and Scanlan on the basis of their Irish birth. 'I told him that they were both countrymen and co-religionists of his own.' He knew that Ned had been born in Australia but said, 'I thought he might be possessed of some of that patriotic-religious feeling which is such a bond of sympathy amongst the Irish people'. Ned was unmoved by his argument. 'My opinion is that he possessed none of this feeling', McIntyre said later. 'On the question of religion I believe he was apathetic.'

Anti-Kelly sentiment also found strong echoes within the Service government's political opposition. When he led the government two years earlier, Premier Graham Berry was responsible for branding the bushrangers as outlaws and had lavished enormous funds on the Kelly hunt. Even the so-called 'advanced liberals' in his ranks had shown little sympathy for Ned.

At least in part, the former government's failure to end the gang's reign had hinged on its weakness in allowing police commissioner Standish to run the hunt. It would appear that Service and Ramsay had recognised this fact in curbing Standish's powers immediately upon taking office. The murky relationship between the Berry government and the police commissioner made it unlikely that any of the former premier's key supporters would speak out against Ramsay's methods of dealing with Ned, particularly with an election in the offing.

11 | WORDS AS WEAPONS

By 1880 Victoria's literacy rate was amongst the highest in the world. The per capita sales of newspapers and journals in the colony were probably as great, if not greater, than anywhere else in the world, including the grand cities of London and New York. Words and pictures were reaching a mass audience for the first time. It was an era when a publication like the *Age* – the largest circulating newspaper in the colony by far, selling around thirty thousand copies a day – could make and break governments. The dour Scots-born proprietor David Syme was widely referred to as 'King David' by friend and foe alike.

The coming of the electric telegraph along with significant technical advances in newspaper production brought a greater sense of immediacy to such events as the Glenrowan siege and resulted in far greater community involvement. Although no strict audits were carried out, it is estimated that Melbourne's *Herald* published more than one hundred and ten thousand copies of the special editions on the day of Ned's capture, about three times its normal daily sales at the time. In addition, there were many thousands of copies of multiple special editions produced by the city's three other daily newspapers, and more again in country and regional centres.

Another powerful influence in print had recently emerged which was also doing much to mould public attitudes. For technical and traditional reasons, the ordinary newspapers did not have illustrations to accompany reported events. The void was now being filled by special journals featuring graphic illustrations. Across the board it was claimed the pictures they printed were fair depictions and, indeed, sometimes this was so, but all too often illustrators owed their work more to artistic licence and a vivid imagination than truth. In most cases they never went near the scenes they portrayed, but the public was not to know this and the popularity of pictorials soared.

As a rule the leading newspapers were in constant conflict with each other, violently disagreeing on political, economic, religious and social issues, giving no quarter and expecting none in return. The *Age* was regarded as a 'liberal' morning newspaper, a workingman's bible that fought for the protection of local industries and the improvement of workers' conditions. It championed democratic reforms seeking to diminish the hold of the rich country landowning classes and their allies who controlled the upper house of the colonial legislature.

Whilst a copy of the *Age* cost a single penny, the *Argus,* which was regarded as one of the best-produced newspapers of its time, cost three times as much. Deeply conservative, its circulation was less than half that of the *Age*. It was seen to reflect the concerns of the elite professional classes and represented rural and merchant interests wanting free trade with other countries at the expense of local industries.

Like the *Age*, the *Herald* had a liberal bent, but focused much more on sporting coverage (especially racing), and had a reputation for representing Roman Catholic interests more than any other paper in the colony. In contrast, the *Daily Telegraph* had a more Protestant outlook. A morning paper, it was conservative like the *Argus* but was much cheaper, selling for a penny a copy.

Ordinarily, the four publications offered very different opinions on current issues. Their treatment of Ned, however, proved to be a special exception. With rare unanimity he was portrayed by every one of them as a dangerous public enemy from the moment reports of the police killings at Stringybark Creek came in. The *Argus* pronounced the killing of the three police officers 'a premeditated and atrocious crime'. According to its great rival the *Age*, the police deaths were 'horrible deeds' carried out by 'assassins' who had to be captured 'dead or alive'. The *Herald* referred to the gang as 'demons' already guilty of 'a most dastardly offence' and praised the act by the colonial legislature that had made them outlaws so that they could be 'shot down like dogs, wherever or whenever met with' for they 'had forfeited all claim to be human'. To the *Telegraph*, they were 'miscreants', 'ruffians' and 'bloodthirsty wretches'.

In a special feature the *Age* devoted almost three columns to the 'History of the Kelly Family', claiming they were 'a source of danger and terror to the surrounding country', living 'like savages and brigands'. Even the 'blackest iniquities' of other bushrangers could be 'scarcely paralleled' to those of the Kelly gang. And in the months that followed there was to be no respite as the papers relentlessly attacked the fugitive outlaws at every opportunity.

One of the most significant stories that the media focused on was the raising of subscriptions for a memorial to the dead police officers at Mansfield. Three weeks before Glenrowan, the *Australasian* – one of the largest circulating weeklies in Australia – recalled the death of Sergeant Michael Kennedy, adding a new, and entirely fanciful, dimension to the now infamous tale. It claimed that for some time the gang kept the wounded sergeant alive and suffering in agony so that they 'might learn from him how to work his Spencer rifle'. Only when Ned was satisfied had he 'shot him through the breast', finally ending his misery.

This was but a prelude to the far more devastating attacks on the bushranger in the immediate aftermath of the Glenrowan siege, elevating him to a new level of infamy. With one voice the press rose up and condemned the leader of the Kelly gang. Reporters and editorial writers openly vied with each other for the most vituperative words and phrases to describe Ned and his companions. The *Argus* cast its normally high-mannered tones aside, describing the gang as 'Men Wolves' and 'cut-throats'. To the *Age* they were 'desperadoes' and 'cold blooded'; to the *Daily Telegraph* they were 'blood-stained villains'. An article in the Methodist weekly *Spectator* described the routing of the gang in terms of an elemental battle between good and evil. It concluded that the bushrangers had carried out 'an accumulation of outrages against divine and human law' and in the inferno of the Glenrowan Inn had 'met their proper and just retribution'.

The killing of Aaron Sherritt was singled out as more than just a vengeful act against a traitor. It was 'as diabolical as any' aimed at producing 'terrorism in the district' said the *Argus*. The *Age* agreed, asserting that, 'The cold-blooded murder of Sherritt was committed solely with a view of striking terror into all who had the hardihood to endeavour to trace them'.

There was a steady stream of grim speculations as to what might have been had the gang's attempt to derail a police train succeeded. The *Argus* called it a 'wicked mischief' when they had planned to take 'thirty or forty lives at a blow', whilst the *Daily Telegraph* proclaimed it a 'demoniacal project' of 'hellish design'. One (anonymous) newspaperman dramatically recalled the moment the special train was stopped just short of Glenrowan, describing how the journalists barricaded the windows of their compartment with cushions and waited in silent terror for the next move: 'We had no arms except one little revolver, and the carriage doors were locked, so that if the Kellys had descended on the train at that time they could have shot us all without any chance of our escape'. After Glenrowan this same journalist referred to the three dead bushrangers 'as cold blooded murderers as ever walked the earth since the days of Cain'. He wholeheartedly applauded their demise, delighted that at last they 'had expiated their crimes on a fiery altar'. As for Ned, he was merely 'lying waiting for the rope to be put round his neck'.

Many other journalists throughout the colonies openly canvassed the necessity for a hanging: 'The only pity is that so many of the gang have escaped the halter, which was their proper doom', but hopefully Ned would survive his wounds 'to expiate his crime on the gallows' intoned the *Argus*. The *Age* declared it wholly just that the ringleader of the gang 'should remain alive to suffer the ignominy of a criminal death' and the *Herald* welcomed 'the suffering and miserable death Ned Kelly has to meet'.

In Adelaide the *Express* and *Telegraph* considered the only certainty about Ned's fate was 'whether he will die of his wounds or recover to perish on the gallows'. In Sydney, the *Bulletin* newspaper founded just a few months earlier added its own unequivocal voice to the demand that Ned be hanged. Normally opposed to capital punishment, and a champion of those mistreated by governments and courts, it had a dramatic shift in attitude when it came to Ned Kelly, whose life 'should be taken coolly with the stern relentlessness of that justice which never dies'.

Such attitudes were not confined to the editorial columns but spilled over into ordinary reporting of the actual events. One Melbourne newspaperman was so biased he felt no qualms in proudly stating that he had personally taken part in the assault on the Glenrowan Inn. After the hostages had been released, he wrote, 'the police commenced to rake the hotel in which I joined . . . From east, west, north and south we poured in volley after volley.'

Although significantly more expensive than ordinary newspapers, pictorial journals had many more readers than sales. It was common practice for purchasers to hand on their copy to others who in turn passed them on, so circulation was high even if profits weren't. What's more, certain editions would be kept for weeks and even months afterwards, much like special souvenir editions today.

But all too often the artists who prepared the featured woodcuts produced grave distortions and even blatant fabrications in their coverage of events.

After Glenrowan one of the worst offenders was the fortnightly *Australasian Sketcher*, the largest-selling Australian pictorial journal at the time. Echoing the conservatism of its parent newspaper the *Argus*, the *Sketcher* found a willing, well-practised exponent of its causes in Thomas Carrington, the artist who was chiefly responsible for the pictorial coverage of the Glenrowan siege and its immediate aftermath. Carrington had a distinct advantage in that alone of all the pictorial journal artists he was specially favoured with a place on the train that carried O'Connor and his Queensland police contingent to Glenrowan. Other artists – like Julian Ashton, who went on to much greater fame than Carrington – did not arrive at Glenrowan until much later. In this way the *Sketcher* artist was able to set the tone of all pictorial representations of the siege.

Five days after Glenrowan the *Sketcher* appeared with its entire front page devoted to a Carrington woodcut of Ned in his armour. Titled 'Ned Kelly at Bay' it showed him as a monstrous figure with his outstretched right hand brandishing a smoking pistol aimed at the police advancing upon him – defiant, unrepentant, murderous to the last. (Ironically, more than a century later this same drawing and its derivatives are used to emphasise the heroic nature of the bushranger's last stand.) In reality, the overwhelming weight of evidence shows that Ned's appearance outside Glenrowan Inn was not like this at all, despite Carrington's claim that his woodcut was made accurately from a 'sketch drawn on the spot'. In sworn evidence, a police officer standing nearby was adamant that when Ned appeared he was obviously 'more dead than alive'. According to Constable James Arthur, the bushranger did not stride boldly but staggered along, utterly incapable of aiming his pistol.

The most serious indictment of Carrington's misrepresentation came from Dr John Nicholson, the Benalla doctor who had accompanied police reinforcements to Glenrowan. Carrington's woodcut and several written reports implied that Ned had carried on a fierce exchange of murderous gunfire with the police (it shows glimpses of officers firing at Ned). Nicholson, however, who was not far away, could only recall seeing Ned fire a pistol 'two or three times'. Furthermore, his detailed medical examination of the stricken bushranger confirmed there was a wound on his right hand and more on his left arm, making it impossible for Ned to aim the weapon. He found no reason to disbelieve Ned when he said these had been inflicted much earlier, at the time of the first police assault on the Glenrowan Inn.

In the next edition the *Sketcher* again featured a full cover page woodcut on the Kelly saga. Since the last issue there had been reports of the possibility of a new bushranging outbreak in Victoria's northeast, led by members of the Kelly family or their associates. These allegations were largely, if not entirely, unsubstantiated – the products of gossip, rumour and, more disturbingly, the flights of imagination of part-time newspaper correspondents who were paid by results (a penny or thereabouts for every line published). The *Sketcher*'s illustration, titled 'Wake at Greta', purported to show the scene at Maggie Skillion's hut soon after the Glenrowan siege. Standing before the charred remains of Dan Kelly and Steve Hart, surrounded by votive candles, Ned's acolytes (resembling Tom Lloyd and Ned's sisters, among others) swear vengeance against their enemies. The priestly figure of a man towers above the corpses with his right hand raised as if invoking some elemental force.

An explosive image indeed, but of course there was absolutely no proof that such a scene actually occurred. Certainly there was much grieving at Maggie Skillion's home, mingled no doubt with anger and talk of revenge in the hours immediately following the siege. But the wake was an intensely private gathering, limited to family members and their very closest and most sympathetic

'Wake at Greta' from the Australasian Sketcher

associates. Not even local newspaper reporters were present, let
alone any representative of the *Australasian Sketcher.*

The *Sketcher's* chief rival at the time in Victoria was the
Illustrated Australian News, another fortnightly, published by David
Syme. Its artists, too, could manufacture illusion, but at least in the
case of Glenrowan they showed a little more respect for the facts

than Thomas Carrington. Syme's journal had no qualms in attaching an evil, other-worldly quality to its illustration of the bushranger's dawn advance through the trees. Larger than life, he looms like a darkly cloaked and helmeted monster, a yesteryear Darth Vadar. Quoting the *Age* in its caption the journal called Ned Kelly a 'fiend' who had laughed 'derisively' as shots ricocheted off his armour.

Yet compared to the *Sketcher*, the *Australian Illustrated News* did at least try to stick closer to the visual facts. Ned was depicted holding his pistol awkwardly askew in his left hand (his right was useless by this stage) with the barrel pointing to the sky, not at those pictured advancing on him. The whole effect was far less threatening, as was indeed the case. It confirmed that Ned had physically reached the end of his tether and that this final confrontation with the police had been a far more one-sided affair than the newspapers and other illustrated journals were acknowledging. It was but a small break in the ranks of the mighty print force ranged against him. As Ned himself continued to regain strength and spirit in his isolated prison cell, the power of his opponents increased by the day, fuelled by a relentless outpouring of words and pictures clamouring for his execution.

12 | OUTLAW NO MORE

Sometime before Aaron Sherritt was killed and Ned Kelly was riding towards Glenrowan, the governor of Victoria, Sir George Bowen, signed an official proclamation in Melbourne that closed the current session of parliament. Constitutionally, the event was of passing significance. In the immediate aftermath of the defeat of the Service government on Friday morning in the Legislative Assembly, the main opposition party led by the former premier, Graham Berry, believed it would be called on by the governor to take over the reins of government in the next few days. Then, quite unexpectedly, the governor agreed to call the poll for the new Assembly. Though the legislature was still in session there were rumblings abroad that the former premier might seek to reverse the decision when parliament met again the following week. To forestall this, the governor closed down the existing session of the legislature on the Saturday morning, pending official arrangements for the poll. Presumably, parliament could then be called at a future date. Nobody perceived for the moment that this had dramatically altered the legal status of the Kelly gang.

Once Ned Kelly had been captured, it was universally believed that because of the special outlawry act, he would be executed without an ordinary criminal trial. There were no official denials suggesting otherwise and the rumours raged unchecked as journals and newspapers promoted the idea that hanging was a foregone conclusion. The fact that it appears no one was aware of the shift in status is demonstrated again and again in the conduct and behaviour of all those connected to the Glenrowan siege and its aftermath. When Ned collapsed for the last time outside the inn at Glenrowan, an officer moved in the moment his helmet was removed and 'put his revolver to his head' intending to execute the outlaw on the spot (as the act allowed). Senior Constable Kelly apparently pushed away the would-be killer's hand, probably taking pity on the fallen bushranger as he shouted, 'Don't shoot me; let me see it out, let me see it out!'

Years later Superintendent Sadleir justified the release of Dan Kelly and Steve Hart's bodies because of the abnormal legal situation created by the act. As 'wild animals' the deceased were no longer recognised to be legal persons and their bodies did not need to be the subject of the usual inquests, so their relatives could dispose of the remains as they saw fit. Standish and McBean similarly justified the swift hearing into Joe Byrne's death and subsequent disposal of his body on the basis of the bushrangers' outlawry. The morning after the body of Joe Byrne had been hastily buried, Robert McBean affixed his signature to the official notification of the bushranger's death. Unaware of the shift in status the previous Saturday, he wrote in his bold copybook hand, the word 'Outlaw' in the space allocated for the bushranger's occupation.

Robert Ramsay warily admitted later that he authorised the dispatch of artillery to Glenrowan on the basis of the act. This was normally legally inappropriate except under 'special circumstances'. With the understanding that Kelly was still an outlaw he was also able to remove Ned to the capital without a court order. And the bushranger himself had no reason to believe otherwise. During his train journey to the capital, the doors to his van were flung open at station after station and crowds on the platform pressed forward to gape, the general consensus being that this would be their last chance to see the notorious criminal alive. When the train stopped at Beveridge, about thirty-eight kilometres from Melbourne, he leaned forward and peered out of the van, remarking to the officer in charge: 'Look across there to the left . . . Do you see a little hill there?' The officer nodded. 'That was where I was born twenty-eight years ago. Now I am passing through it I suppose to my doom.' (Official records state that Ned was twenty-five at the time of his capture. This statement adds to the Kelly family's assertion that Ned was, in fact, three years older than was commonly believed.)

But everything had changed with the closing of parliament, which meant the outlawry act was no longer in force. The reason for this was plain enough, though overlooked by many. Because of the way it intruded on traditional civil liberties, the act had always been of temporary duration, intended to remain in force just so long as it could be used against the Kellys. Most were under the impression that the destruction of the gang was imminent, but as the hunt went from weeks to months, the statute's life had to be extended. In December 1879 it was kept in force until the end of the next session of parliament. When the governor prematurely shut down this session, the statute automatically ceased operation and, with the stroke of a pen, the bushrangers were no longer outlaws.

No official record exists as to who first spotted the lapse. There is little doubt it would have been someone in parliament that day who then passed the information on. When the news reached the Treasury building, initial surprise swiftly turned into growing alarm as the potential consequences of the cessation of the bushrangers' outlawry came under scrutiny by top governmental lawyers. In short, Ned could no longer be hanged as an outlaw; he now had to be subjected to the ordinary processes of the legal system. Those, like Robert Ramsay, who used the pretext of outlawry to justify the way they dealt with the bushranger could no longer legally sustain their actions.

Among all the political grandstanding that occurred during the hasty inception of the outlawry act in the immediate aftermath of the Stringybark Creek killings, very little consideration had been given to any difficulties that might arise. Apart from a few minor technical modifications relating to the administration of criminal justice in Victoria, the legislation had simply been copied from a similar law temporarily introduced to deal with bushranging in New South Wales in the 1860s. But as some lawyers in the northern colony had argued (not without cause) there could be odd legal consequences flowing from the legislation, a warning that went unheeded in Victoria. As the impact of this error began to sink in, the Victorians realised there were serious implications for them.

The demise of the outlawry act did not automatically nullify its validity during the period of its operation and there were at least two potential consequences from this that could seriously affect ordinary court proceedings against Ned. One was the way the ancient law recognised that when a person was outlawed for specified crimes for which the penalty was hanging, it was legally regarded as a conviction. In Victoria, as in England, the legal system forbade anyone being placed on trial for an offence for which they had previously been 'convicted' and were no longer liable to be subject to ordinary court proceedings. This opened up the possibility of a complicated legal paradox. Ned could no longer be hanged as an outlaw because of the cessation of the outlawry legislation, but he could also no longer be tried in the ordinary way as he was an outlaw when the alleged offences were committed.

The other consequence was that as 'wild animals', outlaws could also be regarded as not legally responsible for what they said and did during the period of their outlawry, that they were, in effect, legally incapable of making cognisable statements in future court proceedings. In Ned's case it meant he could not be tried for any offences alleged against him from the time immediately after the Stringybark killings until the termination of the outlawry legislation. Nor could he be made legally accountable for anything he might have said during this period. All in all, it was a legal mine-field and a potential nightmare for Ned's accusers.

On the other hand there was one advantage for them in the accidental end of the act. As lawyers in New South Wales had pointed out, the legislation made no provision for the circumstances where an outlaw was captured alive. It was assumed that if this happened the only penalty that could be imposed on them was to hang them as outlaws or, alternatively, they were entitled to be set free.

It was little comfort to the government lawyers for whom the capture of Ned Kelly had come as an unexpected shock. Many believed the Kellys had fled to other colonies following their disappearance in early 1879. Others claimed they had most prob-ably escaped overseas. For those who believed the gang was still in Victoria, the assumption was that they would not be captured but shot down. As a result, even the most basic documents required for a legal process had been thrown out or mislaid, and indeed some records may never have come into existence in the first place as it was presumed they would not be required. Needless to say, there were no public disclosures of these complications and certainly no official announcement that the outlawry act had ceased operation. Confirmation that it had expired can only be found in an obscure enactment passed by the legislature in 1879 that was designed to keep it in force with some other legislative provisions.

Most of Melbourne's newspapers and journals maintained a stony silence on one of the most remarkable coincidences in Australian legal history. The day after Ned arrived in Melbourne, just ten lines appeared in the *Herald* that briefly touched on the expiration of the act. Without any identifying headline, the item reported: 'A widespread impression prevails that Kelly being an outlaw, he can and will probably be summarily executed, or at most only after a magisterial inquiry as to his identity ... This is incor-rect.' It stated as matters of 'fact' (as if any further comment might invite legal difficulties) that 'on the best of authority that now being in legal custody, he is under the protection of the law, which must be precisely carried out'. After this brief mention, the *Herald* said no more on the subject.

There were compelling reasons why those in positions of authority would have wished to keep it this way. If this situation had been aired more publicly, the belated discovery that Ned was no longer an outlaw had the potential to cast grave doubts on the legality of some of the actions that had been carried out by the police and others during and after the Glenrowan siege. So successful was the press silence that for years to come many could honestly claim they believed he had never ceased to be an outlaw and felt the authorities showed great magnanimity in subjecting his case to ordinary legal processes when they could have saved themselves a lot of bother and hung him immediately. Months later the Adelaide *Advertiser* reaffirmed the widely held view that Ned had not deserved such generosity and should have been 'put to death without any form of enquiry'. But it was not benevolence – it was the law.

There's no doubt there were people in the community who were aware of some if not all of the potentially explosive effects of the outlaw act's demise. Years later, when Thomas McIntyre penned his memoirs, he displayed a remarkable astuteness in understanding Ned's legal situation at the time of his capture. As he explained, in the absence of making any provision for outlaws being captured alive, the legislation might still allow an accused person to plead what the law called *autrefois attain* – making it impossible for 'dead persons' (that is, outlaws) to be charged and convicted for serious criminal offences in ordinary court proceedings. McIntyre also pointed out that the local outlawry statute had been modelled almost entirely on an earlier one enacted in New South Wales. Since then, the northern colony had re-enacted the statute and it became a permanent part of New South Wales law for the

remainder of the nineteenth century. The former constable com-
mented on the irony that if Ned had been captured in New South
Wales, he could have pled *autrefois attain* and could conceivably have
been set free on that basis.

We will probably never know conclusively whether prior to
this discovery the government contemplated hanging Ned Kelly
without an ordinary criminal trial. In accordance with the traditional constitutional practice at the time, no official records exist of
any cabinet discussions that would almost certainly have occurred.

Outwardly, Ramsay continued to treat the bushranger as a
special case. On Friday he paid the prisoner a short visit after which
the only concession he authorised was to recommend that Kelly be
allowed further visits from his mother. Ellen was in the women's
section of the gaol where she was nearly two years into her three-
year sentence. She had been permitted to spend a few minutes with
her son the day after his arrival in Melbourne and we can only
speculate as to what went on in that first meeting between mother
and son. Otherwise, Ned was still denied all forms of contact with
the outside world without the chief secretary's express permission.

The outlaw act was little more than an annoyance, though
legal fallout from it in the future was a niggling cause for concern.
For now, all Ramsay's efforts centred on gathering the team to try
Ned in what would be considered 'regular' court proceedings.

13 | PROSECUTION CASE

Max Kreitmayer of the Melbourne Waxworks on Bourke Street was labouring around the clock on the 'spectacular' new display that he hoped to launch the day after Separation Day, the holiday marking 1 July 1851, when Victoria officially ceased to be a part of New South Wales. Like all good showmen, he knew that time was of the essence if he was to fully capitalise on the enormous public interest in the Kelly gang. The jewel of his new display featured a model of Joe Byrne at Glenrowan. 'A marvellous imitation of nature to be offered for public display at no extra charge!' announced the billboards.

Competition was fierce and he was keenly aware of another impresario who had already begun to draw big crowds to his own Kelly entertainment at the popular St George's Hall venue. Photographs from the siege were being projected onto a large screen interspersed with graphic scenes from the recent Russian–Turkish war. Not to be outdone, another entrepreneur at the nearby Eastern Arcade was preparing an illuminated pictorial display – a 'Pantechetheca Exhibition' – on the happenings at Glenrowan. He was confident he would attract a surge of interested customers on Saturday, the busiest day of the week.

Like Madame Tussaud's Waxworks in London with its famed Chamber of Horrors, the depiction of crime in the local waxworks

'At the Waxworks' from the Australasian Sketcher

was one of its most popular attractions. The Kelly display was designed to have an air of finality, as if the last chapter had already been written in the story of the gang. It seemed the bushrangers were to be relegated to the pages of history as the waxworks portrayed them: branded forever as notorious malefactors even though one of them was still languishing – very much alive – in Melbourne Gaol.

For those charged with conducting the case against the bushranger, it was a different tale. The general euphoria following Ned's triumphant capture at Glenrowan had given way to growing fears about the diminishing prospect of sending him to the gallows. The lapse of the outlawry act quashed any expectation that the bushranger would be hanged quickly and quietly. Now the only recourse was to seek his execution through the colony's normal legal processes, although it would unquestionably entail numerous complications.

At his government offices, the colony's Crown solicitor, Henry Gurner, had personally taken responsibility for the case against the bushranger. In his early sixties, paunchy, balding and comfortably jowled, he had a deceptively kind and grandfatherly demeanour. But behind the genial facade was a steely determination to see Kelly hang. A longstanding member of the Melbourne Club, he reflected the deeply conservative values of the majority of its denizens, one of the most notable being Redmond Barry, who was the longest serving judge on the colony's Supreme Court. Together they were among the oldest to still maintain their official positions, with records in government service that originated in the days when Victoria was still part of New South Wales.

Gurner's standpoint could be traced back to his childhood in Sydney, where his father had worked his way up from lowly court official to become a prosperous and well-respected lawyer. John Gurner had instilled strong views in his son, nurturing a decidedly negative attitude towards men like Ned, who he believed should be regarded as incorrigible criminals. In his household, convicts were inferior beings.

Gurner lived in an era when most lawyers had little to do with the criminal law, but he stood out as a notable exception. Since his appointment to the Crown solicitorship in 1851 he considered the trying of criminal cases an integral part of his responsibilities. He had even written a prominent text called *The Practice of the Criminal Law in Victoria*, published in 1871. It was deeply influential in dictating the conduct of criminal proceedings, not least with the judges in the colony. As the accepted bible on the working of local criminal law, there were few in the colony (including judges) who were prepared to countermand its precepts, even if the author was known to favour the Crown's interests against those charged with criminal offences. To this Gurner added more than half a lifetime of experience in manipulating the law and its procedures to serve the Crown's interests.

As soon as his role in the Kelly trial was confirmed, Gurner brought Charles Smyth – a prominent barrister and Victoria's best-known Crown prosecutor – into the fray. He was a quiet, enigmatic gentleman from a middle-class background, with a large proportion of his face concealed behind a long bushy beard. A tough adversary, he had proven his mettle repeatedly at scores of important criminal trials. Smyth and Gurner were sufficiently cynical and case-hardened to know that criminal trials could be won or lost by actions that had little to do with the strict letter of the law and its procedures. First and foremost, they understood the importance of ensuring their cases were heard before judges known to favour the government.

The prosecution case was further enhanced by a breakthrough report in Friday's *Argus*. 'NED KELLY THE MURDERER OF CHERRY', the headline blared. The article claimed that Martin Cherry, the railway platelayer who had been a hostage in the Glenrowan Inn, was shot when he refused to hold back a curtain so that Ned could fire at the police through the window. But it turned out that whoever had placed the story, which originally emanated from the police at Benalla, had erred disastrously. 'His mate told me he had been shot by the police', the priest who attended the dying hostage telegraphed to Melbourne. And a telegram from a newspaper correspondent in Benalla confirmed: 'The statement Cherry was shot by Ned Kelly is contradicted by a large majority of those who were in the building during the encounter'.

Swallowing his disappointment over this false report, Gurner began to explore the case against Ned. Technically, there were a number of circumstances in which the bushranger might be charged with hanging offences. Even the death of Aaron Sherritt could result in a death penalty provided Ned's association with the murder could be proved. There were several other possibilities, too, that could ensure Ned would be imprisoned for the remainder of his natural life. But as Gurner well knew, working with the criminal law could be a fickle enterprise. Ultimately, if Ned was to be dispatched to the gallows, the law required a unanimous guilty verdict by twelve male jurors drawn from the community. A single individual voting the other way could result in a hung trial, leaving the Crown with no option but to bring new proceedings against the accused, or risk trying him again on the same charge. It was an unhappy prospect for the Crown solicitor.

While Gurner and his staff continued to work through the weekend, he made every effort to promote the impression that there was more than enough material when it came to the weight of evidence against Kelly. As the *Herald* reported on Monday: 'Altogether there is such an array of capital offences as never could have been mounted up against any prisoner of the Crown in Victoria ... It is doubtful whether such a variety was piled on the head of any of the worst bushrangers of old times in Tasmania or New South Wales.' In its exuberance the paper clocked up at least twenty hanging offences it claimed could be applied to the bushranger, but according to the office records of this busy Saturday, the Crown solicitor was confronted with quite a different situation. In truth, the range of options available for successfully prosecuting the bushranger on a capital charge had significantly diminished.

During the past thirty years the number of hanging offences in Victoria had been greatly reduced. Only a handful might now be used against Kelly for his activities prior to the events at Glenrowan, and serious doubts could be raised in terms of establishing his guilt in relation to any one of them. Even robbery under arms – once a much-favoured hanging charge against bushrangers – no longer automatically incurred the death penalty. The perpetrators could only be hanged if a robbery was accompanied by violence resulting in injury.

There was still the warrant issued in 1878 to arrest Ned for attempting to murder Police Constable Alexander Fitzpatrick. This was indeed a capital offence but the possibility of convicting him on the charge had become extremely remote. Two months before Ned's capture, Fitzpatrick had been sacked ignominiously from the Victoria Police for 'generally bad and discreditable behaviour'. By his own admission he 'could not be trusted out of sight and never did my duty': an acknowledgment that would belie the truthfulness of his evidence in a criminal trial. What's more, medical doubts had been raised as to the nature of the wound he claimed the bushranger had inflicted upon him. John Nicholson (the same doctor who attended Ned at Glenrowan) was unable to confirm with absolute certainty that Fitzpatrick had been wounded by a gunshot.

By far the greatest public condemnation of the Kellys came after the deaths of the three police officers at Stringybark Creek, but prosecuting Ned for murder in these circumstances was not as easy as it may have appeared. Proving his guilt was ultimately going to depend on the evidence of one man: the mounted police constable who had managed to escape from the bushrangers and lived to tell the tale. Thomas McIntyre was strong-minded, physically robust and a keen observer. Ordinarily his evidence would have been irrefutable, but he had witnessed the deaths of his fellow officers in fading light with gunfire erupting all around him. It was extremely difficult for him to know with absolute certainty what had happened. Furthermore, he had escaped while the third victim was still alive. Kennedy's bullet-riddled body was discovered five days later well away from the scene of the other killings, so there was no way McIntyre could have seen how he finally died.

In the following four months the gang carried out two highly publicised raids on country towns: Euroa in December 1878 and Jerilderie the following February. A variety of charges could be laid as a result of Euroa. There was enough evidence to send Ned to gaol for many years for stealing and other offences, but none had the death penalty attached. As for Jerilderie, it was a cross-border raid and therefore beyond the jurisdiction of Victoria's courts. In both cases no one was wounded or killed but the Kellys had stolen large sums from the local banks. Since then, none of the gang had appeared publicly until the killing of Aaron Sherritt. If this was the best the Crown could come up with, it was going to be extremely hard to charge Ned with a hangable offence prior to the siege, and there was no guarantee there would be capital charges arising from Glenrowan.

The police were being criticised on a daily basis for their conduct of the siege. In Benalla, the *North-Eastern Ensign* proclaimed that Superintendent Hare had 'lacked both judgment and courage in the way he had taken part in the affray'. The superficial wounding of Hare and the lengthy gunfight were hardly going to be enough to convince a jury that Ned had committed a capital offence at Glenrowan.

Even Police Commissioner Standish had to grudgingly admit the proposed charges deserved further investigation to test their legality, a marked turnaround to his decision at the Benalla hearing earlier in the week. Not only had Ned been unable to use a weapon effectively at the time, as Dr Nicholson affirmed, but the medico's report on the subsequent examination also suggested that Ned was in such a debilitated state, it was quite plausible that he was not fully responsible for his actions during the siege: 'He was shivering with cold, ghastly white and smelt strongly of brandy'. He said that well before he emerged from the hotel, Ned had already suffered a considerable loss of blood and imbibed a large quantity of brandy.

As the circumstances of the gunfight looked increasingly ambiguous, Gurner decided to write a letter to Standish ordering more detailed inquiries be made into the bushranger's involvement in the sabotage of the railway line at Glenrowan. In itself, causing the break in the line was not a capital offence. Indeed, the maximum punishment for such a crime was fourteen years imprisonment, but it could well lead to charging the bushranger with the capital offence of attempted murder. Ned himself had told one journalist at Glenrowan that if the railwaymen and other civilians on the special train had suffered injury or death 'It served them —— right'. He had also told a group of police and journalists: 'I had the rails pulled up so that those —— black trackers might be settled'. Gurner requested that witness statements confirming these comments be sent to him as soon as possible.

However, Gurner's primary concern was time, or the lack of it. As the law stood, the bushranger was required to be brought before a court within seven days of being remanded from Benalla – a deadline that posed huge problems for the Crown solicitor. He desperately needed to avoid making any firm public commitments on the nature of the charges he would bring against Ned, given the legal and practical problems facing him. He also needed to stall any lawyers who would eventually be called in to represent the bushranger. Above all, it was imperative that Ned be denied visitors who would aid him with legal representation, or who might publicly raise issues to promote the bushranger's cause.

In his letter to the police commissioner, Gurner exhibited his determination to keep Ned isolated from any meaningful assistance for as long as possible. Provided no court interfered, the chief secretary's ban on outsiders meeting with Ned could then be taken to remain in force, even if gaol regulations read to the contrary. He ignored the fact that if Ned was physically unable to make an open court appearance, it was possible to hold a hearing elsewhere – even at his bedside in Melbourne Gaol. But as Gurner made clear, he intended to stave off any meaningful proceedings against him 'for about three weeks' by having his case adjourned every seven days without any formal charges being brought against him. And for this, at least in the beginning, he required the active assistance of the gaol's doctor, Dr Shields, to back him up. He directed the commissioner to arrange for him to be available on Monday to give evidence confirming that Ned could not appear at the City Court.

Meanwhile, Gurner took comfort in the knowledge that the magistrates were unlikely to cause any difficulties. The men who usually presided at its hearings were government employees, subject to official direction, and removable at will by the government. A constant reminder of their vulnerability would have been the example set on the day known as Black Wednesday, which was still fresh in their minds.

In January 1878, the Berry government tried time and time again to pass legislation on fiscal and constitutional matters through the Legislative Assembly. Every attempt it made was vetoed by the rich landholders and merchants who held a monopoly of power bestowed upon them in the colony's constitution enacted in the mid 1850s (much like the Senate refused supply to the Whitlam government in 1975).

Finally the government responded with an unprecedented cull of senior civil servants, magistrates and middle-level judges – roughly two hundred in all – and justified its actions by saying richer members of the community should not be exempt from the emergency measures required. If the Legislative Council refused to provide the funds needed for the running of government, then the Council itself must be reduced to free up the funds. Needless to say, denizens of the Melbourne Club and publishers of the *Argus*, among other conservative elements, were outraged. The majority of men who managed to remain in office were well attuned to the whims and will of the police and the Crown law authorities. And if any honorary justices of the peace were present at hearings concerning Ned (where they too could exercise judicial-style authority) it was assumed their social backgrounds would preclude any sympathy for a man of Ned's class.

No sooner had the letter been dispatched to the police commissioner than Gurner was suddenly confronted with a new crisis. An urgent message arrived informing him that the police commissioner had received a telegram from Margaret Skillion, Ned's most forceful and articulate supporter. Maggie was coming to Melbourne on Monday for the express purpose of seeking assistance for her brother.

14 | FAMILY LOYALTIES

Two plain-clothes police detectives mingled inconspicuously with the afternoon crowd at Spencer Street railway station. The men were on a top priority assignment, under strict instructions to meet the northeast train due at two o'clock. In a few minutes Maggie Skillion and two male companions would be arriving in the Victorian capital and the officers had orders to maintain surveillance on them around the clock. Precise details of every move they made would be relayed back to police headquarters.

Like Ned, Maggie was no stranger to the city and she was already familiar to local detectives. During the hunt she had come to Melbourne to obtain desperately needed ammunition for the fugitive gang. Her presence had inspired a full-scale police alert but, ever resourceful, she had managed to ensure the supplies were smuggled north by someone who would not attract suspicion (believed to be Kelly sympathiser Michael Nolan).

Of all Ned's relations, his eldest sister was the one the police and government were most wary of. Highly intelligent, proud and defiant, she was her family's most devoted champion. Her sudden appearance on horseback at the scene of the Glenrowan siege had been recorded in the newspapers with a sense of high drama. 'Dressed in a black riding habit with a red underskirt and a white Gainsborough hat' she had ridden directly to the front line of the

Maggie Skillion

gun battle. There she had stormed the police line in a bid to enter the Glenrowan Inn and persuade her brother Dan and his mate Steve Hart to end the fighting. Unsuccessful in her attempt she was later seen to weep bitterly over their remains.

She did, however, manage to have the bodies released and escorted them to her home at Eleven Mile Creek near Greta. In the days that followed she stood guard over the dead, defying all (including Police Commissioner Standish) who attempted to reclaim them during the course of the two-day wake. In this instance she was aided by a surprising gesture of sympathy from two magistrates at Wangaratta who bypassed Standish's order to recover the bodies for further investigation by giving the dubious excuse that they couldn't find an official vehicle for the purposes of transporting the gruesome cargo. The two bushrangers were mourned and interred in an unmarked plot in the Greta cemetery, surrounded by family and friends.

If Maggie hoped she might experience similar displays of compassion in Melbourne, she was quickly disillusioned. When the train finally ground to a halt people began rushing up and down the station platform, peering into carriages as porters unlocked the doors. The news had spread that Catherine Kelly, Ned's seventeen-year-old sister, was arriving in Melbourne to visit her brother. The spectators were disappointed when Kate did not materialise but the detectives quickly recognised Maggie. In a plain black dress with matching hat and veil, she calmly made her way along the platform. Slightly built and just over five feet tall, at twenty-four she was no longer a 'slip' of a girl, but still regarded by many as the most hand-some of Ned's sisters. In 1874 she had married William Skillion and had two children by him, but she had been left to fend for the family when he was gaoled for six years due to his involvement in the Fitzpatrick skirmish at Greta.

It was common knowledge that Maggie was in sole charge of her family's affairs. In the telegram to Standish she informed him that she would be taking responsibility for acting on her brother's behalf with the police and government authorities. Ned's other brother, James, was nowhere to be seen. For several years he had deliberately distanced himself from his family, particularly his eldest sibling. Early that year he had been released after a long gaol term for cattle stealing in New South Wales. He had also served an earlier sentence for horse stealing in Victoria at the age of fourteen. There were some who claimed he might have been at the Glenrowan siege, but at least one newspaper reported he was employed in a factory in Melbourne at the time, working as a bootmaker – a trade he learned in prison. He did, however, make a brief appearance at the Greta funerals.

History tells us very little about James. Closer in age to his younger brother, he seems to have had a much stronger affinity with Dan than Ned, and the fact that he left the colony for New South Wales while still a teenager suggests he wanted to escape the shadow of his domineering older brother. After Glenrowan there was talk that James had been heard muttering about avenging the gang, but for the rest of his life (he was well into his eighties when he died) he gave no sign of following through on such a threat. One of the few statements attributed to him was recorded by a police officer soon after Ned's execution, in which he gave every indication that he was far more interested in pursuing 'the good life' than the high drama and uncertainty of a life of crime: 'I will not enter the bush. I have got a good trade. I can earn three pounds a week by making boots. And I am too fond of going to theatres, and taking girls in the gardens at night, for the work [sic]. But should I ever be interfered with by the police I will not do what Ned has done, I will shoot every man and have satisfaction.'

Of one thing we can be sure, James scarcely figured in the events of the Kelly Outbreak, having spent most of the 1870s working far from home and serving time in the neighbouring colony.

During the long absences of Ned and Jim in the previous decade, Maggie had been left to shoulder her family's heaviest burdens. It was she who was constantly on hand, giving comfort and support to her mother after the death of Maggie's father, Red Kelly, and helping her manage the children from Ellen's marriage to the American George King, who had since disappeared. When her mother was gaoled over the Fitzpatrick incident, it again fell to Maggie to take charge of the younger members of her mother's family as well as caring for her own brood.

Accompanying her on the Melbourne trip was a cousin named Tom Lloyd, son of one of her mother's sisters. The two had recently begun a personal relationship that would result in the birth of several children, and she would remain his common law partner for the rest of her life. Tall and good looking, many suspected he was not far away when the police killings occurred at Stringybark Creek, though there is no evidence to back this up. Maggie's other male companion was John McElroy, married to one of her cousins. His loyalty to Ned was based more on his long-term friendship with the family than on any direct involvement with his criminal activities.

For Maggie, the two men were among the few relatives she could trust. Hers was a constantly warring clan and she could never be sure that even her closest relations would stay loyal to her brother's cause. One of her uncles by marriage had been a major police informer in the early 1870s, receiving a very large sum for his information about the family. He had even insisted that 'Quin' (apparently a reference to his wife's family name, which was normally spelled 'Quinn') should be used to describe him in official records, so that others could be blamed if word ever leaked out of his association with the police. Unbeknown to Maggie, another 'Quin' was top of the list of informers who had assisted the police in the months of the hunt for the Kellys. The records of the period do not confirm beyond doubt that this was one of her immediate kin, but if it was, it would hardly have surprised her under the circumstances.

When Maggie reached the hotel, she faced the first of many setbacks. Upon learning of her imminent arrival, Crown Solicitor Gurner had been busy reshuffling the schedule relating to Ned's case. On Sunday 4 July, it was at No. 27 on the list of magisterial hearings that were to be held in Melbourne's City Court. In the normal course the case would not have been called until late in the day. Everything changed on the Monday when Gurner and Crown Prosecutor Smyth appeared in court at the start of proceedings. Ned's case was immediately called and the bench deferentially agreed to their demands, ignoring all proper consideration of the bushranger's legal situation. Minutes later Gurner and Smyth departed, completely unchallenged.

The bench had readily agreed to their statement that the bushranger's injuries precluded his presence in court. No mention was made of the possibility that he might be entitled to legal assistance in his absence or that he was entitled to a special hearing at his bedside in Melbourne Gaol. No objection was raised when Smyth intimated that formal charges would not be brought against Ned for three weeks or more. No reference was made to the fact that Ned's sister was due to arrive in Melbourne and would be expecting to visit him. The court ruled there was to be no further mention of Ned's case for another week, leaving the bushranger completely isolated in Melbourne Gaol as before. Perhaps suffering pangs of conscience, the presiding magistrate personally visited Ned late that afternoon to inform him of the outcome of the hearing, but it was hardly compensation for the manner in which Ned's rights had been disregarded.

When Maggie learned of the ruling, she and her companions dashed across town to police headquarters where they confronted Police Commissioner Standish in his office. Just a few metres away from Melbourne Gaol, Ned's sister pleaded with the commissioner for permission to visit her brother. It was here she experienced her first real taste of the government forces arraigned against Ned. Standish told her the simple fact that he did not have the authority to allow it. Nor did the gaol governor, he informed her curtly. Later he recorded on a secret police memorandum: 'I told them he could not be interviewed without an order from Mr. Ramsay'.

More bad news reached her in the form of information leaked from Melbourne Gaol. One of the two men who had been convicted along with Ellen had reportedly made a sworn statement that directly implicated Ned in the Fitzpatrick altercation, despite his staunch denials that he had been in the neighbourhood at the time. This informer could only have been one of two men: either long-time family associate Brickey Williamson or her own husband, William Skillion. As a family member, it's unlikely to have been Skillion, but this further display of disloyalty among the ranks would have been disheartening.

The next morning Maggie was waiting on the doorstep of the Treasury building when it opened. For more than an hour she remonstrated with government officials about her brother's situation. She demanded to see the chief secretary, but was told he was not to be found. Undeterred, she set off with her two companions to seek him out at his private office on the other side of the city. He finally agreed to meet her provided she was alone. Maggie 'argued and wept' at their meeting, so the *Daily Telegraph* reported, but 'Mr. Ramsay was firm', and he refused permission for her to visit her brother. The chief secretary later told the paper he had no intention of allowing Ned 'to be at liberty to circulate lying stories which find their way into print'.

According to police surveillance records, throughout the rest of her stay in Melbourne Maggie had no contact with anyone who might directly assist her brother's cause. A detective trailing her claimed that during this time Maggie was subject to personal harassment and even threatened with physical harm on at least one occasion. He told of how on her second night in the city she took a stroll along the main streets with Tom and McElroy. After a time people began to recognise the trio and several 'hooted' at them. Soon they were being followed by an increasingly rowdy mob and they were forced to make an escape, hailing a passing cab and ordering the driver to speed away.

It was also noted in the report that Ned's sister sought a brief respite on the final afternoon in Melbourne. With detectives following her at a discreet distance, Maggie visited the St Francis Roman Catholic Church, an unpretentious building nestled in the heart of the city where her parents had married in November 1850. People saw this as a sign that Maggie could be returning to the religion she was born into after having turned her back on it when she married William Skillion by the rites of the Primitive Methodist Church.

After a short period of contemplation, she left the church and made her way to Melbourne Gaol, where she had a brief reunion with her mother. It was to be the one and only concession Ramsay granted her. No report exists of the meeting, for the newspapers considered it 'improper' to reveal details of such an intimate family encounter.

15 | HOMECOMING

Barely forty-eight hours after they arrived in Melbourne, Maggie Skillion and her two companions were going home. Departures from the drab Spencer Street railway terminal were never auspicious even at the best of times. Its sprawling network of tracks and huddles of ramshackle buildings were perpetually enveloped in gritty coal smoke from the steam engines and bathed in the putrid winds blowing from the West Melbourne Swamp and the fetid Yarra River.

The journey was uneventful and when the train finally pulled into Glenrowan station, passengers peered into the darkness for a glimpse of the two brick chimneys that were all that remained of the Glenrowan Inn. For Maggie Skillion it was a dismal homecoming. The charred skeleton of the hotel was a vivid reminder of the recent battle and her little brother's horrific death. It also flung up images of the hundreds of people who had flocked to Glenrowan from nearby towns and the surrounding countryside to witness the grisly spectacle. Many had jeered at the small band of Ned's relatives and associates who had gathered near the railway line while, one by one, the gang members died inside. To Maggie it was a culmination of the years of hostility and abuse her family had suffered at the hands of her community.

Anti-Kelly sentiment was at least partly due to Ned's widespread reputation for bullying and his penchant for threatening physical harm at the slightest provocation. But the clan as a whole was viewed with suspicion and often fear. On the day of the siege a number of Kelly supporters had gathered at McDonnell's, the other local hotel, separated from the Glenrowan Inn by the railway line. The wife of the hotel's licensee was so alarmed by their presence that she hid from public view for several hours until the bar emptied. She told a reporter later that she feared being 'molested' in case they suspected she was siding with the police.

For many locals antipathy towards Ned ran far deeper. It was particularly so for landholders both rich and poor who had suffered from the depredations of the highly organised wholesale horse and cattle stealing that had plagued the area in recent years. By his own admission, Ned Kelly was one of the chief operators in this illicit trade. He and his stepfather George King had transformed stock theft into organised crime on a grand scale with tentacles reaching into New South Wales and even as far as Melbourne. Wealthy landed proprietors lost valuable animals but in comparison, the smaller landholders suffered catastrophic losses. Their draughthorses were readily saleable and hard to trace. As records from the period show, the thefts left many near destitute, unable to replace the animals that were the mainstay of their farming operations. A number of these unfortunates were so intimidated that they deliberately failed to report their losses and seek compensation because the thieves had threatened to destroy their fences and burn their haystacks if they did so.

The public face of the situation was markedly different. For more than a year the newspapers shrieked about the growing number of Kelly sympathisers. They were depicted as a swarming malignant force ready, willing and able to aid Ned's cause with money and active assistance. In truth, the figures were greatly inflated by government officers and none so much as Commissioner Standish, who desperately needed to justify his failure to rout the gang and his vast expenditure on the fruitless hunt. At best, police records listed about one hundred 'sympathetic' households throughout northeastern Victoria, and most of these were included by virtue of the fact that they contained distant relatives of the gang or people suspected of engaging in horse and cattle stealing in the area. In the Benalla district alone it was a small proportion: merely a hundred people among more than five thousand residents.

Even the official listing of gang supporters was proved seriously defective when in 1879 Standish ordered the arrest of a number of men (including John McElroy, who accompanied Maggie to Melbourne) on the pretext that they were actively aiding and abetting the fugitives. Despite their anti-Kelly stance local newspapers pointed out that at least some of the men were wrongly imprisoned and yet the local magistrates left them stranded for weeks without instigating formal proceedings. Finally, without a shred of concrete evidence, the embarrassed government authorities released the group and, officially, no more was said about it.

Many of those who appeared to be onside with the gang revealed themselves to be fair-weather friends. So far, cash handouts from the bank raids had sustained their loyalty, but unless these funds were regularly replenished their so-called 'support' steadily evaporated. For several days after the siege newspapers reported a strong local presence rallying for Ned and his clan, but as Superintendent Sadleir confirmed, this was greatly exaggerated. By the end of the week Melbourne's *Herald* was saying that even the tempers of the most loyal sympathisers had 'cooled down'. Some, it seemed, had even gone to the trouble of communicating directly with the police in an anxious bid to ensure they would not be arrested for their previous association with the bushrangers.

Maggie's isolation was exacerbated by the fact that her brothers had alienated many old friends who might once have been willing to give her help and advice. This was typified by a group of families that had once been very close to the Kellys. Four brothers named Whitty had emigrated from Ireland in 1840. Although illiterate and with no capital to speak of, they had managed to work their way to a position of reasonable prosperity. Before moving further north, they had lived near Ned's family at Avenel. One of the Whitty boys had gone to school with Ned for a time and the wife of one of the Whitty brothers had reputedly helped to look after the Kelly family after the death of their father.

In more recent times, however, the Whittys had become staunch enemies of the Kelly clan. Despite the close and friendly association, their landholdings had not escaped the wholesale raiding attributed to the Kellys. In response, Ned's old schoolmate Charles Whitty joined the police service and enthusiastically participated in the hunt for the gang. Shortly after, another brother also joined the police and begged to be allowed to participate in the hunt. He was duly transferred to Benalla to meet his request.

In Maggie's immediate neighbourhood, the 'Greta Mob' – mostly young Kelly relations and their retinue – had created a serious divide between the Kelly clan and the local populace. Ordinarily there was a level of tolerance for groups of youths coming together like this. It was seen as providing an outlet for displays of physical prowess such as boxing and horsemanship when the less desirable alternatives were sexual adventures and excessive consumption of alcohol. The Mob had proudly strutted around town with their own insignia (chinstraps on their hats caught beneath the nose) and its members attained an unprecedented reputation for violence and intimidation. The hostility these youths inspired helped to make Greta and the surrounding neighbourhood a fertile source of inside information that was passed on to the police during the months of the Kelly hunt.

From a historical perspective, it appears there were times when, with few exceptions, the Kelly family was universally reviled by the community. For a woman in increasingly dire circumstances like Maggie, the lack of support could only have made her situation more desperate. Not only was she looking after her own children, but also her mother's four youngsters, including the infant daughter Ellen had been forced to abandon when she was sent to gaol. Most of her neighbours were hostile, and being under constant police surveillance – with regular invasive house searches in which, as Ned described in the Jerilderie letter, 'they would destroy all the provisions and shove the girls in front of them into the rooms like dogs' – would have taken its toll.

Maggie's hut was small and rudimentary. With her husband serving six years hard labour she had no visible means of ongoing financial support. She would have received a goodly portion of the proceeds from the Kelly hold-ups, but that could not have lasted long with so many mouths to feed and expenses to meet. Security would also have been an issue as hers was a household exclusively of women and children, though various male members of the extended Kelly clan, like Tom Lloyd and Wild Wright, stayed as often as possible to protect them. An extraordinarily resourceful and resilient woman, even she would have struggled in the face of such hardship and seemingly relentless ostracism and persecution.

But recently an astonishing act of kindness has come to light revealing a most unexpected ally. Soon after Ned and his brothers fled into the bush and their mother was sentenced to three years gaol, it became apparent that the Kelly girls had been left all but destitute. Seeing their desperation, the same Senior Constable Kelly who guarded Ned in Benalla organised a fund so that the local storekeeper would provide them 'with any necessaries they might require'. 'It was impossible to shut my eyes to the fact that they were struggling against the pressure of want', he recalled many years later. To his credit the senior constable did not broadcast the level of poverty that prompted the charitable gesture, knowing full well it would have been a crippling blow to Kelly pride. Ned was fully aware of what the policeman had done and freely acknowledged his gratitude. On one notable occasion during the later Beechworth hearing, the magistrate ordered all witnesses to leave the court during testimony and Ned piped up that he had no objection to Senior Constable Kelly being allowed to remain.

This is but one of several instances over the years that indicate there was a civilised aspect to the Kellys' relationship with the police that has been frequently overlooked. On at least one occasion, the young Ned sought police protection at Greta following threats from his own kin (two uncles who suspected him of collaborating with the law). Furthermore, his sister Anne gave birth to a child commonly believed to have been fathered by married police officer Ernest Flood in a romance that seems to have attracted no active condemnation from family members. But Flood never owned up to the liaison which ultimately ended in disaster, turning the family firmly against him. Anne died two days after she gave birth to a daughter in 1872 and the little girl succumbed to diphtheria just over a year later. (At Stringybark Ned told McIntyre that from a distance he believed him to be Flood at first. 'It is a good job for you that you are not, because if you had [been] I would not have shot you but roasted you upon the fire.')

As Maggie Skillion resumed life at Greta after her return from Melbourne, two new arrivals slipped into the neighbourhood. Humping blanket and swag and dressed for the road, they gave every appearance of belonging to the small legion of itinerant workers who tramped rural districts seeking employment. In fact they were undercover detectives from Melbourne, carefully disguised and operating with assumed identities. One was attempting to ingratiate himself with the locals by pretending he was a 'new chum' who had just arrived from England. They sought to independently immerse themselves in the community: drinking in the pubs frequented by friends and associates of the Kellys and calling at homesteads to ask for work and to pass the time of day with the occupants. Their special orders were to gather intelligence about the Kelly clan and its supporters and specifically to seek out those who had been responsible for the manufacture of the armour the gang had worn at Glenrowan. They had no direct contact with the local police except at the very highest level, and their reports were to be sent immediately to Melbourne by post.

Some days they tramped for miles on the pretext of looking for employment, and if they were unable to obtain accommodation they were obliged to sleep rough. Now and again they managed to meet secretly to share information and report on their individual progress, but most of the time they were on their own, a vital part of the ever-growing army of information gatherers.

16 | HIS OWN WORST ENEMY

At police headquarters in Melbourne the majority of available officers were working on the Kelly case, assembling information and interviewing witnesses about anything and everything related to the gang. A flood of orders continued to issue from above. The dispatch of the two undercover detectives to Greta was on 'the express request of the government', as the head of the police detective force revealed in internal department correspondence. Henry Gurner and Charles Smyth called for new police inquiries on an almost daily basis, and Commissioner Standish zealously issued special directives demanding material with which to attack Ned and his supporters.

At Benalla officers were charged with accumulating evidence for the Crown prosecutor that related specifically to Ned's state of mind when he confronted the police outside the Glenrowan Inn. Smyth had still not ruled out this episode as a basis for proceeding against the bushranger for the hanging offence of attempted murder. The Crown prosecutor needed to know if at that most crucial point in time Ned had been in the act of surrendering or had intended to continue the fight. Despite published statements that the bushranger had not shot the hostage Martin Cherry, several contrary witness statements were collected. At Beechworth members of the coroner's jury inquiring into the death of Aaron Sherritt

DETECTIVE REPORT.

SUBJECT { *Re Surveillance of Mrs Skillan Tom Lloyd & John McElroy*

POLICE DEPARTMENT,

Melbourne Detective Office, 6 / 7 / 80

We have the honor to report for
your information that Mrs Skillan
and the two above named men left
the Robert Burns Hotel at 11 am went
to Mr Burmans Photographic Rooms #8
then to the Law Department where
they remained a good while and returned
to the Hotel at 1.5 pm left again at 2pm
then to the Treasury, then down Collin
St to 74 Queens St and back to the Hotel
at 4.30 pm, left the Hotel at 7.30 pm
they walked to Elizabeth St and about
one hundred people followed them
and began to hoot them a cab was
passing at the time and the Skillan
party stopped it and got into it
and drove away at a rapid pace
and turned up Russell St &, we
got another cab but could not
overtake them, and we believe they went
to St George Hall, after searching
for them for about an hour and not-

F. H. Secretan Esq
Officer in Charge
of Detectives

Police Detective Report

complained that the bushranger should have been called before them in person to determine whether he might be arraigned for direct involvement in his murder.

Despite a lack of firm evidence, the Fitzpatrick incident at Greta was once again under the spotlight. The sworn statement taken from either Bill Skillion or Brickey Williamson had raised new hopes that the government could proceed against Ned for the claimed 'attack' on the disgraced police officer. As Senior Constable John Kelly reported, he had discussed the matter with Ned at Benalla and during the conversation the bushranger had freely admitted that he had shot at the former constable. 'Ned, what about Fitzpatrick? Was his statement correct?' the policeman inquired. The bushranger replied: 'Yes, it was I that fired at him'. To this, Senior Constable Kelly was prepared to swear under oath.

The sabotage of the railway line was still being regarded as a potential reason for charging the bushranger with hanging offences. One by one, the railwaymen who had been forced to make the break in the line were confirming Ned's personal involvement in the incident. Most damning of all was the statement given by Thomas Curnow, the lame schoolteacher who had halted the 'special', who could vividly recall the situation in precise detail. Before managing to escape from the Glenrowan Inn he was convinced of the bushrangers' murderous intent when it came to the passengers and crew of the train.

Although it seemed every effort was being made to collect all available pieces of evidence, there were also instances where the police deliberately withheld information from the authorities in Melbourne. And with good reason. A number of local officers were guilty of serious offences that, if they came to light, could have reduced them to the status of common thieves in the eyes of the public. One, a Constable George Gascoigne, 'appropriated' a piece of Ned's armour though it was an important exhibit listed for court proceedings (recently it was sold to the Kelly Exhibition at the State

Museum of Victoria). Another, Thomas McHugh, had souvenired a
Webley pistol that Ned used at the siege. It would have provided
vital evidence linking Ned to the Stringybark killings, for clearly
etched on the pistol's handle was a number identifying it as part of
the police kit issued to Sergeant Kennedy. A packhorse saddle found
at Glenrowan had been the property of one of the police officers
who died at Stringybark Creek, but it too disappeared. And a gold
ring Joe Byrne was wearing on his left hand when he died had
previously belonged to one of the dead officers. It vanished when a
member of the police service was guarding Byrne's corpse.

Nevertheless, the Stringybark killings were still at the forefront
of proceedings against Ned on capital charges. As long as the difficulties relating to his outlawry were kept in the background, these
apparently cold-blooded murders lay at the core of the public
opprobrium against the surviving gang leader. The circumstances of
the police deaths and the publicity attending them ever since were
more than enough to ensure many potential jurors would be
severely prejudiced against the bushranger even before a word of
evidence could be presented.

Technically, by focusing on the Stringybark murders, Gurner
could also exploit a considerable procedural advantage because
Thomas McIntyre was available to give sworn evidence about the
events. Paradoxically, the bushranger was banned from giving
evidence himself despite being the only other living witness to the
events. Due to a principle of English criminal law harking back to
the Middle Ages, Ned was only permitted to give an unsworn statement in court, unprompted by defence counsel and without
cross-examination. Furthermore, a jury could also be directed by a
judge to ignore any parts of his statement if they were in conflict
with sworn testimony. Otherwise, the old principle dictated, he
might be 'tempted' to lie under oath in court, and this, as medieval
theologians propounded it, would lead to his eternal damnation!

This was not the only age-old rubric in Victoria's criminal law

system that would favour the Crown. Time and again, as newspaper reports and eyewitness accounts confirmed, Ned had displayed a dangerous penchant for bragging about his exploits, especially the Stringybark killings. And as the solicitor-general wrote in 1872, both public and private admissions of guilt could amount to 'confessions' for the purposes of the law. The legal impact was such that careless utterances could be regarded 'as the strongest and most satisfactory proof of a person's guilt'. This extraordinary law again had its origins in medieval times, when theologians had placed a great deal of weight on the validity of personal confessions. They preached that owning up to the commission of crimes and other sins was a 'soul-cleansing' act and should be admitted to evidence as a form of self-condemnation.

Numerous legal precedents demonstrated that such confessions could arise from ordinary conversations between police officers and accused persons. What's more, they could be admissions of guilt made to private individuals despite there being no one else present. None of these 'confessions' were required to be taken down contemporaneously in writing: a consequence of circumstances in earlier times when the majority of the population, including law enforcement officers, could neither read nor write. All that really mattered was that any witness who attested to such pronouncements was believed by judge and jury to be speaking the truth. Their credibility was simply a matter of their position in the community and their ability to withstand cross-examination by defence counsel. As a result, Victorian courts recognised these idle disclosures as proof in themselves of an accused person's guilt. In a bizarre paradox, Ned could emerge as the most damaging witness for the prosecution. Henry Gurner and Charles Smyth knew that in employing this form of confessional evidence, the accused man was a gift for their case. His tendency to brag was not simply to gain notoriety and adulation, but was a classic symptom of his stock in trade – a way of trying to intimidate those who threatened him on both sides of the law.

The Crown could also use such evidence for another purpose. In legal theory, the possibility that Ned had committed crimes that were not the subject of charges brought before a court was not allowed to be mentioned. Otherwise, as the law prescribed, jurors could be made unfairly biased towards the accused because of allegedly criminal episodes that were not the subject of the proceedings. There was, however, a way in which this principle could be subverted at least partially, with the use of confessional evidence. For the rule did not *necessarily* exclude self-incriminatory statements made out of court by an accused in the course of carrying out allegedly criminal acts. This could even extend to the presentation of testimony on the background situation of a crime that indirectly reminded jurors of other possible criminal activities of the accused. It's no surprise, then, that a large portion of funds was allocated to seeking out those who could and would be willing to testify that the bushranger had made remarks that might be used against him.

Day by day, names were added to the list of those who could attest to the bushranger's 'confessions'. From Benalla, Senior Constable John Kelly confirmed that following his capture Ned had admitted he was present at Stringybark Creek and that he had taken a valuable presentation watch from the body of Sergeant Kennedy. Another officer who had been in charge of the bushranger for several hours on the night after his capture had recorded how Ned spoke of his role in the police shootings, and agreed with portions of Thomas McIntyre's version of what had happened. Crown law officers could also utilise self-condemnatory statements Ned made at Glenrowan when he told a journalist that he intended to kill all of those on the special train regardless of whether they were police or civilians.

The search was on to secure formal statements from witnesses who might testify to Ned making admissions about the Stringybark deaths during the raid on Euroa. Locals who had encountered the bushrangers – including those made hostage – were formally interviewed. These statements contained confessional testimony that could not only be used against the bushranger in relation to Stringybark Creek, but could serve to remind jurors of Ned's involvement in the criminal activities the bushrangers had committed in Euroa.

Similarly, although the raid on Jerilderie was beyond the jurisdiction of Victorian courts, the New South Wales police were helping to locate witnesses to the events there who might have heard Ned brag about his previous illegal exploits and could be called upon to incriminate him. It was an arduous and time-consuming task as many potential witnesses had moved away from the scene of the raids and were difficult, if not impossible, to trace, but every effort was made to locate them.

And finally, urgent priority was placed on the recovery of a 6000-word document that by all accounts contained statements authored by Kelly himself. At some point during the raid he had handed a bundle of pages to a local resident, describing it as his 'autobiography'. This was to become known as the Jerilderie letter. He told Edwin Living, an accountant at the bank, that it must be published in the town newspaper. His demand was never met.

What happened to this document, which holds a somewhat mythical status in the annals of Australian history, has been the subject of exhaustive speculation and conjecture. Living first gave evidence of its existence in an article that appeared in the *Herald* just after the hold-up and large portions of it were printed, again in the *Herald,* prior to the Glenrowan siege. The story goes that Living handed it over to the authorities when they started gathering material for the court case. A copy was duly made and it is this document that now resides in the National Museum of Australia. As for the original, circumstantial evidence suggests that it was probably stolen from police records soon after Ned's execution. When Thomas McIntyre prepared his memoirs in 1890, he claimed to know who had the letter and said they had allowed him access to it, though he never revealed who the person was. It was donated anonymously to the State Library of Victoria in 2001.

Since Ned Kelly's capture, McIntyre had been kept deliberately out of the public eye at the Melbourne depot of the mounted police. Years later he was to describe this as a particularly dark period in his life – 'an incessant round of drill, grooming horses and burnishing accoutrements' – until he finally managed to secure temporary employment as a clerk at police headquarters in Russell Street. It began to look like he would have no more direct involvement in the Kelly case. And then, without warning, on 13 July he was summoned to present himself to an officer compiling statements for Henry Gurner and asked to sign two important documents. The first stated that 'Edward Kelly feloniously, wilfully and with malice aforethought did kill and murder Thomas Lonigan.' The second repeated the charge word for word, except for the name of the victim: Michael Scanlan.

McIntyre now faced the very real prospect that he would be a leading witness when Ned Kelly was put on trial for his life. With some reluctance, the constable found himself among those who were expected to provide information on confessional evidence that the Crown was planning to use against the bushranger. He faced a difficult dilemma: on the one hand, he was a proud and loyal member of the police service; on the other, he had made a personal resolution to keep his early morning interview with Ned at the Benalla gaol a strictly private occasion. In the end, he reached an uneasy compromise. He agreed to testify but neglected to reveal the full sting of the bushranger's remarks made to him when they spoke in his cell the morning after Glenrowan. Years later he continued to justify this decision. 'I did not wish to press the charge against Kelly with unseemly severity', he said.

Three weeks after his capture, Ned Kelly dictated a short letter to which he laboriously affixed his signature mark. All he could manage was a crude 'X', for his injuries had rendered him severely incapacitated. Since Glenrowan it had been impossible for him to use either of his hands, and because he received no further proper medical treatment, he would be unable to write for the brief remainder of his life. The wound to his right foot – sustained during the final shoot-out with police – had reduced his confident swagger to a hobbling limp. Nevertheless, the letter was proof that he was of sound mind and physically capable of taking part in local court proceedings.

Addressed to the chief secretary, the wording was very much 'officialise', reflecting the language of the gaol visitor who had penned it for him. (This visitor would have been one of several lay persons who were regularly allowed into the cells to give assistance to inmates.) 'I beg respectfully to request your permission to send for my sister to meet me at the hospital', it read. Ned wanted to see her so that he could 'confer with her respecting the provision of a Solicitor to prepare my defence at my forthcoming trial and likewise for her to procure me the necessary clothing to appear thereat'. He then requested permission for a second visit from his mother.

Meanwhile, Charles Smyth had made his third appearance in the City Court in relation to Ned's case. Though the excuses for the bushranger's continued non-appearance were wearing thin, he made no apologies. Newspapers had begun to hint at the surprising lack of opposition to Smyth's stonewalling. As a report in the *Herald* stated, the submissions were received 'without demur'. For the third Monday in a row, the decision of the bench was to leave Ned isolated in his cell based on Smyth's untested assurance that Ned was 'not quite well enough to leave gaol'. When Ned's letter found its way to the chief secretary, Ramsay surprisingly raised no formal objection to Ned meeting with his sister, but stipulated that it could take place only in his presence. Before sending it on to the gaol governor he wrote on it: 'Permission granted but special care must be taken as I have already verbally explained to the Governor of the Gaol'.

The following Monday a senior police officer announced to the City Court that Ned would be brought there in a week's time to determine whether he should be placed on trial for the murders of Constables Lonigan and Scanlan at Stringybark Creek. 'Kelly will be able to appear on Monday next', the gaol doctor confirmed. Witnesses were summoned to Melbourne for the hearings. Special contingents of police were enlisted to guard the bushranger at the City Court. Unbeknownst to most of them, however, the proceedings had been brought forward and the gaol kitchen had been hastily transformed into a makeshift courtroom. No formal public notification was given and it seems to have been hurriedly planned in the previous twenty-four hours. The paucity of reportage on the event suggests no regular newspaper representatives were invited. In the manner of the times, particularly with respect to minor courts, no detailed official record was made of any remarks. Later, a *Sydney Illustrated News* woodcut purporting to be a pictorial representation of the scene appears to have been just another fabrication by an artist on the payroll, an image dreamed up after rudimentary discussions with a few of those present on the day.

By the early afternoon of Saturday 31 July, the majority of working men in the Victorian capital had downed tools and begun to enjoy their weekend leisure activities. Large crowds assembled to watch competitive matches based on the code of football dubbed 'Victorian Rules'. Local racetracks filled up with men and women drawn to one of the country's favourite pastimes: betting. Almost all reporters were off duty because there were no Sunday newspapers and the main edition of the city's only evening newspaper was already on the press. Later editions customarily focused on expanded reportage of the afternoon's sporting events. It was as if all matters other than sport ceased to have any significance for the next twenty-four hours (an attitude that many locals would have to agree hasn't changed much in a hundred and twenty-five years!).

Meanwhile, at Melbourne Gaol a group of a dozen or so men was being ushered inside for an event shrouded in the utmost secrecy. When newspapers later reported on what had happened, the best description they could give was that a magistrate, Mr Call PM, had entered the gaol with Henry Gurner, Charles Smyth, Robert Ramsay and 'other persons'. These were Ramsay's final days in office as chief secretary: he was to relinquish his position the following week due to the defeat of the Service government in the recent poll. Just after 2 pm Ned was escorted into the makeshift court. The only visitor he acknowledged was Thomas McIntyre, who had been called as a witness to formally identify him. The bushranger smiled at him and 'welcomed me as an old acquaintance', McIntyre recalled later.

Conspicuously absent was William Zincke, a Beechworth lawyer who earlier in the week had been engaged by Maggie Skillion to undertake her brother's defence. In his early sixties, he had risen to prominence after recently being elected as the second member for the Assembly electorate of Ovens. A staunch ally of the Service government, he was in Melbourne for the opening of the new parliament, and his political connections meant he was able to visit the bushranger almost immediately after Maggie retained his services. He had represented the Kellys before, without much success, but at least he knew the family and their history and Maggie possibly saw this as an advantage. Little is known of this first meeting and whether or not Ned was satisfied with his legal representative. It seems he was happy to defer to Maggie on these matters, confident that she would have his best interests at heart.

Ned was nonplussed by Zincke's absence from the hearing. In the brief, heavily abbreviated version of events that have survived, he was reported to have inquired if he had been brought to the gaol kitchen to be 'placed on trial'. He was visibly relieved when he learned the purpose of the gathering was simply to move the planned committal proceedings in Melbourne to Beechworth, and the bushranger readily agreed to this new arrangement. The magistrate then ordered his transfer to the northeastern town where the proceedings were slated to begin in six days time.

The bushranger was unaware that his newly appointed lawyer had certain prior knowledge of the hearing and deliberately absented himself from the proceedings. He had slipped away to Beechworth, which indicates that he had no doubt about the probable outcome of the hearing. He was obviously not troubled by the fact that anything raised during the proceedings that might harm his client would go unchallenged. He also made no effort to meet with Maggie and Tom Lloyd, who had arrived in Melbourne on Friday night, and certainly did not inform them of the Saturday hearing. It was unprofessional to say the least, and suspect legal behaviour by any standards.

The Beechworth *Ovens and Murray Advertiser* seems to have been the only newspaper that was forewarned of the impending committal hearing. This particular publication had earlier questioned the legality of Ned's removal to Melbourne, so it was somewhat of a vindication that he was being brought back to the area for the next stage of legal proceedings. Government records were strangely mute concerning the event, but as Thomas McIntyre acknowledged twenty years later, it was to have a fundamental significance in overcoming legal difficulties that might jeopardise the Crown case. This was proof to him that the authorities were prepared to manipulate the legal system to ensure that any technicalities that might have impeded their efforts were glossed over or ignored altogether. In his words: 'A technicality was not likely to cause the discharge of a man it [the Crown] had taken such infinite pains to arrest'.

At police headquarters on Russell Street arrangements were being made to transport Ned to Beechworth. Orders were drafted for Superintendent Sadleir to pack his bags for Benalla, leaving first thing in the morning. Senior officers in the Victorian Railways were pledged to secrecy and placed personally in charge of guarding Ned on the journey. They were advised to give the railway workers no prior warning about who would be on the train. The Beechworth hearing was not due to begin for almost a week but Ramsay wanted Ned out of the capital the very next day. He was to surrender office in three days time and was reluctant for his successor to get his hands on Ned in case he questioned the enforced isolation that Ramsay had so carefully maintained.

Across town, Maggie and Tom Lloyd remained oblivious to the goings-on at the gaol. First thing that Saturday morning, Maggie made her way to St Francis Church for another spell of quiet contemplation. By eleven o'clock Tom had joined her at the Treasury building, where they sought out officials who might help them in their cause. This time the personnel were far more solicitous towards her and remained on duty beyond their working hours as they engaged her in discussion until well after 2 pm. When Maggie and Tom finally left, trailed as always by two detectives, she still had no idea about the hearing that was currently underway. She would only come to know of it the next day when a newspaper reporter informed her.

For the rest of the evening Maggie and Tom strolled through the city along with the crowds of people that were drawn to the centre in search of entertainment. This was the most colourful night of the week as the populace enjoyed all the diversions the capital had to offer. Vendors were out selling a delicacy particularly popular with children at a penny a plate: ladles of peas smothered in mint sauce. Sugary sticks of 'Turkish lolly' were also doing a roaring trade. Spruikers took their places outside shopfronts, loudly regaling passers-by with enticing patter about the amusement to be had within. It would have been a welcome distraction for Maggie and Tom after their frustrating lack of success. As they took in the sights that night, however, they must surely have experienced pangs of foreboding when they caught sight of billboards set up around the city streets advertising the season of a new theatrical performance: 'The Theatre Royal has much pleasure in announcing the premiere of a new play – *Sentenced to Death*'.

18 | FALLEN

The main gates of Melbourne Gaol swung open to admit a horse-drawn cab just after eight thirty on the morning of Sunday 1 August. The Sabbath was a day of holiness and contemplation, a stricture that was drummed into Robert Ramsay from infancy. But on this day the outgoing chief secretary would defy the cardinal rule that he had broken only once before, when the battle of Glenrowan had forced his hand.

During the night, operators of the railway telegraph service had arranged for a special train to transfer Ned to Beechworth on the one day of the week when normal country railway services were stringently suspended. Only a handful of police officers and two senior railway officials knew of the secret rendezvous point where Ned would be taken aboard: the Newmarket railway station, just over fourteen kilometres away. The Flemington racecourse and the city's animal saleyards dominated the area, so it was expected there would be few people about to witness the bushranger's departure from the Victorian capital.

Three of the four officers in plain clothes who arrived in the cab to escort Ned to the station and then to Beechworth were well known to him – flesh and blood reminders of some of the darkest moments in his life. The officer in charge was Sergeant Arthur Steele from Wangaratta, the man who had been publicly acclaimed for felling the bushranger at Glenrowan. Thomas McIntyre was also present, though under duress. He believed it was a serious impropriety for the chief witness against the bushranger to be part of his escort, but he had been informed in no uncertain terms that it was 'his duty'. The third officer known to Ned was Constable Hugh Bracken, who was stationed at Glenrowan at the time of the siege. He had been seized as a hostage, then managed to escape and give valuable tactical information to the authorities.

Ned entered the courtyard of Melbourne Gaol flanked by prison guards, with Governor John Castieau walking close beside him. The bushranger stumbled along painfully on crutches, his right boot cut open to accommodate his badly swollen foot. He was no longer the weather-hardened, taut-muscled bushman he had been at Glenrowan. After spending the better part of four weeks in the gaol hospital, he looked pale, sallow and undernourished. For a while he had been placed on a prescribed diet heavy in carbohydrates – a 'farinaceous diet', as it was called – but he was still a long way from his previously robust physical condition. His crippled left arm had received no medical treatment since Glenrowan, and it hung limp at his side, all but useless. He had also suffered a great deal from the cold and damp, further depleting his reserves of energy, until Castieau waived regulations and allowed a small fire in the prisoner's cell to give him a modicum of comfort during the night.

Ned was in civilian attire but not of his own choosing. His letter requesting that Maggie Skillion replace his gaol wardrobe had never reached her. As a result, he was no longer the well-dressed 'bush dandy'. Clothing he had worn at Glenrowan – including a fashionable white shirt with black spots, yellow corduroy trousers and matching waistcoat – had either 'strayed' or were beyond repair. These stylish items had been replaced with the dull, conventional garments supplied by Castieau. The bushranger's own very costly custom-made boots, high-heeled with shining patent leather tips, had been cut from his feet when they treated his wounds at the siege. One of the newspaper reporters at Glenrowan had taken them as souvenirs, leaving Ned with a very ordinary pair of plain black boots.

'I suppose you fellows are going to hang me!' Ned called out as he approached the police officers waiting for him. 'There is McIntyre and I know he is going to do it ... This is better than a wombat hole, eh, McIntyre!'

The constable smiled wanly. For McIntyre, the bushranger's remarks were more than just a crude attempt at gallows humour. Years later he recalled that his impression of Ned that morning was 'A fallen foe fast approaching the end of his career', and many others shared his opinion. Certainly, there were odd moments when he had shown signs of his old bravado. And he still persisted in making the best of his appearance, as indicated by the plain white hat he wore that he deliberately fixed at a jaunty angle, with the brim carefully turned up on one side. But overall he had maintained a sober air of resignation about his fate: an attitude that could be traced back to Glenrowan. In the moments before he left the confines of the inn for the last time, Ned said later, he had come perilously close to taking his own life.

'I had half a mind to shoot myself', he told reporters and, in preparation, 'I had loaded my rifle, but could not hold it after I was wounded'. He later repeated to Maggie that he had indeed left the comparative safety of the besieged hotel with the intention of ending his life once and for all. 'It's a wonder you did not keep behind a tree', she admonished him, and he told her, 'I got away into the bush and found my mare and could have rushed away but I wanted to see this thing out'.

After Ned had fallen, Dr Ryan was made aware of his suicidal intentions, reporting that even as he administered to his wounds, the bushranger 'gave me the idea he wished to die'. And during the early days in Melbourne Gaol, Ned's gloomy air of resignation indicated to one and all that he was preparing to sever his earthly ties. Then, over a number of weeks, another factor began to come into play. By all accounts religion had no meaningful part in Ned's adult life. Nevertheless, at Glenrowan he was given the last rites of the Roman Catholic church. The priest then made a point of telegraphing Melbourne to ensure the bushranger would receive further spiritual guidance when he arrived in the capital. As a result, the bushranger met with the gaol's Roman Catholic chaplain shortly after he took up residence, and would continue to receive him frequently.

Ned's mood seemed to lift early on, for after several days Castieau let it be known that the bushranger was no longer expressing suicidal thoughts. It had never been the gaol governor's choice to keep Ned isolated from outside influences and he disdainfully rejected the thin excuses made by police that Maggie might bring in poison to help her brother commit suicide. Nevertheless, it was more than his job was worth to go against specific orders.

Castieau and his family lived in a house within the gaol walls so it was easy for him to drop by Ned's cell at any time. He continued to visit Ned on a regular basis and it was noted they would often converse for hours at a time. During these sessions it became apparent to Castieau that there was a marked change in the prisoner's attitude. Apparently the religion of his childhood had re-emerged to play a role in his final days, sustaining him with the hope that whatever his mortal sins, judgement upon him in the afterlife would be far more lenient. It was not just representatives of Ned's childhood faith who were seeking to claim responsibility for his spiritual reawakening. With government approval, a Protestant evangelist by the name of Dr John Singleton had spent many years visiting incarcerated men in order to provide them with moral guidance. It stood to reason that the country's most infamous prisoner would not escape his attentions.

John Castieau

During his first encounter with Ned he introduced the prisoner to his personal notion of good and evil. The way to repentance that would surely lead to eternal life in heaven was by the open confession of earthly sins, he declared. Singleton gave him a copy of the New Testament, which the bushranger promised to read, and he arranged for the provision of a variety of religious pamphlets. Afterwards he described Ned's forthright response to his ministrations: 'I believe in this man', the prisoner had declared. But they were not to meet again. Years later, Singleton revealed that from then on he was the subject of a religious tug of war which excluded him from having any further contact with Kelly. He also claimed the gaol authorities had confiscated the New Testament before Ned could read it.

After Ned's conviction, Singleton sought permission from the government to visit the bushranger again and received a letter agreeing to this, provided the condemned man concurred. But when Ned signed a letter to this effect, John Castieau exploded, telling Singleton: 'If you were to see him, such a disturbance would be raised as has never yet been seen in this gaol'. He directed him to speak to the Roman Catholic chaplain of the gaol, Dean Donaghy. Singleton asked him to authorise his visit to Ned, promising 'not to interfere with any of the dogmas of the Roman Catholic Church'. But it was not enough for the priest. Singleton recalled: 'The Dean, in his reply, said he had every objection to my seeing him, and that I ought to have known from my experience that everyone should be left to mind his own religion'.

Although physically diminished, the prisoner who emerged from the grim fortress on Sunday 1 August had certainly regained some of his spark. He seemed to have recovered his talkative nature, encouraged perhaps by the religious discussions he had recently participated in. As Ned was helped into the cab, Castieau had some last words for him: 'Now, Kelly, your best game is to be quiet'.

'Damn it, ain't I always quiet?' joked the bushranger.

Most probably the inclusion of Arthur Steele as a travelling companion was a deliberate ploy to provoke Ned to an unguarded outburst. And the journey itself would provide some strong visual triggers for the fallen bushranger. Along the way they would pass the scene of one of Ned's great outlawing triumphs: the gang's daring raid on Euroa. Later they would pass through the grim landscape of disaster and defeat at Glenrowan. No doubt Commissioner Standish had hopes he might be prompted to let slip further admissions that could be used against him in court, and it was this possibility that the gaol governor was probably warning him against. Along with the friendly advice, Castieau slipped Ned a bottle of gin and water to ease the pain he would unavoidably experience on the bone-rattling journey to Beechworth.

19 | ONE FOR NED

Barely eleven hours before Ned was to appear in the Beechworth court on Friday 6 August, the governor of the local gaol, Henry Williams, set up vigil at the railway station. This was the second night in a row he had had to meet the last branch line train from Melbourne. The night before he was there to take delivery of an urgent letter about the tenuous state of Ned's representation. Kelly's lack of legal counsel had been a niggling preoccupation for the last three days. Williams found himself embroiled in a series of complex manoeuvres involving Maggie Skillion, two lawyers, the new colonial government and the prisoner who had been placed in his care on Sunday afternoon.

On this night he was relieved to see the blazing headlamp of the locomotive appear in the distance, but there were still no guarantees that Ned would have a lawyer when the court hearing was called at 10 am. It was not to be a trial, though some newspapers had proclaimed it to be that. Ned's guilt or innocence on serious charges could only be determined in a full-blown trial before a senior judge and jury, but still these preliminary proceedings were an important part of the process. A local magistrate had been called upon to determine whether there was a reasonable case to prove the bushranger's guilt on the charges made against him, a necessary preliminary to any further action. This, however, would be the only

David Gaunson

occasion before trial when key witnesses against Ned could be cross-examined by Ned's lawyer. It would also be the only chance he would have prior to trial to test other elements of the Crown case in a public place.

Williams scanned the arrivals as they alighted from the train. To his relief he recognised David Gaunson, the Melbourne lawyer who had taken charge of Ned's defence. Twenty-four hours earlier, William Zincke had finally announced he would no longer be associated with defending Kelly. Upon hearing of the lawyer's failure to appear at the Melbourne hearing, Maggie Skillion had discharged him forthwith. Less than three hours before the last train connecting to Beechworth left Melbourne, Gaunson was confirmed as Ned's new lawyer.

At thirty-six, tall and spare with a long thoughtful face and carefully trimmed beard, Gaunson was approaching the peak of his political and legal career. Highly intelligent, sharp-witted and an effusive talker, he had long ago cast off the more obvious influences of his Presbyterian upbringing despite the fact that he had once served as a choirboy in a leading Sydney church where his father was an elder. He had played a prominent role in the defeat of the Service government and rightfully expected to be rewarded with a position in the new Berry cabinet. But it was no great surprise when he was fobbed off with the position of chairman of committees in the Legislative Assembly. His independence of mind had done little to endear him to the political and legal powers in the colony, so the promotion did not eventuate, leaving him free to take up Ned's case.

Whilst in Melbourne, Maggie Skillion and Tom Lloyd had visited Gaunson to discuss him taking charge of her brother's defence. It's unclear who approached whom. Gaunson had a reputation as a radical that would have appealed to Maggie, but he also enjoyed the spotlight and may have volunteered his services for such a high-profile case. Either way, the fact that William Zincke had not told her of the secret gaol hearing, had failed to represent Ned there and had obviously known in advance of the plan to transfer him to the northeastern town but neglected to inform her, was more than enough to convince her he should be replaced. She had also learned that Zincke had appeared publicly on the first floor verandah of Beechworth's Empire Hotel to watch her brother's arrival in town, standing beside Aaron Sherritt's widow and her mother. Maggie had every reason now to distrust him.

When the Crown solicitor loudly voiced his objections to Gaunson taking over, the impasse was only resolved with the direct intervention of Graham Berry, the new premier and chief secretary. He had no particular desire to aid the bushranger's cause – far from it. In fact, one of his first official acts was to inform Gaunson that he would not allow Mrs Skillion to visit her brother. But he also recognised that William Zincke had been collaborating with Gurner and Smyth.

Berry arranged for the defendant himself to be consulted by ensuring Ned received a letter from Maggie advising him to switch representatives. At 10.30 am, Henry Williams telegraphed Berry that the bushranger had told him: 'I want Mr Gaunson to defend me', and to ensure there was no mistake he added: 'Kelly has given me this in writing'. The new premier passed on direct orders that allowed Gaunson immediate and continued access to his client, finally granting Ned the proper legal assistance he had been denied since capture.

As soon as he got word, Gaunson wrote to Ramsay on the chief secretary's last full day in office, informing him that he would be acting for Kelly. Time was short and it was touch and go whether the lawyer would make the train so that he would be there for Ned at the hearing.

Whatever Gaunson's defects he could not be faulted on the enormous energy he showed when pursuing the causes he espoused, and Ned Kelly's predicament was certainly one of them. With no opportunity to prepare his case but a dogged determination spurring him on, he managed to get on the last train that would deliver him to Beechworth that night.

Meanwhile, his new client languished in his cell. Close to high mountain country with snow-capped peaks glowering in the distance, the prison was a cold, miserable and forbidding place. Like the other inmates, Ned was bedded down early in the evening. For much of his time there he remained in bed anyway, nursing his painful foot and suffering with the bitter cold in his unheated cell. Inadequate milk in his diet was one of his many complaints and the location of his cell had added to his discomfort because the entrance was just below the prison's gallows. It was said he had exclaimed on arrival: 'What a pity that such a fine fellow like Ned Kelly should be hung up there'.

And yet the bushranger was far more reconciled to his situation than might have been expected. Newspapers had reported that

Ned was unsettled and rowdy on his journey to Beechworth, but as Thomas McIntyre related in what appears to be the only surviving eyewitness account of the trip: 'He was a little truculent but anything that was beyond decorum I would have described as bluster'. Ned had apparently passed a good deal of his time on the seven-hour rail journey singing loudly, frequently interspersed with apologies for his 'lack of musical ability' and 'poor voice'. He also seemed to have taken to heart Castieau's warning about the dangers of conversing with the police. McIntyre recounted, 'He would talk freely enough, but immediately he was asked a question he would cease talking and look at his questioner with a cunning leer, which evidently meant "you can't get anything out of me"'.

Williams and his staff found Ned behaved with more 'equanimity' than they expected, given his fearsome reputation. And again, he was allowed regular visits from a local Roman Catholic priest, which appeared to contribute to his placid state of mind. In fact, according to the men guarding him, his main preoccupation seemed to be ensuring that he would look his best when he appeared in court. During a short spell outside in the gaol yard, he sat gazing into the mirror-like surface of a bucket of water, admiring his reflection as he meticulously combed his hair and beard. He also succeeded in getting a message sent out of the gaol asking Maggie Skillion to buy him a more stylish hat, a new shirt and a bottle of hair oil.

As soon as Gaunson stepped off the train on Thursday night he was greeted by Williams and taken directly to the gaol. When he entered Ned's cell, he sat down on the end of the bed and said, 'Well, Kelly, I do not want to keep you up too late tonight'. He then proceeded to take notes of all that passed between them, a habit that continued throughout his relationship with his famous client.

Before leaving Melbourne Gaunson had organised with the *Age* newspaper to provide detailed reports of his work with Kelly, including a description of all their meetings. This practice was not

unusual. Several other lawyers – including Alfred Deakin, future
Victorian premier and Australian prime minister – also wrote for
the newspapers. They viewed such articles as an important tool for
gaining public support for their clients. Today they are invaluable
historical documents.

Gaunson hoped that publishing Ned's own words might
redress the unremitting propaganda war against him and encourage
readers to give him a 'fair go': 'Until now, the police have had all the
say, and have had it all their own way ... All I want is a full and fair
trial, and a chance to make my side heard.' Ned also spoke about
how he had suffered at the hands of the authorities, how he had
been treated like a 'wild beast' and forcibly kept away from his
family and from any legal advice since his capture. Such criticism
was welcomed by the *Age* editors as they had vehemently opposed
the previous conservative government peopled by men like Henry
Gurner.

At the same time, Ned appeared to be indifferent to the outcome of the proceedings: 'If I get a full and fair trial I don't care
how it goes', his lawyer recorded. What seemed to matter most to
the bushranger was that he would have an opportunity to raise
issues in public. He wanted people to know that he had been
'hunted and hounded on from step to step; they will see that I am
not the monster I have been made out', and 'What I have done has
been under strong provocation'. Needless to say, such statements
would not go far in defending the charges against him.

Before leaving the gaol an hour later, Gaunson arranged to
have another meeting with his client at the courthouse at 8 am, a
little over six hours away. Incidentally, it was revealed years later that
these so-called 'private meetings' he had with Ned in a confidential
visitors' room were in fact nothing of the sort. One of the courthouse officers apparently regarded it as his responsibility to listen in,
and he did in fact report all that passed between the prisoner and
his lawyer to his superior officer.

Meanwhile, Ned wasn't the only one who was suffering from the lack of amenities in the local gaol. On Sunday afternoon Thomas McIntyre was ordered to take up residence there for the duration of the hearing. Ironically, he was assigned sleeping quarters in the cell where condemned prisoners were held just before being led to the scaffold. The constable had scoffed at the suggestion that he might otherwise be 'assassinated' if he was allowed to stay anywhere else around the town, but because the orders had come from high up, he reluctantly complied.

On Friday 6 August the residents of Beechworth woke to the prospect of a crisp and sunny winter's day. From early in the morning hundreds converged on the courthouse for the first day of hearings on the deaths of Constable Thomas Lonigan and Constable Michael Scanlan. In their finest dresses and most stylish hats, women from all walks of life made their way to Ford Street, accompanied by tradesmen and shopkeepers who'd opted to close their businesses for the day and enjoy the spectacle. Everyone was hoping to catch a glimpse of the infamous Ned Kelly.

As the crowd steadily grew, local magistrate William Foster slipped away for a few moments of solitude, taking a brief stroll in the bushland on the edge of the town. 'I wanted to think before I opened the court at 10 am', he reminisced many years later. As a public servant he owed his primary responsibility to the government and had good reason to fear for his job if he did not act in accordance with the wishes of the authorities in Melbourne. In 1878 he was one of those dismissed from magisterial office by the previous Berry administration on Black Wednesday. He was lucky enough to regain his position, but only after strenuous representations on his behalf by powerful political allies.

Meanwhile, the mood was sombre at the Hibernian Hotel where David Gaunson had arrived in the early hours of the morning after his first interview with Ned. For the time being this was the unofficial headquarters of the Kelly camp, where Maggie Skillion and Tom Lloyd were staying. It was a modest establishment situated just over a block from the courthouse.

So far they were the only visible supporters of Ned in town but the police continued to harass them. A few days after Ned arrived Maggie tried to deliver a new shirt for her brother at the gaol, but she was turned away. As newspaper reports confirmed, she had also gone to the local police station to deliver a new hat for Ned. An officer took it from her but refused to pass it on as he claimed it could contain 'a sign of some dangerous import' for the prisoner. Maggie pleaded with them, proposing that police officers accompany her to the local shops where she would purchase clothes for Ned without even touching them, but she was rudely rebuffed.

By 8 am the courthouse was starting to look like a fortress under siege. Erected in 1858 during Beechworth's heyday as a gold rush town, it is a small sandstone building which still stands in excellent condition today. Armed police officers were stationed at every door and a conspicuously large number patrolled the grounds. This demonstration of military-style force was unlike anything Ned's lawyer had encountered in his legal career. It reinforced Maggie and Tom Lloyd's warnings about the single-minded ruthlessness of Ned's enemies and increased Gaunson's foreboding about their seemingly relentless zeal. The overwhelming scale of the police presence could only mean one thing: the police commissioner was in town. Indeed, Standish had left Melbourne, without obtaining permission from the new government, and arrived in Beechworth the previous afternoon, accompanied by Henry Gurner.

There were no immediate signs of trouble as Ned's lawyer passed through the doors of the courthouse. A scattering of onlookers waited patiently for admittance and provisions were being made for women to be ushered into the upstairs gallery especially reserved for female observers. The abundance of uniformed representatives helped to create an aura of danger around the bushranger, although he was in fact as weak as a kitten in his injured state. And as Melbourne's *Herald* reported the next day, if there were any Kelly supporters around they were conducting themselves with 'much propriety'.

Though the press was hoping for some sort of confrontation, there was little drama to be had that day. The main Beechworth newspaper, the *Ovens and Murray Advertiser*, had long been an outspoken and sustained opponent of the Kellys, and its journalists were counting on a juicy story. But with no signs of excitement in the offing, they focused on the fact that an 'alarming number' of boys who had evidently skipped school were spotted trying to gain admission to the court proceedings. The paper claimed to have grave concerns that the boys might treat Ned as a 'Hero of Romance', and so it was demanded that immediate steps be taken to keep the impressionable youngsters away. This must be done, the paper told its readers, to 'prevent the creation of an amount of sympathy with Kelly'.

Just before ten o'clock a hush fell on the courtroom as the town's clerk of court and his assistant took their places in front of the elevated bench. David Gaunson indicated that Maggie Skillion and Tom Lloyd should move back to the seats reserved for them in the main area. Their presence on the courtroom floor was one concession he had been able to extract from those in charge of the proceedings. At the newly constituted bar table Henry Gurner sat facing Charles Smyth and Arthur Chomley (the barrister employed to assist him).

Gaunson sat on his own, quietly convinced that Henry Gurner had no intention of giving him the slightest leeway. The portly Crown solicitor's grandfatherly demeanour had slipped more than a little when he learned Gaunson was replacing Zincke in representing Ned. 'He has no right to be here', he spluttered angrily, and in doing so he paid the lawyer a distinctly backhanded compliment.

Until Gaunson's appearance on the scene it looked like plain sailing for the Crown, at least at the Beechworth hearing. Zincke was far from being a formidable opponent. He was an average lawyer and certainly no orator, as his barely audible maiden speech in parliament had demonstrated the week before. His connivance in the previous Saturday's secret court proceedings had also clearly marked him as a likely collaborator with the Crown law officers. In contrast, Ned's new lawyer was well drilled in the rough and tumble world of Melbourne's police courts, and had a reputation as a persistent and skilled advocate.

As the post office clock chimed ten times, the clerk of court signalled for all those in the crammed courthouse to be upstanding for the impending arrival of the local police magistrate. A multitude of colourful hats and bonnets rose among the sober hues of male attire. More than a hundred women had already taken their seats in the court's balcony before 9 am. Another thirty or so had found places on the ground floor, leaving very little room for others. Among them was a scattering of mature matriarchs who saw themselves as the more respectable representatives of the local community. The vast majority, however, were 'very young – mere girls', as the *Age* recorded the next day.

Like many of his bushranging predecessors, Ned acted in an almost courtly fashion around females, a fact that was especially noted in his encounters with women during the raids on Euroa and Jerilderie. His behaviour was not uncommon, though: in Australian frontier culture, where women were frequently outnumbered by men, there was already a deeply rooted tradition that women were to be regarded as deserving of special care. Nevertheless, ladies in the 'polite' reaches of society were not supposed to have any sexual proclivities of their own, at least as far as the public was concerned. Nor were they supposed to have meaningful opinions of their own, as the *Ovens and Murray Advertiser* implied the next morning, dismissing the women in the courtroom as members of the 'softer sex'.

Senior Constable John Kelly and Constable Thomas McIntyre stood side by side waiting their turn to give evidence as Crown witnesses. It was an enormous effort for McIntyre to make it to court that day as his enforced sojourn in the Beechworth gaol had debilitating consequences. He found the 'penetrating draughts' in the corridors of the prison had seriously damaged his health. 'The removal from the comforts of home to the chilly atmosphere of the gaol', he later recalled, 'gave me a severe attack of pleurisy in which I found it impossible to draw inspiration without suffering acute agony'.

Gaunson was uneasy about the task ahead. Even with McIntyre's evidence to hand, he was not well-versed in the events concerning the Kelly gang. For two years he had been immersed in political storms and the necessity of earning a living as a lawyer, leaving him little time to keep up with the circumstances of Stringybark Creek or the Fitzpatrick incident. He had virtually no knowledge at all of the parade of witnesses the Crown solicitor was planning to use to prove their case against Ned.

Most worrying, though, was that Gaunson knew he probably faced one of the great dilemmas in the professional life of a lawyer. His early morning meeting had revealed that Ned was somewhat ambiguous about defending himself in the public sphere. It seems he was quite prepared to acknowledge his guilt in the Stringybark deaths, and he repeated what he had told Zincke in an interview earlier in the week: that he was willing to face up to 'all that he had done'. He argued that he had been entitled to attack the three police officers for what he claimed were 'outrages' that had been committed against himself and members of his family. Zincke told journalists that the bushranger had specially cited the episode at Greta involving Alexander Fitzpatrick, and was adamant in his claim that the 'tyranny' of the police had 'compelled him to take up arms'.

Gaunson desperately needed more time with his client to understand the motivation behind Ned's incriminatory revelations about Stringybark. If Ned was actually acknowledging his guilt, the most that the Melbourne lawyer could do for him at this stage was to test the cases and closely scrutinise the evidence against his client. As the clerk announced the arrival of the bench, Gaunson steeled himself for a fierce struggle ahead. His discussions with Ned and Maggie, the siege-like atmosphere in the neighbourhood and the obvious enmity of Gurner and his cohorts gave him little to be confident about.

A moment later, his problems increased exponentially as, dumbfounded, he watched the entrance of not one but two magistrates. Together they strode to their places at the bench and sat down side by side, claiming the positions of highest authority.

Most of the spectators in the room did not glance twice at the man who sat next to the local magistrate – they were all eagerly awaiting their first sight of the bushranger. But within minutes the representative of Melbourne's *Herald* had dashed off his first report for the day. There was, he wrote, 'some surprise' that Police Commissioner Standish had joined William Foster at the bench.

By the journalistic standards of the day these were strong words, though in today's terminology 'sensation' or 'shock' would have been more appropriate to describe the gravity of this turn of events. As the reporter recognised, it was an affront to any standards of ordinary legal propriety that one of Ned's greatest antagonists was going to sit in judgement on him. But William Foster was in a straitjacket. He had no doubt where his ultimate duty lay as a government employee. He wrote later: 'We all knew how determined the authorities were to convict Kelly, now they had him at last'. The commissioner, he explained, was the only other 'justice' in the court, so it was a matter of courtesy that he sat beside him in the place of ultimate power, though Foster was careful to emphasise that in all ways he was in charge of the proceedings. Foster was unwilling to admit that Standish's presence would undoubtedly intimidate witnesses, especially the members of the police force – effectively the commissioner's subordinates – who had been called to testify.

When Ned finally limped into view, Gaunson immediately demanded that the prisoner not be forced to stand in the dock. It was common practice at the time to seat the accused, injured or not, despite a long outmoded English rule to the contrary. 'Was it a genuine limp I wondered', Foster recalled years later, remembering the scene, 'or assumed to gain sympathy?' To him, the limp might well have been no more than another example of Ned's 'showmanship'.

As Ned took his seat, Gaunson loudly voiced his most important request of the day: 'I have to ask that a remand be granted to give me an opportunity to prepare Kelly's defence'. In all fairness it was a sound plea. As the law intended, such a hearing was supposed to give a person accused of serious charges the opportunity to test the evidence against them, even have the charges dismissed if they proved inadequate to lead to a conviction. Gaunson explained that his late entry as Kelly's lawyer meant that he simply did not have enough personal knowledge of the events at Stringybark Creek to do a satisfactory job and the proceedings must be delayed, preferably for at least a week. In addition, he needed more time to ascertain his client's wishes on his situation, not least because Ned himself had been denied any legal assistance for more than four weeks and had no idea what he was up against.

It seemed reasonable enough, but Gaunson knew his request had fallen on deaf ears when Crown Prosecutor Smyth rose grim-faced and addressed the court. Deliberately avoiding any mention of Ned's isolation in Melbourne Gaol, Smyth laid the blame for Gaunson's difficulties squarely on Ned and his advisers: 'The prisoner was informed last Saturday, before he left Melbourne, that he would be brought here today, and he was told he must go on'. He failed to mention that Ned had been given no choice in the matter and that his previous lawyer, Zincke, had abandoned him in Melbourne without any legal advice.

With similar contempt, the Crown prosecutor attacked Gaunson for claiming he lacked sufficient knowledge to conduct

Ned's defence at the hearing: 'The witnesses have been examined long ago, and the evidence has been reported in the newspapers' – although later it was revealed that he used documents that day containing information that had never been revealed publicly. Smyth did, however, close his remarks with an offer to grant a concession to Gaunson and his client. He pronounced that after all of the Crown witnesses had given their evidence and been cross-examined, he had no objection to Gaunson calling witnesses of his own. Gaunson shouted in frustration: 'How can I examine without knowing all the facts of the case?'

After more than an hour of this kind of legal wrangling, Foster finally intervened. Taking his cue from Smyth, he stated that Ned's treatment so far in custody was not to sully the proceedings, but that he would allow an immediate adjournment to enable Ned's lawyer to 'prepare his case'. This apparently magnanimous gesture ended up as no more than extra time tacked on to the normal lunch break. Gaunson had requested a week; he was granted an hour. The court would resume at two o'clock.

When he returned to the courtroom that afternoon, Gaunson lugged a thick file of newspapers that he dumped with a resounding slap on the table before him. It was a forceful rebuke. In the ridiculously short time he had been granted, he was only able to find copies of Melbourne's *Argus*. He had no proper access to the frequently conflicting reports on the Stringybark events that had been published in other journals.

Immediately after the court reconvened he was on his feet demanding a further adjournment. With the pile of newspapers conspicuously swamping his section of the bar table, he told the magistrate he was 'in a more difficult position than ever by the immense mass of facts' he had to master. Certainly, he complained, there was no way he could make any use of the newspapers at this stage, 'as the many columns of reportage in close, small-spaced type would take many hours to read, amounting to hundreds of thousands of words'.

Gaunson continued to be anything but conciliatory during the afternoon session. He described the actions of Robert Ramsay, who insisted on holding the bushranger in isolation, as patently illegal. He said Ramsay was denying the bushranger rights to which he was entitled and preventing him from organising a defence of the charges against him. Merely an arm's length away, Henry Gurner and his two barristers made no attempt to respond – there was simply no need. Unmoved, William Foster ignored the accusations and again denied David Gaunson a further delay in the proceedings. He then called for Thomas McIntyre to be summoned to the box as the first witness for the prosecution.

Despite his incapacitating respiratory infection, the constable gave evidence for more than two hours, frequently interspersed with long pauses as the clerk painstakingly annotated the details of his testimony in longhand and then checked every line back with him. He described in detail how after Constable Lonigan was shot, he crawled for cover in a seriously wounded state. Ned had passed his rifle from his right hand to his left and, reaching behind him for the revolver tucked in his belt, he finished off the injured constable with a couple of well-aimed bullets.

Foster moved to adjourn the proceedings just before five, saying that McIntyre would continue his evidence first thing in the morning. In a last-ditch effort to gain some ground, Gaunson demanded that Maggie Skillion be allowed to visit her brother, otherwise 'might has been right and the law has been disregarded'. Foster replied that he was only prepared to discuss this matter in private, and with no further comment he swept from the court.

For Gaunson, the day was not yet over. It was fortunate that he was accustomed to operating on the minimum amount of sleep, as numerous sallies in the Legislative Assembly in the early hours of the morning had demonstrated. The lawyer had an enormous task ahead of him, but it had become increasingly obvious that the most troubling factor was his client, whose behaviour in court that day had been as baffling as it was destructive.

*'After an all-night sitting in the Legislative Assembly –
the morning view'. This is how the* Australasian Sketcher
artist saw David Gaunson (centre).

Immediately after the proceedings closed, Gaunson went straight to Foster's office to demand yet again that Maggie be permitted to visit her brother. Foster refused. Undaunted, Gaunson sent a telegraph to Premier Berry, pleading with him to intervene because the ban on family visits was 'illegal, arbitrary and unjust to a man standing on trial for his life'.

After his immensely frustrating day, Gaunson returned to the Hibernian Hotel to find a journalist waiting to berate him about his professional conduct. This must have been the last straw. Nevertheless, the lawyer vehemently defended himself, asserting that there was nothing unprofessional about his replacing William Zincke at such short notice. So outraged were his protests that witnesses were convinced he was on the verge of resorting to blows when suddenly, in the heat of his tirade, Gaunson turned on his heel and stalked out of the hotel. He'd had enough combat for one day.

Meanwhile, after-court gossip spread that the bushranger was strangely relaxed during the short journey back to the gaol though the day had gone badly for him. He even went so far as to reminisce with a local detective about an incident at Wangaratta several years earlier: the policeman had been present when Ned found himself on a horse that stubbornly refused to move an inch; though it was a potentially embarrassing moment, Ned made a joke of it and everyone had responded with good humour. The prisoner went on to surprise another officer with the candid comment that 'McIntyre had given his evidence better than he expected'. It was as if he had no interest at all in the battle to save his life. And it was this attitude that was now Gaunson's chief concern. He was acutely conscious of the fact that Ned had made no attempt to hide his detachment from the day's proceedings. The *Herald*'s reporter wired to Melbourne that soon after the bushranger appeared in court he displayed a 'cool demeanour' towards all those present. At the bench where a large contingent of journalists gathered there was a growing consensus that Ned displayed 'apparent indifference to his position'. William Foster later recalled, 'Kelly sat there in the dock appearing, at times, as if he had gone to sleep'.

Though Ned was not paying much attention to the legal manoeuvrings, local folklore affirmed he paid conspicuous attention to a particular section of the crowd. 'He appeared to derive great satisfaction from the large attendance of the ladies at the court', a police officer later confirmed. There was talk that he had directed flirtatious winks at a number of ladies present, and years later local women were still boasting that they had 'not been ignored' by the bushranger in court that day.

If Gaunson hoped to extract some helpful information from his client when he visited him that evening, he was to be sorely disappointed. The lawyer needed details to counter McIntyre's graphic description of the murder of Thomas Lonigan. Instead, Ned wanted to focus on the events at Greta that led to the imprisonment of his mother, William Skillion and Brickey Williamson, claiming it was the false evidence of Alexander Fitzpatrick that led to their convictions. 'It was this unjust treatment that exasperated him and led to his taking to the bush', said Gaunson's report of the meeting in the *Age* the next day.

More revealing in this account, though, were signs that Gaunson was beginning to have serious doubts about the truthfulness of his client's statements. Ned repeated sentiments contained in the Jerilderie letter, telling Gaunson that he had not been near the scene of the Greta affray. This was a claim not borne out by contemporary evidence or statements by his mother and others who were present at the actual event. Gaunson avoided the issue, choosing to call it merely 'an assertion'. The report ended on a decidedly lame note: 'In Beechworth many people discredit every statement made by the Kellys and their friends'.

An element of disquiet in his report concealed what must have been a growing awareness that Ned had no desire to defend the charges against him. Gaunson had to face the very real prospect that all he would be able to do on a professional level was test the evidence against his client without presenting any counter-defence.

Beechworth shopkeepers were lamenting the sharp drop in takings due to the Kelly hearings, but business was booming for the local publicans. The proprietor of the Hibernian had no rooms left to accommodate the brothers of Joe Byrne and Steve Hart, who had arrived in Beechworth that afternoon. Maggie Skillion and Tom Lloyd moved out of the hotel soon after in order to keep them company at another establishment. The journalist who had so provoked Gaunson seized this opportunity to file a report stating that the congregation of four relatives of the gang had a dangerous purpose: 'The four living together is regarded as significant'.

Like most other newsmen covering the hearing that day, he made no mention of the fact that the police commissioner had sat at the bench alongside William Foster and that Gaunson had vigorously objected to it. A strange omission when one considers that an enormous amount of newsprint was devoted to the proceedings. The police commissioner's presence was simply acknowledged with the words: 'The police officers present were Captain Standish, Superintendent Sadleir and Sub Inspector Baber'.

When the telegraph office closed at midnight, Gaunson had still not received a reply from the premier about Maggie's visiting rights. Before retiring to his room, he arranged an early morning meeting with Ned and imbibed a whisky or two. Signs that wet weather was on its way only compounded his already damp spirits.

The next morning Beechworth was awash from an overnight deluge and heavy downpours continued throughout the second day of proceedings. Numbers in the courtroom were noticeably down and most people agreed the weather was to blame. But there were those, like the journalist from Melbourne's *Herald*, who claimed more cynically that 'the principal interest in the trial seems to have been got over' because 'many who came to see Ned Kelly, having gratified their peculiar curiosity, have left Beechworth'. Police stationed at the courthouse were more diligent and organised than the day before, closely questioning everyone who sought entry. David Gaunson described the spectacle of these mini-interrogations as 'simply ridiculous'.

Gaunson's one significant foray into questioning McIntyre's statements arose when the constable began to recount details of his meeting with Ned in the cell at Benalla. 'It was a blackguard proceeding', Gaunson declared to the court, saying this evidence was tainted because Ned was badly wounded at the time and he had not been warned that anything he might say could be used against him in court proceedings. Nevertheless, the magistrate had no compunction in permitting McIntyre to continue, and though he did go on to reveal the larger portion of what they'd talked about, McIntyre remained true to the personal vow he had made to himself at Benalla and deliberately left out parts of his account of the meeting that he believed were significantly condemnatory.

The court concluded at four thirty after McIntyre had spent more than six gruelling hours in the witness box. In all, the court's longhand report of his evidence and cross-examination filled seventy-seven foolscap pages and took an hour and a half to be read back to him. He had provided a mass of testimony that by law could never be rebutted with sworn evidence by any other witness. In the end, McIntyre's account of the Benalla meeting was somewhat superfluous given the range and depth of evidence he had otherwise presented. He had provided enormous detail proving Ned's guilt in the deaths of his three late colleagues and, despite his fear of cross-examination, he had stood up extremely well to Gaunson's attacks.

At one point Ned's lawyer questioned him about his acquaintance with Alexander Fitzpatrick, seizing this opportunity to remind the court that Fitzpatrick had been dismissed from the police service. But McIntyre would not be drawn on the man's character and was emphatic in his reply: 'I never saw anything wrong with Fitzpatrick'. Moments like these demonstrated how firmly resolute he was in telling the truth of the events as he saw them and that if unreasonably pressed, he could prove even more dangerous to Ned's cause.

McIntyre admitted there were faults in the way the fateful police expedition at Stringybark had been organised and carried out. He recognised that he did not know if Sergeant Kennedy or either of his other unfortunate colleagues had in their possession official warrants to apprehend Ned or his brother – documents that might be considered a legal necessity under the circumstances. He acknowledged there could be those in the community who viewed with disfavour ordinary police officers wearing civilian clothes as they went about their duties, but maintained that surely this did not justify the bushrangers invading the police camp with guns at the ready.

In the interval between McIntyre stepping down from the witness stand and the clerk reading back his testimony, another powerful blow was delivered to Gaunson's case. Dr Reynolds, who had carried out the autopsy on Constable Lonigan's body at Mansfield, took the stand and reaffirmed that the deceased officer had received at least three non-fatal wounds on the lower part of his body before the bullet that entered his brain through one of his eyes finally killed him. Gaunson resisted a detailed cross-examination of the medical practitioner but the damage was done. His description undeniably

NED KELLY IN THE DOCK.

A SKETCH BY OUR SPECIAL ARTIST, MR. DAVID GAUNSON, IN THE BEECHWORTH
POLICE COURT.

'Ned Kelly in the dock' from Melbourne Punch

corroborated McIntyre's account of the events. Gaunson managed to draw from him the possibility that a graze on the deceased officer's forehead might not have been caused by a bullet, but he knew full well it was an extremely minor concession.

Yet all things considered, Ned's lawyer put up a brave fight. At one point he roundly rebuked William Foster for what he regarded as his continuing bias. When the magistrate said to McIntyre, after receiving his evidence, 'You have given your evidence intelligently, and, as far as I am able to judge, fairly and honestly', Gaunson was understandably indignant: 'I need not say it is very unusual to make such a statement before a prisoner is dealt with'. But Gaunson knew his efforts had been largely ineffective and at the end of McIntyre's testimony had conceded: 'I will now leave the witness to be turned inside out by a better man in the Supreme Court'. By this, he publicly accepted that Ned's committal for trial in the higher court was now just a formality.

Despite excitable predictions that Maggie and Tom Lloyd might cause a scene, Ned's supporters sat silent and obedient in the court. Halfway through the afternoon they were obliged to leave to catch the last train home. Kate Kelly had single-handedly shouldered the domestic responsibilities of the family for the past week and it was time her sister relieved her. Maggie left town without ever speaking to her brother. None of Gaunson's pleas had borne fruit and his telegraph to Berry had yielded the reply: 'The Chief Secretary declines to vary the order of his predecessor at the present time'. Gaunson immediately sent off a telegram of protest to the premier.

Ned's lawyer would have been further incensed to learn that William Foster was also campaigning to maintain the policy that kept Ned isolated from his family. The magistrate sent a telegraph to Melbourne: 'Urgent and Confidential for the present at least order prohibiting Kellys relations from seeing him should not in my opinion be relaxed in any degree or in favour of anyone'.

It appears he was paying heed to the rumour that Maggie's real intention in wanting to visit Ned was to learn the location of a hidden cache of stolen money. And this was despite the citizens of Benalla and Beechworth being well aware 'that the Gang had spent all the proceeds of the two bank robberies, and were almost without money before the Glenrowan affair', as reported by the *Herald*.

The second day in court would have made it painfully clear to Gaunson that he was heading for a showdown with his ever more perplexing client, who seemed hell-bent on undermining his own defence with his bizarre courtroom antics. In the morning Ned complained to Foster that freezing gusts in the courtroom were causing 'great pains in his wounds'. Court officials scurried around searching for a suitable blanket and eventually located a large possum rug dyed a lurid red. Ned wrapped himself in the garment with a noisy show of satisfaction and proceeded to cover his head with it, deliberately concealing his face from an artist who was trying to draw him.

For many in the courtroom this display was further proof of the incorrigible nature of the bushranger. To one reporter he looked like a 'true brigand' and led all those present to believe he was proud of the description of events at Stringybark Creek that had led to the death of Thomas Lonigan. For others it confirmed Thomas McIntyre's personal view of the bushranger, that his disrespect in court showed his sense of morality had become 'dormant' and he had no regrets about the death of the policemen. Gaunson, however, saw it as final proof that Ned did not regard the proceedings against him as important or meaningful and that he'd already resigned himself to the inevitable.

The next day locals gathered after the various Sunday services to swap stories and pick over the events that had drawn so much attention to their little town. The traditional after-church tea meetings were abuzz with gossip about the hearing. Despite the intermittent rain, children ran about playing boisterous games (no doubt 'Troopers Against Outlaws' among them).

Meanwhile, David Gaunson was making the best of this day of grace. Nightly meetings at the prison revealed little more about his client, nor had the hasty exchanges with Ned in the cell at the Beechworth courthouse. On this free day courtesy of the colonial legislature's rules of the Sabbath, he was hoping for a lengthy dialogue that would increase his client's trust in him and loosen his tongue a little. Gaunson had no doubt that Ned would stand trial for the murder of Thomas Lonigan and Michael Scanlan and there was nothing he could do to stop it, for McIntyre and Dr Reynolds had presented unimpeachable evidence. His most pressing task now was to discover how best to help the bushranger help himself.

Two days in court had done nothing to improve Ned's sombre mood. He was outraged when forced to strip off all of his clothes in freezing conditions after his return from the courtroom. He complained unceasingly of the lack of warmth in his cell and the poor standard of prison food. It did not augur well for the afternoon interview.

Fortunately, the lawyer possessed an easy, winning manner and an ability to communicate with men from all walks of life. Over the past few days he and his client had gained a little confidence in each other and were even able to share the odd joke. Gaunson told later how, during one interview, he handed his client a copy of the *Australasian Sketcher* that featured an etching of Ned. They both chuckled at the absence of likeness and the bushranger remarked wryly: 'It is a mere fancy sketch of a bushman and no way like me'.

The Sunday interview lasted the whole afternoon, with Gaunson's resulting scrawl totalling more than two thousand words. Operators at the local government telegraph office were kept busy that evening transmitting Gaunson's report of the interview to the *Age* for inclusion in the next day's publication. Critics were eager to attack the author's formal language in the *Age* reports, but he made no apologies. Apart from the difficulty he would have had in translating his own handwriting (an occupational hazard) he must also have decided that Ned had neither the literary capacity nor the ability to express ideas clearly without assistance. As his lawyer, he would have taken it as a professional responsibility to 'translate' Ned's words and views as accurately and concisely as he could before presenting them to the public.

During the hunt Ned had twice attempted to publish his side of the Stringybark story in the Cameron and Jerilderie letters, but was thwarted on both occasions. Aside from a couple of paragraphs dealing with peripheral matters, the 'document' that appeared in the following Monday's *Age* constitutes the only fully authenticated expression of Ned's thinking and attitudes produced since the police killings. It's a vital account, containing significant additions and omissions that paint a clearer picture of what Ned experienced that evening in the clearing.

In both the earlier letters, the bushranger contended that the shooting of Constable Lonigan was a form of 'self-defence': 'Lonigan ran to a battery of logs and put his head up to take aim at

me, when I shot him, or he would have shot me, as I knew well'
(Cameron letter). Gaunson's account made no reference to this.
Instead Ned spoke of the fact that Lonigan was a long-time enemy
who, during an altercation in Benalla several years earlier, had
roughly grabbed Ned's genitals in an attempt to subdue him. This
brutal act had deeply affected him and he had never forgotten the
insult of it. Time and again, Ned claimed that the bushrangers' aim
upon entering the clearing was to seize the officers' weapons so as
to prevent the police from hunting them down and shooting them
in cold blood. He was not so adamant when he spoke to Gaunson:
'They may have intended to apprehend us, but I firmly believe they
only wanted the slightest pretext to shoot both my brother and
myself'.

The most remarkable feature of the lawyer's newspaper report,
however, was that Ned took a very different moral stand on the
police deaths. Previously he had justified the attack on the police
because of their unceasing harassment and oppression of his family
members, not least the barbaric treatment of his mother following
the Fitzpatrick incident. He made no mention of this to Gaunson
that afternoon, telling him simply that he did not 'wish to avert any
decree the law may deem necessary to vindicate justice ... I do not
pretend I have lived a blameless life, or that one fault justifies
another.'

And finally, Gaunson extracted the reason for his client's
strange behaviour: 'For my part I do not care one straw about my
life nor for the result of the trial'. What mattered to him most, he
said, was having the opportunity to give his own explanation for his
criminal activities. 'Let the hand of the law strike me down if
it will, but I ask that my story might be heard and considered ... If
my life teaches the public that men are made mad by bad treatment,
and if the police are taught that they may not exasperate to madness
men they persecute and ill treat, my life will not entirely be thrown
away.'

When the report hit the streets the next morning, many were of the opinion that it was solely the lawyer's work which surely threw the document's authenticity into question. They regarded the account as no more than a blatant attempt to make the best of Ned's rapidly deteriorating legal situation by concentrating on claims of police persecution. It was feared this might arouse sympathy among those who believed they had suffered at the hands of their local constabulary, potential jurymen among them.

Although the bushranger's revelations were hardly going to help him win the case, at least Gaunson now knew where he stood with his client. Ned believed that he had no effective defence against the charges, and that 'justice' would be served if he was found guilty. His lawyer's task, therefore, was to challenge unfair evidence and to seize every opportunity to expose police duplicity in their dealings with the bushrangers. It would also be incumbent on him to draw attention to the background circumstances that Ned claimed had led him to take up arms against the police in the first place. Though not legally recognised as a defence of the charges, Gaunson acknowledged his client's need to express the root cause of his criminality and felt obliged to help him do so at all costs.

After dispatching his report to the *Age* on Sunday night, Gaunson toned down his aggressive stance in court, with his characteristic retorts and provocative remarks now few and far between. He continued to agitate for Ned's visitation rights without success.

On Monday Premier Berry replied to his follow-up telegram with a curt dismissal: 'Your second telegram received, but under all the circumstances of this case, I must decline to vary the order of my predecessor'. It was a strong indication that Ned and his lawyer could expect no succour from the new government, despite Gaunson's long association with Berry and other members of his fledgling administration. It also added to his growing fear that the new premier shared Robert Ramsay's determination to ensure that the ultimate punishment would be served on the bushranger.

There were no further incidents in court like Ned's petulant display with the red possum rug. To Gaunson's relief, he behaved with detached decorum for the remainder of the proceedings. The order of business on Tuesday included the appearance of a number of 'confessional' witnesses, among them a former bank manager captured by the gang at Euroa, who swore unequivocally that Ned said to him, 'Oh, I shot Lonigan'. Later, Gaunson tried to test the credibility of two government employees who had also been caught by the gang in the same raid, but to no avail. Both were firm in their accounts of how the bushranger cheerfully boasted of his direct involvement in the Stringybark deaths. Gaunson managed to extract from another witness that he had sometimes been in the employ of the police as a 'private detective', which immediately threw his credibility into doubt, but he was followed by two witnesses who proceeded to corroborate his entire testimony, confirming that they too heard Ned brag about killing Thomas Lonigan.

In the closing stages of the Lonigan hearing, the Crown began to lay the foundations for a crucial piece of 'confessional' evidence in the form of Ned's 'autobiography' – the Jerilderie letter. Although a small portion of it had been published prior to the Beechworth hearing, the entire manuscript was now in the hands of the Melbourne police. The prosecution planned to make full use of the more damning passages of the document, including a boastful admission that Ned considered himself to be a 'great horsestealer' and a lengthy description of the killing of Sergeant Kennedy.

After the last piece of evidence pertaining to Lonigan's death was presented, William Foster asked the accused if he had anything to say before he was committed for trial for the murder of Thomas Lonigan. He replied, 'No'. His lawyer then confirmed his client's wishes that he would say nothing 'except through his counsel in the Supreme Court'.

The Scanlan hearing was next and Thomas McIntyre was recalled to the witness box to give evidence once again. His testimony was largely a repeat of what he had said earlier in relation to Lonigan. As to the details of Scanlan's death, he believed that at least three shots were fired almost simultaneously at the victim as his horse 'tossed-up' and a single blast soon after: 'I will swear that Scanlan did not fire a shot, and he was incapable afterwards, as he fell to his knees'.

Dr Reynold's evidence confirmed McIntyre's version and, as in the previous hearing, Gaunson found no reason to challenge it. The medico had gone with the initial search party to Stringybark

Creek and personally viewed the constable's body lying face up near the clearing. The wound he saw was consistent with the victim being shot under the right arm as he attempted to slew his horse away from his attackers: 'I could see the blood on the right side, under his arm'. The autopsy he conducted later at Mansfield affirmed this as well as the three other shots that McIntyre described.

The final witness in the Scanlan proceedings was Senior Constable John Kelly, who told of a conversation he had had with Ned in Benalla on the night after Glenrowan. He said he asked him about Fitzpatrick, 'Was his statement correct?', to which Ned had replied, 'Yes, it was I who fired at him'. If Gaunson had not previously harboured doubts about using the Fitzpatrick affair to justify Ned's actions, he certainly had them now.

At the close of proceedings on Wednesday afternoon, Ned was committed for trial on a second charge of murder.

Years later, William Foster admitted that his negative feelings towards Ned were of a deeply personal nature. He recalled the bushranger's first appearance in court: 'Kelly's hatred of the police was well known, and as he cast a quick glance in my direction, I knew he felt the same about me'. His eight-year-old daughter Molly had been badly shaken by her encounter with the bushranger in the Beechworth Gaol when she accompanied her father to the cells earlier in the week. The two had gawked through the prison bars with not the slightest self-consciousness, much as if they were viewing an animal in a zoo. Foster was baffled as to why Ned had taken umbrage. 'I'll get your father when I'm out of here', Ned snarled, frightening the little girl out of her wits. Lily, her ten-year-old sister, also had a tale to tell about Ned. The two girls were part of the large crowd at the local railway station who had come to witness the prisoner's arrival. Lily rushed home immediately after and breathlessly told her father: 'He had a great beard, and black beady eyes, and he spat at us, I felt it!'

Personal bias aside, William Foster was very impressed by the range and depth of the evidence presented. 'No expense spared', he noted in his remarks on the Crown cases. In the end he confessed that the sheer volume of it became tedious and 'dragged on' somewhat: 'The police department has collected every bit of information about the Kelly Gang from the time of the Wombat Forest shooting up to the capture of their leader'. Is it any wonder that Gaunson was unable to make headway in the face of such a mountain of 'confessional' evidence against his client?

As for the prisoner, his last afternoon in the Beechworth court appears to have had a negative effect on him and there were reports he was showing signs of severe depression. On the face of it, his committals to trial for the murders of Thomas Lonigan and Michael Scanlan were an unhappy though not unexpected outcome. More significant, though, was the emotional impact of being confronted for the first time by the spectre of his loved ones; people he might very soon be forced to leave behind forever.

During the court's last session, Kate Kelly took a seat in the main body of the court accompanied by Kate Lloyd, his 'sweetheart' as the reporter of Melbourne's *Herald* claimed (though with a touch of chivalry, he declined to mention her name). When the court proceedings came to a close, his sister rushed over to Ned and kissed him on the cheek, then, in an odd gesture of formality, she shook him by the hand. Not much was said of Kate Lloyd apart from reports that she waved to Ned at one point and he responded by blowing her a lingering kiss.

When the hearing was closed a flood of orders poured from police headquarters to Beechworth Gaol, the government telegraph office and the local railway station. Although there had been no signs of the anticipated trouble from Ned or his sympathisers, the authorities were taking no chances. Top-secret arrangements were made to move the bushranger to Melbourne first thing in the morning. A false trail was set indicating that Ned would be taken from Beechworth on a special train. Instead he would go by road to Wangaratta where one of the best locomotives in the Victorian Railways would be waiting with a special van attached to transport the prisoner.

Later that evening David Gaunson was an impromptu partici-pant in a local celebration that could only have been a welcome respite from the disappointments and humiliations he had endured in the past week. As night closed in a torchlight procession wound its way slowly through the streets, heralding an event that was entirely unrelated to the court case that had besieged the town. A concert by Beechworth's 'United Minstrels' in support of the local fire brigade was to be held at the Oddfellows Hall. The parade was a colourful prelude, drawing many spectators as it snaked along, including Ned's lawyer, who was free (momentarily at least) from any immediate obligations to his client. Before the night was over he made his own special mark on the gathering when he stood up before the assembled crowd and sang 'I Fear No Foe', in a voice that the *Ovens and Murray Advertiser* reported was 'good but not powerful'. The irony of his choice of refrain was not lost on his audience and could have been seen as a deliberate public statement that he was determined to continue representing the bushranger's cause to the very best of his ability.

His warm reception at the Oddfellows Hall was in sharp contrast to his treatment in the Beechworth court and suggested that whatever the locals might think of Ned and his family, a good number in the town were prepared to show Ned's lawyer the fairness and respect he deserved.

William Foster set down Ned's trials to be held at Beechworth in early October. Gaunson could take solace from the fact that the proceedings would most probably be presided over by George Higginbotham, the newest appointment to the Supreme Court. As a parliamentarian and minister of the Crown, Higginbotham was one of the most liberal influences in the public life of the colony.

Whatever he might think of Ned, there could be no doubt from his record of service as a lawyer and in government that the accused and his legal representative would not be subjected to another mockery of justice.

A month later Gaunson's hopes for a fair and unbiased judge were decisively crushed. On 18 September it was announced the trials had been transferred from Beechworth to Melbourne, a move that ensured George Higginbotham would not be presiding.

On the instructions of Henry Gurner, Smyth had instigated a special 'chambers' hearing before Sir Redmond Barry of the Supreme Court. Their aim was to move the trial to Melbourne and although David Gaunson protested vehemently, the judge overruled him on every point, agreeing with the Crown that jurors might well be subjected to intimidation and physical threat if the trials were held in the northeastern town. He said the situation 'demanded' the hearings go on in the Victorian capital where he himself would be presiding over all criminal sittings in the month of October. There was nothing Gaunson could do.

Successfully moving the trial was a major victory for Henry Gurner and Charles Smyth. It was a fundamental given in the profession that a lawyer's first consideration in approaching court proceedings was 'the predominating character of the presiding judge'. Of all the Supreme Court judges, Barry was the one most likely to be amenable to the Crown lawyers' cause. Like the Crown solicitor, Barry's legal thinking and social attitudes were strictly conservative and many were of the opinion that he would relish the opportunity to condemn the bushranger to death. He had made his anti-Kelly sentiments quite clear when he imposed a savage three-year sentence on Ned's mother over the Fitzpatrick incident, made even more severe because she had recently given birth to a daughter who would spend the first crucial years of her life without her mother.

And yet for all his reactionary values, Barry was a highly contradictory figure. In the august circles in which he mixed it was no secret that since 1846 he had cohabited with a woman who was not his wife and that she had borne him four children. Despite this growing family he continued to live at the exclusive Melbourne Club and joined wholeheartedly in the bachelor lifestyle favoured by the police commissioner, whose gambling and sexual adventuring were legendary amongst their cohorts. Throughout his life Barry stubbornly maintained there was an entirely different moral code for the class to which Ned Kelly and his family belonged and the class to which he belonged.

As the law stood at the time, legal rulings of a judge at a criminal trial could not be challenged before other judges unless the judge himself gave personal permission – an unlikely eventuality under the circumstances. If Ned was convicted of murder, the judge could be the deciding factor in determining whether the sentence of death that would be necessarily imposed on him was actually carried out. If he made favourable remarks about the prisoner, it might convince government authorities to replace the death penalty with imprisonment. Tradition also dictated that he would attend the colony's Executive Council when the final decision was made as to whether a condemned prisoner should be granted life or death. In essence, Redmond Barry would have influence over every stage of the legal processes that would decide Ned Kelly's fate.

Barry set the date for the opening of the trial when the month was more than half over. It was a welcome development for Premier Berry and the rest of Melbourne's dignitaries, for they were anxious that this trial did not overshadow one of the most illustrious and important events in the colony's history. The first day of October 1880 would mark the opening of the Melbourne International Exhibition and the eyes of the entire nation would be upon them. Years in planning, it would bring in tens of thousands of visitors from around the country and abroad, and was designed to promote the colony as one of the most socially advanced regions in the world. Special trains from country areas offered cheap tickets to bring in provincial visitors. A public holiday was called for the first day and a grand procession would mark its opening. In addition, the busy city thoroughfare known as Stephen Street was renamed Exhibition Street. Home to one of the largest per capita brothel districts in the English speaking world at the time, its numerous 'establishments' were moved to less conspicuous locations like Little Lonsdale Street so as not to advertise the seamy side of the host city to the rest of the world.

This was the first Australian international exhibition and was modelled on the London event that had been so successfully orchestrated by Prince Albert in 1851. The Exhibition Building and Gardens were impossibly grand for the time, and visitors strolled through the lavish exhibits from many countries designed to show-case local products spawned by the industrial revolution. There were daily concerts and numerous other entertainments to keep the punters happy.

Authorities knew that the stories of poverty, desperate men and frontier-style conflicts which would most certainly abound in the Kelly trial would do nothing to enhance the image they hoped the exhibition would project. When the trial was slated for Monday 18 October, there must have been a collective sigh of relief from society's upper echelons. By then the exhibition would be well underway, minimising any potential damage.

When proceedings finally commenced on that bright spring Monday morning, the courtroom was filled with at least eighty potential jurors awaiting the selection process. Maggie Skillion was there, tucked away in the second row of the gallery reserved for women. A reporter from Melbourne's *Herald* thought he saw Tom Lloyd in the crowd, but in the heavy crush of newsmen around him he could not be sure and it was never confirmed.

One notable absentee was Charles Standish. His raffish demeanour and insubordinate ways, and his fondness for dabbling in blackmail, had finally caught up with him. In mid-September he 'resigned' as police commissioner, presumably to save face. Melbourne's newspapers only touched on it briefly but a Sydney journal could see the writing on the wall, predicting a few days before the resignation that his manifest unfitness as police commissioner would soon result in his downfall.

Far more significant was the absence of defence counsel at their allotted side of the bar table. On the other side was Henry Gurner, Charles Smyth and Arthur Chomley, ready to do battle. Seated in the dock, the bushranger appeared to be in a state of 'bewilderment', as one newspaper described him. He had to be asked twice to raise his right hand to plead to the charge of murdering Thomas Lonigan. He glanced in vain at the bar table as if hoping his lawyers might appear miraculously from thin air to advise him. After a third request he raised his right hand 'slightly' and murmured, 'Not guilty'.

As the second murder charge was being read out by the judge's associate, a young man, wigged and gowned, suddenly burst into the court and hurried over to the bar table. The atmosphere in the room noticeably shifted and the clerk abruptly fell silent.

This was novice barrister Henry Bindon's first solo appearance before a Supreme Court judge. He had recently returned to Victoria after completing his legal education in England. Without further ado he announced to the court that he knew nothing about the case he had just been charged with, and he was there to explain why the accused had no legal representatives present.

Redmond Barry

At that time in Victoria only those who qualified as barristers could address Supreme Court hearings. South Australia, New South Wales and Tasmania did not hold with this excessive bureaucracy, but in Victoria the system favoured any opportunity for lawyers to increase their income, in this instance by doubling up on the number of lawyers required in major court proceedings. As a solicitor, Gaunson couldn't speak for his client even though he was by far the most knowledgeable when it came to Ned's situation. It was this professional division, complained Bindon, which was denying Ned proper legal representation at his trials.

Bindon explained to the court that the previous Friday in a special hearing before Redmond Barry, senior barrister Hickman Molesworth had temporarily represented Ned in seeking a postponement of his trial for another month. He'd made it very clear that he was not actually briefed to represent the accused as Ned's lawyer had yet to reach a satisfactory financial arrangement with him. Bindon went on to read laboriously from a long affidavit by

Gaunson describing complicated negotiations over the weekend that had still failed to secure Molesworth's services. The sum the barrister was seeking was far in excess of the amount the law of the colony provided for such services, and Maggie Skillion was unable to meet the shortfall. They needed more time to raise funds, he protested.

There was no mention of why it had taken more than the two months since the Beechworth hearing for the question of Ned's legal representation to finally erupt on the eve of his first trial. For those familiar with the workings of the legal profession at the time, there was in fact an eminently plausible explanation. Bindon's dramatic entry that day had been well stage-managed. The ploy was a last-ditch effort to prevent Redmond Barry from presiding over the trial. Under normal circumstances, when a lawyer representing a party was not able to be present, the presiding judge would be obliged to postpone proceedings until the situation was rectified. If not, he risked appearing to act unfairly. Most likely Gaunson was hoping that if they could postpone the proceedings long enough, the trial would not begin until November, when another (hopefully less biased) judge would be obliged to take over the list.

Bindon finally wound up the affidavit and sat down. All eyes turned to Charles Smyth who, following a brief whispered conversation with the Crown solicitor, rose to address the court. The time had now come for the Crown prosecutor to give a little. Gravely he told the court he was 'very unwilling that there should be even the slightest reason for saying hereafter this prisoner has been improperly prosecuted or harshly treated'. With an air of grave magnanimity, he agreed that a stay of proceedings would be appropriate.

It was a self-serving act, though, for if Ned had no legal representation and continued to act with the same bewilderment he had shown earlier, there might be difficulties for the Crown in conducting their case. An accused with no lawyer would have to be given considerable latitude in questioning witnesses. Jurors could also begin to sympathise with the defendant, helplessly cast adrift in a complex and unforgiving legal system. On one issue, however, Smyth was adamant: the terms of adjournment in regards to Barry's involvement. If Ned's cases were postponed until November another judge would take charge of Melbourne's 'criminal sittings' under the Supreme Court's administrative arrangements, therefore excluding Barry.

Barry discussed the situation at length with Crown Prosecutor Smyth. The judge had unbreakable commitments but it soon emerged there was just enough time for him to rearrange his schedule. Ned's trial for the murder of Thomas Lonigan could begin again in ten days time, with just three court sitting days remaining before the end of the month. No reference was made to the fact that if it went on for several days, the holiday for the running of the Melbourne Cup would intervene on the following Tuesday. When Smyth willingly agreed to the arrangement Barry intoned smugly, 'It is very becoming on the part of the Crown.' The recommence-ment date was set for Thursday 28 October. Gaunson's defence ploy was a resounding failure.

News of the delay in proceedings was swiftly conveyed to the large crowd waiting outside. Angry and disappointed, there were wild scenes as impatient onlookers scrambled for a sighting of Ned being led back to gaol. Several were pursued by police as they attempted to scale a building that overlooked the pathway leading to the cells. Others hugged the ground in an effort to see under the prison gates. Police officers drew their batons and began to rap the knuckles of the more agile ones climbing the fence to peer over the prison walls. So unruly and desperate were they, the correspondent of a Ballarat newspaper noted, that several women caught up in the swarming crowd were roughly shoved and jostled.

A far more subdued group lined the pathway leading from the courthouse. These were the potential jurors who had been summarily excused from participation in the bushranger's trial.

No doubt they were feeling disgruntled at their dismissal as they watched Ned being led in handcuffs back to his cell surrounded by armed warders. As he had in the courtroom, Ned seemed calm, composed and unmoved by all the fuss. Later he told his warders that he wasn't really perturbed about the difficulties concerning his legal representation and he would have been well satisfied to let the proceedings go on without defence lawyers. Apparently his state of mind had altered little since Beechworth.

Although the defence had gained some time before the resumption of the trial, there was still the problem of securing a barrister willing to act for Ned. Molesworth remained adamant that he would not defend the bushranger for the meagre fee of seven pounds seven shillings despite the promise of further 'refreshers' should the proceedings extend beyond the normal timeframe. This was a unique form of legal aid for the era, and was rarely (if ever) equalled in the nineteenth century English speaking world. It was set up by Victorian law to enable those facing capital offences (who were usually fighting for their lives) to have barristers represent them at their trials. Nevertheless, Molesworth flatly refused and Gaunson could not tempt any other experienced barrister to take on the job. So much for the ethical tradition among barristers that monetary interests were supposed to play no part in such circumstances.

For Gurner, Smyth and Chomley the postponement was little more than an inconvenience. Their most important weapon was Barry and his position as presiding judge of the trial was still secure. They had also achieved another victory that day. In a further development of the outlaw act loophole, the possibility that it might be brought to light and damage the prosecution case had been dealt a decisive blow. According to the reading of the ancient law, the moment Ned was called upon to plead to the charges against him, which he did by answering 'Not guilty', he nullified the possibility of his previous status as outlaw being used as a potential defence.

The trial for the murder of Thomas Lonigan resumed on the last Thursday in October – two days after the second anniversary of Stringybark Creek. A few days earlier the prosecution had opted not to proceed with the charge of Scanlan's murder for the simple fact there was no eyewitness because McIntyre had already fled the scene. Many believed the trial would continue for at least a week. Melbourne's *Herald* voiced fears that unless the proceedings were allowed to go on after normal court hours, the trial would spill over into the Melbourne Cup holiday on Tuesday and 'His Honour is averse to having the jury locked up during the race time'. Their concerns were unwarranted. The trial moved rapidly to its conclusion on the second day despite new Crown witnesses and lengthy addresses by the judge and lawyers. Final judgement was passed on Ned Kelly in a determination still described in law books as a manifestation of the will of 'God and Country'.

Throughout the trial Ned remained silent. His only formally recorded utterance was 'Not guilty' at his first appearance almost two weeks earlier. He made no unsworn statement from the dock as the law allowed him, and so forfeited the right to give the court his personal explanation for what happened at Stringybark Creek. No defence witnesses were called, nor evidence produced to support Ned's claims of police intimidation despite his assertions that their oppression justified the gang's subsequent actions. All matters of defence were left to David Gaunson and the young barrister Henry Bindon.

By all accounts Gaunson had done his best to persuade the government to increase the statutory fee so that he could obtain a more experienced advocate for his client. The demand had been flatly refused by the attorney-general, who was not prepared to make an exception in the bushranger's case despite Gaunson's heartfelt entreaties. Nor had Maggie Skillion succeeded in raising funds to secure better legal representation for her brother. Just as happened when her mother was gaoled two years earlier, Maggie received no support from other members of her family or the people who claimed friendship with the Kellys.

Bindon was inexperienced, but he was undoubtedly ambitious and fast gaining a reputation as a bit of a legal nonconformist for his espousal of liberal views. He had recently sought election to the Legislative Assembly supporting Graham Berry, which alienated many conservative middle-level judges still smarting from Berry's Black Wednesday cull. The novice barrister was more than willing to take on what was shaping up to be an important case, but he could hardly be blamed if he sometimes appeared less than adequate in pursuing Ned's cause. Only after Gaunson had exhausted all efforts to obtain an experienced barrister was the case formally passed to Bindon on Monday night, so he had only two days to prepare – not nearly enough time to familiarise himself with the bushranger's situation. He remonstrated with Redmond Barry to this effect, seeking another adjournment of the trial. But the judge was determined to preside over the entire trial. He dismissed the plea, ruling that the proceedings must continue because more than eight weeks had elapsed since the bushranger's committal for trial at Beechworth.

At ten past five on the Friday afternoon, the court rose as Redmond Barry left the bench. Two gaol warders took Ned to the prisoner's room and all eyes turned to the twelve men as they were escorted to the jury room to consider their verdict. There was no strict time limit set for their deliberations. They could be cloistered away for a matter of minutes or for many hours.

None of the jurors was especially notable. In their own way they were representative of the expanding middle classes that had come to exercise a growing influence on the conduct of political activities in the colony. Every one of them had a modest property holding, a requirement that formed the basic qualification for jury service. Three of the jurymen were farmers who lived on the fringes of the Melbourne metropolitan area. Three were ordinary working men: a gardener, a bricklayer and a grave decorator. Four others were engaged in more skilled occupations: a carpenter, a book-binder, a blacksmith and a bootmaker. The final two were described as a dairyman from the inner suburb of Carlton and an ironmonger from West Melbourne.

The task before them was critical. If they reached a unanimous verdict on Ned's guilt or innocence it could not be further chal-lenged in the courts, whatever the opinions of judges and lawyers. Nor were they required to give reasons for reaching their decision, except in very special circumstances. This was based on an English principle dating back to the thirteenth century when the use of juries in criminal matters had first taken hold in the working of the law. Juries were described as custodians of the judgements of 'God and Country' and it was unconscionable to challenge the authority of God or impugn the probity of the community. Five hundred years later and several continents away, the practice was unchanged.

As the jurymen filed out the lawyers scanned their faces, hoping to gain some sense of the prevailing attitude. The Crown lawyers were far too experienced in the unpredictable nature of juries to be overconfident. A single dissenting voice on the panel would result in a hung trial and the hearing would be aborted. If this occurred, Ned could be tried on the same charge before a

different jury, and tried yet again if needs be, for there was no strict
limit on the number of times this could occur. The Crown lawyers
had come prepared to meet an adverse verdict and had in their
possession entirely separate briefs to proceed immediately against
Ned for the murder of Constable Scanlan. In the end they were not
necessary, but unlike so many other records they still exist and are
housed in the Sir Thomas Ramsay Collection at the Scotch College
library, Melbourne.

Had the Crown been forced to use the addenda to the Scanlan
brief, it would have caused considerable embarrassment to the local
constabulary for they contained decisive proof that some policemen
had souvenired pieces of evidence at Glenrowan. A witness statement from Constable McHugh tells that he had in his possession a
Webley revolver 'which I picked up in the bush about 100 yards
from Jones's hotel'. Not only did he still have it as 'the only
memento I have of the affray', but he did 'respectfully ask that
I be allowed to keep it'! And Sergeant Steele speaks of a revolver
that he took from the prisoner Kelly and passed to a Mr Marsden
... 'but some person took it out of [Mr Marsden's] hand to
look at it and did not return it, I cannot therefore produce it'. The
prosecution would most certainly have been reluctant to impart this
information.

An interesting feature of the Smyth Crown brief and the brief
housed in the Victorian archives that was probably used by Smyth's
junior counsel, Arthur Chomley, is that both men indulged in a bit
of 'doodling' on the pages. While Smyth sketched a couple of rough
pen portraits of people in the court, Chomley fashioned most
notably a flower, a cottage and an elaborate letter K. It's strange to
think that both men had the time and opportunity to mentally
wander off and engage in idle scribbling during such an important
criminal trial. Perhaps the prosecution team felt the outcome was
such a foregone conclusion that there was no need to give the
proceedings their full attention?

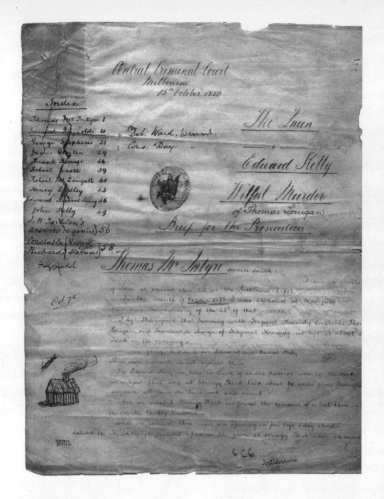

Top: Portion of Crown brief (probably) used by Arthur Chomley
Bottom: Portions of Crown brief used by Charles Smyth

As for the doodles themselves, there's one in particular that speaks volumes. Dick Briggs, the curator of the Sir Thomas Ramsay Collection, was particularly taken by three C's on the Chomley brief. A long-time aficionado of fine tobacco, he immediately recognised the symbol that identifies the highest quality of tobacco leaf available: CCC stands for 'Claro Claro Claro' roughly translated from the Spanish as 'Clear Clear Clear'. It doesn't take a huge leap of imagination to consider that at some stage junior counsel Arthur Chomley's thoughts were elsewhere – the man was longing for a smoke!

Ned's lawyers had acquitted themselves well enough. In line with tradition, Gaunson and Bindon were positioned close to the dock, allowing Gaunson to consult with his client on a number of occasions during the course of the proceedings. The best they could hope for was that the jury might feel a small measure of sympathy for the accused. Even an aborted trial would be a victory.

Evidence presented on Ned's 'confessions' had inevitably revealed comments he made about the deaths of the officers at Stringybark Creek. Bindon had tried to prevent these revelations for he could see the trial was turning into an investigation into the deaths of all of the Stringybark victims, not just Lonigan. This was particularly so in the case of Sergeant Kennedy, whose death had provoked such an outpouring of grief and rage in the community. Redmond Barry overruled his objections, saying he held that this kind of evidence pointed to the bushranger's state of mind at Stringybark. He then refused Bindon's request to allow his ruling to be tested in a special hearing before other judges, opening the way for an avalanche of this type of evidence that reminded the jury of the range and scope of Ned's criminal activities.

Facts relating to Euroa and Jerilderie had necessarily summoned up the gang's armed hold-ups. Although the attempt to derail the police train at Glenrowan was not the subject of criminal charges, Sergeant Steele reminded the court of the potential horror of such a disaster had the plan succeeded. He told of Ned's remarks at the time of his capture: 'I asked him what he intended to do with the wreck of the train and Ned replied "Shoot every bloody one that escaped"'.

In the end Bindon's only tangible victory was preventing the presentation of material from the Jerilderie letter. The document brought into court seems to have been an abridged version of the original, but it contained material that would serve as a vivid reminder of the sordid nature of Kennedy's death. Charles Smyth was forced to admit the document was not in Ned's handwriting and Redmond Barry had no choice under the circumstances but to rule that it could not be admitted into evidence.

Ned's dress and conduct did not help his cause. As always, in a major criminal trial the presentation of the accused was of considerable significance for the jury. Ned appeared in the dock at the start of the second day of the trial wearing a large silk handkerchief with a vivid multicoloured flower pattern draped around his neck. To the hard-working, soberly attired members of the jury it was like a badge of defiance confirming him a member of the indolent, lawless class which preyed on the community. It was also widely noted that Ned responded with a knowing wink directed at the jury after a witness's remark that he had acted in a 'gentlemanly fashion' in front of women. In an age dominated by stern opposition to drinking alcohol and indulging in sexual licence, these jurymen drawn from the conservative classes would surely not have been impressed.

Once the jury had withdrawn, many spectators quit the stuffy courtroom for a breath of fresh air. It was a hot dusty day and the majority in attendance believed they were in for a long and tedious wait. But less than fifteen minutes later shouts could be heard ordering the court to reassemble. The jury had reached a verdict.

Barristers quickly returned to the bar table and Ned was escorted back to the dock. Thomas McIntyre, Sergeant Arthur

Steele and Senior Constable John Kelly remained side by side, no doubt bound together by their experiences and the understanding that this verdict would have a lasting impact on their lives.

One particularly significant spectator did not return. Throughout the day Maggie Skillion sat quietly in the place that had been specially allocated for her on the ground floor of the court. Kate Lloyd, Kate's friend Bridget McAuliffe, Tom Lloyd and two other supporters from Greta accompanied her. But as Redmond Barry returned to his place at the bench, only Kate and her companion entered and resumed their seats. Maggie had unswervingly fought for her brother's rights throughout his period of incarceration, suffering enormous financial and emotional hardships. Now, at this most critical moment, she chose to hear the news away from court and the glare of public scrutiny.

By five thirty-five the jurors were back and the courtroom was filled to capacity. The dairyman from Carlton who had been elected foreman announced the jury's decision. Guilty.

Newspaper reports of the reaction in the courtroom give little away, so we can only guess at the uproar that ensued. Days later, the foreman disclosed to Thomas McIntyre that 'The guilt of the prisoner was not the subject at all as the jury made up their minds before leaving the court on that matter'. He explained the delay in the announcement was due only to two jurors who had initially opposed a guilty verdict because they were against capital punishment. It had taken the other jurors several minutes to convince their dissenting colleagues that they were sworn to determine the outcome of the case without regard to any sentence the law might impose. This had finally persuaded them to join in the unanimous decision.

With their verdict passed, the jury was discharged forthwith. In accordance with English legal practice, the clerk of the court asked Ned if he had anything to say about the verdict. By tradition, this was an occasion when those convicted of hanging offences could plead what was known as 'benefit of clergy', a process whereby a first-time capital offender might suffer the punishment of branding, but then be allowed to go free. By the time of Ned's trial, it was nothing more than a meaningless ritual. Nevertheless, Ned took this opportunity to finally speak up after sitting sullen and mute in the dock as his fate was decided by strangers.

There are varying reports of what he actually said that day. All agreed that he blamed himself for not making an unsworn statement to the court, and that he regretted he did not personally question those witnesses who attacked him with their testimony about his 'confessions'. Finally, he once again indicated that he was reconciled to his situation. 'It is not that I fear death, I fear it as little as to drink a cup of tea. On the evidence that has been given, no juryman could have given any other verdict.'

The resulting clamour brought shouts of 'Silence!' from the court officials. It was now the moment for the judge to carry out the final ritual of pronouncing the 'awful sentence of death' as it was described in the newspapers. It was also Barry's opportunity to express his personal views on the trial and on the prisoner. He had only just begun to speak when Ned interrupted. What followed is one of the most infamous courtroom exchanges in Australian history.

With constant interjections from the prisoner, Barry launched into a vehement character assassination, revealing once and for all his personal bias against Kelly. He told him he was a member of the class that had completely cut itself off 'from all decencies, the affections, the charities and all the obligations of society', making him as 'degraded as a wild beast of the field'. In cruel reference to the fact that he would have ultimate control over the appeals that would determine whether Ned lived or died, he said, 'I can hold out to you no hope ... I do not see that I can entertain the slightest reason for saying you can expect anything'. In addition, he believed the prisoner should have had all his other crimes taken into account as further justification for the death penalty, though they had not been the subjects of criminal charges.

At one point Ned protested that it was his understanding that in English law 'a man is innocent until he is found guilty'. The judge ignored the comment. A little later Ned reaffirmed, 'I do not fear death ... I dare say the day will come when we shall have to go to a bigger court than this. There we shall see who is right and who is wrong.'

Finally, Barry pronounced the sentence of death, concluding with the traditional utterance: 'May the Lord have mercy on your soul'. Reports differ on the exact wording of Ned's famous riposte: either the pleasingly dramatic 'Yes, I will meet you there', or the more clumsy 'I will go a little further than that, and say that I will see you there where I go'. Either way, it forms a sensational high point in the many retellings of the Kelly myth, and a sobering portent of Barry's imminent demise.

As the condemned man was led from the court, he scanned the excited chattering crowd. When his eyes lit upon the face he sought, he called out, 'Goodbye. I'll see you there.' Accepting his fate, Ned Kelly believed his next meeting with Kate Lloyd would take place in another world. History does not record her response.

It was only ever an assumption that Ned was referring to hell in his final words to Barry. In a book published in 1893, evangelist John Cowley Coles wrote about a number of brief meetings he had with Ned in the days before the hanging. The condemned man heard him preach on the subject 'Prepare to meet your God' and apparently told him afterwards: 'I believe it all. Although I have been bushranging I have believed that when I die I have a God to meet.'

The fact that he made similar remarks in his letter to the Executive Council and as a final farewell to Kate implies he would meet them all again in the same place. As Ned prepared to leave his earthly existence, he fully expected to eventually see friend and foe alike in heaven. There, final judgement by God would be made upon them all.

When Ned returned to his cell after the verdict, he was no longer just a prisoner – he was a prisoner condemned to death. As he entered the gaol he shouted they would need forty thousand troopers to rid the colony of the Kellys, but his show of defiance was short-lived. Immediately the civilian clothes he had worn in the dock were taken away. As the rules decreed, metal bracelets – or 'leg irons', as they were called – were sealed around his ankles with rivets and linked together with a sturdy chain. He was made to wear a specially designed set of trousers with buttons running up the legs to accommodate the chain arrangement. Another chain was attached to a belt, inhibiting movement so that the prisoner could only shuffle around by holding on to it.

Once again the gaol governor did what little he could to help preserve Ned's personal dignity. Castieau allowed the bushranger to keep his beard and waived the normal requirement for his long hair to be cropped.

Ned's legal situation had entered another phase. All further recourse was now vested in the Executive Council, a body presided over by the governor. In constitutional reality this was essentially a rubber stamp for legitimating decisions made by an incumbent premier and those in his cabinet. Aside from the governor they were the only individuals customarily summoned to the meetings, and the proceedings were cloaked in secrecy, much like those of Britain's Privy Council. The determinations could be made on any grounds and were completely unchallengeable in any ordinary court proceedings.

The council directed to the minute when a sentence of death would be carried out. It also had the authority, based on English constitutional precedents, to rule that any sentence of death could be commuted to a sentence of imprisonment for the term of a prisoner's natural life. It was regular practice for the council to seek the advice of the judge who had presided at a trial where the death sentence had been imposed, although it was not bound to this. In the absence of official shorthand transcripts of criminal trials, the judge was expected to provide copies of his own notes or other material that might help in the council's deliberations. In tendering advice a judge was not obliged to act in a judicial capacity. He could either limit his involvement to legal questions or go to the other extreme by expressing his own personal opinions on how the authorities should act in their treatment of a condemned prisoner.

In Redmond Barry's case there was not a shred of doubt about which way he would go. His advice to the council was, as expected, thoroughly damning. Ned's manifest sins as he understood them – whether proven against him or not – were more than enough to send him to the gallows. As Barry wrote in his report, 'the history of the prisoner during the last two years' should not be ignored by the Executive Council when they considered his case. According to the bushranger's own admissions he had committed 'numerous' criminal acts that rendered it unnecessary for him to say more than that the case against him was 'amply proved'. He could therefore 'see no reason whatever' why the sentence of death against Ned 'should not be carried into execution'.

Both the liberal *Age* and the conservative *Argus* echoed Barry's sentiments, viewing Ned's conviction for the murder of Thomas Lonigan as a means of finally punishing the bushranger for a range of crimes that extended far beyond those discussed at his trial. 'No greater criminal name is recorded in the annals of Victorian crime', the *Age* told its readers. In 'self-defence' the community had no choice 'but to exterminate him'. In turn, the *Argus* featured a lengthy retrospective of Ned's life of crime and looked forward to his death upon the scaffold.

Premier Graham Berry and his cabinet now held the ultimate power of life and death over Ned Kelly. Berry did not align himself with the 'top hats': men who paraded their self-proclaimed superiorities over the rest of the community at every opportunity. On one occasion he had even been compared to the bushranger in terms of his 'radical' outlook when he fought to overcome the veto power of the colony's Legislative Council in 1878. He keenly felt the injustice of a constitution that had been entrenched under British authority to preserve the power of the wealthiest classes in the community at the expense of the far more democratically elected Legislative Assembly, and fought to take away their veto power by attacking their property rights. But despite his strenuous efforts, including a visit to England in an attempt to get the British government to alter the constitution, he was ultimately unsuccessful.

Such democratic leanings should not, however, be seen as an indication that he sympathised with the bushranger in any way. As a long political career had demonstrated, his affinities rested with the thinking and aspirations of the ever-expanding 'middling classes' in the colony – the solid, hardworking, self-improving artisans, small farmers and businessmen who had voiced strong opposition to the activities of the Kelly gang. It was this solid base of electoral support that had enabled him to be such a prominent figure in local politics for almost twenty years.

Berry met with David Gaunson's brother, who was also a lawyer, on the morning after the verdict. In the weeks since Ned's return to Melbourne, William Gaunson had become increasingly involved with the bushranger's defence, gradually taking over from

his brother. Exactly why David chose to all but withdraw from the
scene in Ned's final days has never been clear, though it was probably for a combination of reasons. There's no doubt he was an
ambitious politician, hell-bent on securing ministerial office, so he
was probably not prepared to sacrifice his chances of achieving this
by becoming too involved in the very public protests against the
impending execution. Perhaps more importantly, during his
meeting with Ned in Beechworth Gaol, Ned himself had virtually
admitted his legal if not his moral guilt. This would explain why
Gaunson subsequently concentrated on dismantling evidence given
by the prosecution witnesses rather than attempting to mount a
strong defence. It was the duty of a lawyer in these circumstances to
do no more than attack the case against his client when he knows
the client is legally guilty.

As to why David's brother William stepped into the fray there
is no anecdotal evidence to draw upon, apart from the fact that he
shared similar views to his brother and perhaps had less to lose.
William soon found that Berry had no moral qualms about using
capital punishment as a penalty for murder and other capital
offences (unlike Premier Henry Parkes of New South Wales). This
became abundantly clear when he agreed to Gaunson's request to
immediately lift the ban on Ned's visiting rights. The premier fully
expected that Ned would not occupy the condemned man's cell of
Melbourne Gaol for much longer.

That Saturday morning, the people of Melbourne were
turning their attention to an event that drew spectators from across
the land. Cabs, charabancs and a motley collection of other horse-
drawn vehicles were beginning to clog the streets as they set out for
the Flemington racecourse for the first day of Melbourne's spring
racing carnival. On a single day more than fifty thousand people
would be transported to the track on special railway services. Most
official business would be at a standstill until the Melbourne Cup
was run on the following Tuesday afternoon. By then, more than a

third of Melbourne's residents would have spent at least one day at
Flemington, along with the governor and the majority of government officials. In between, balls, parties and a host of other social
events would provide a pleasant diversion for the men who would
ultimately determine Ned's destiny. Their final decision would be
made in haste, leaving little time for any effective appeals on Ned's
behalf.

After his audience with the premier, William Gaunson went to
the Robert Burns Hotel where Maggie Skillion, Kate Lloyd and the
other Kelly supporters were staying. For the time being, at least, he
and his brother had no intention of conceding defeat. There was
nothing more they could do for him in the courts, but the Gaunsons
were strong proselytisers for certain causes, and one that both could
pursue in good conscience was to demand that Ned should not be
hanged because of the barbarity of capital punishment.

Even at the eleventh hour, William was determined to do
whatever he could to prevent the bushranger's looming execution.
Ned's supporters were comparatively few, but Gaunson knew there
was a moral issue that could aid his cause. Two of the jurors who
had convicted the bushranger of the murder of Thomas Lonigan
had initially opposed his execution in good conscience because
they did not believe in capital punishment. There were others,
among them prominently placed women, who most certainly
harboured similar views and were willing to speak in public about
the issue. Even George Higginbotham, the new Supreme Court
judge and a future chief justice of Victoria, had been recorded in
the past openly questioning the desirability of retaining the death
penalty in the colony.

William Gaunson's first task was to report to Maggie Skillion
that after four long months the ban on visiting Ned had finally
been lifted. With a simple stroke of the pen, Graham Berry revoked
this arbitrary restriction revealing the charade that had been so
vigorously pursued by men like Charles Standish and William

Foster. Miraculously, fears that poison would be conveyed to him or that a riot would be incited – some of the 'dire consequences' that had been concocted to justify Ned's unnatural state of isolation – vanished without explanation. Those in government service who had carefully filed away the document giving Robert Ramsay's approval for Maggie to be allowed to visit her brother without informing her of it, breathed a sigh of relief. The subterfuge would not be revealed until government papers were released for public scrutiny several decades later.

Now, for the first time since her fleeting encounter with Ned at Glenrowan, Maggie would finally speak with her brother. Kate Lloyd also had Berry's sanction to see the prisoner. As her presence in the courtroom had confirmed, her devotion to him had not wavered. Despite Ned's grim prediction they would only meet in another world, they were now to be allowed a few quiet moments together before the sentence parted them, in this world at least, forever.

28 | THE FINAL BATTLE

Two days before the Cup was run, Premier Berry announced the Executive Council would 'most likely' meet in seven days time to consider the bushranger's situation. With the help of Maggie Skillion, the Gaunson brothers joined a public campaign to seek the commutation of Ned's death sentence. Their plan for the next few days was that the bushranger would produce a document containing his side of the story and informing the council of his views relating to his precarious situation. Upon learning of this, the premier's immediate response was to expedite Ned's hanging and bring forward the Executive Council meeting to the morning after the Melbourne Cup. He knew if he left it any longer they would have to wait until at least the end of the week because the governor was solidly booked up for the Oaks Day of the racing carnival on Thursday.

While more than one hundred thousand people attended the Flemington racecourse, the documents required for the yet to be scheduled meeting were hastily prepared. Those working in Redmond Barry's chambers had no chance whatsoever of joining in the holiday spirit as they toiled to produce a copy of the official judge's lengthy notes made at the trial. Historically, the resulting document has often been described as a 'transcript' of the proceedings, but it was more like a summary of what occurred. (In terms of accuracy, the closest surviving 'transcript' of the trial would have to be the many columns of reportage in the newspapers.) Barry's heavily abridged document of the evidence omitted the remarks of counsel, made no mention of the judge's address to the jury and left out Henry Bindon's plea for a higher court to rule on the legality of several aspects of the proceedings.

Ned only learned of the change of plans on the morning of the meeting. Hastily he dictated to a gaol warden: 'I have not had time to put all the facts as I would have liked to have brought under your notice because I have had to write this morning to be in time for the Executive Council'. He affixed his mark to the letter and it was sent under urgent cover to the governor.

In line with tradition, no minutes were taken during the meeting and the members were sworn to secrecy. All we know of this pivotal meeting is the final decision. The prisoner himself was among the first to learn of the outcome. John Castieau personally informed him the Executive Council had shown no mercy and determined the prisoner would be hanged in eight days time. The bravado from Friday night had completely evaporated and when he was told how long he had left to live, his comment was simply, 'It is short'.

To make matters worse, Castieau had to tell the prisoner that despite his best efforts, the letter Ned had hastily dictated that morning had not been received in time to be read out to the Executive Council. In truth, the letter would have done little to help his case. Now held in the state archives, it is a rambling unstructured piece that could very well have been used to further condemn him. A large part of it reiterated Ned's claims about the iniquities relating to the Fitzpatrick incident, but one section contained information that went directly against the contents of the Cameron and Jerilderie letters.

With no explanation for his change of heart, Ned acknowledged that all four bushrangers had been present throughout the events at Stringybark Creek and he now believed he should not be held fully responsible for what had occurred. In a bizarre turn-around, he accused Thomas McIntyre of contributing to the deaths of Michael Kennedy and Constable Scanlan because he failed to warn his colleagues as they entered the camp that the bushrangers wanted only to disarm them, not to harm them. Finally, he requested yet again that his mother be released, stating that it 'could not make any difference to the government, for the day will come when all men will be judged by their mercy and deeds', and then he asked permission for 'my friends to have my body that they might bury it in Consecrated ground'.

Even as Castieau was breaking the news to Ned, arrangements were being made to carry out the order decreed by the Executive Council. A petty criminal named Elijah Upjohn was being trans-ferred from Pentridge Gaol in Coburg to serve as the bushranger's executioner. It was to be the first time he ever carried out a hanging and there was a good deal for him to learn in the next few days if he was to perform efficiently. In accordance with a custom that dated back to the beginning of British occupation in Australia, when convicts had often been employed as public executioners, Upjohn would receive a partial remission of his current prison sen-tence. In a departure from tradition, though, he would also be rewarded with a small payment for being Ned Kelly's hangman.

When Maggie and Kate Lloyd finally met with Ned the morning after the verdict they did their best to comfort him. Time and again they reiterated that he had their support no matter what happened, but it was hard to ignore the shackles, the iron grille between them and the constant presence of a gaol warden hovering within earshot. Maggie continued to draw in supporters and at this crucial juncture she redoubled her efforts to bring immediate family on board, however painful it might be for them.

Kate Kelly, who had been left behind in Greta to look after the children, was summoned to Melbourne. A couple of Ned's old mates, including the tough, loquacious Wild Wright, were on their way in the hope they'd be granted a final audience. And even James Kelly paid Ned a visit after he had so conspicuously shown no interest in his surviving brother since Glenrowan.

At the Robert Burns Hotel, news of the Executive Council decision was greeted like a fresh call to arms for the Kelly supporters. This plain and unpretentious little establishment located a short distance from Spencer Street railway station had become the headquarters of the recently dubbed Reprieve Committee. Newspaper reporters came and went at all hours and casual drinkers hung around the bar in a bid to catch a glimpse of Maggie and Kate Lloyd, who had both rapidly attained celebrity status.

Behind the scenes, serious business was being conducted on the premises. The group was planning to distribute thousands of petition forms calling for the commutation of Ned's death sentence. Arrangements were also in hand for a public meeting on the coming Friday night to drum up support for their campaign. The cost of producing and distributing the petition forms was far beyond the means of the Kelly clan, and was considerably more than the meagre funds that had been outlaid for Ned's legal defence. Thousands of handbills printed to advertise the meeting had to be paid for, along with special tickets for 'ladies' to be granted admission. In addition there was the cost of hiring the Hippodrome, a large open-air stadium used primarily for sporting events near the centre of the city. In the end the campaign was only made possible with the backing of the local Society for the Abolition of Capital Punishment.

The notices proclaimed the gathering was to be presided over by Archibald Hamilton, the society's president and highly vocal leader of the relatively small but growing movement. With the crusading zeal that marked the society's activities, many members quickly volunteered their services, ensuring that copies of the petition were distributed as widely as possible throughout the colony.

The wording of the petition was skilful and succinct. It could conceivably be signed in good conscience by the two jurors who had originally opposed Ned's conviction, for it expressed no opinion on his legal guilt or innocence in relation to the death of Constable Lonigan: 'The humble Petitioners (having carefully considered the circumstances of the case) respectfully pray that the Life of the Condemned man Edward Kelly may be spared'. For those opposed to capital punishment it could be read as merely a statement of support for their cause. For those more personally involved, it could be taken as a protest against the way the authorities and the working of the law had treated the bushranger unfairly.

As the main thrust of the campaign, the petitions met with David Gaunson's firm approval. His was the only name on the forms and he was designated to be the ultimate recipient of the documents once they were signed. The fact that they did not set out to proclaim Ned's legal innocence in the killing of Lonigan was attuned to his own personal view. He appears to have had no doubt about Ned's formal guilt in relation to the policemen's death, at least not since his marathon Sunday interview with Ned at Beechworth. He agreed that Ned's bid for a reprieve would rest on moral and not legal grounds, and that first and foremost, capital punishment should be opposed. The other possible argument was that Ned could well have believed that his companions' lives were in dire jeopardy had they not attacked the police at Stringybark Creek. This in turn could have justified his actions to some extent. Whether Gaunson believed Ned in this, he did not disclose. Perhaps his legal ethics prevented him from stating publicly whether or not Ned had acknowledged to him his guilt in relation to the deaths.

Graham Berry was not overly concerned with the activities at the Robert Burns Hotel. The vast majority of the populace supported the Executive Council decision and even some of those normally opposed to capital punishment, like Sydney's *Bulletin*, were making a special exception in Ned's case. The journal had informed its readers that the life of the bushranger should be taken 'coolly and deliberately, with the stern relentlessness of that Justice which never dies'. Nevertheless, with the Gaunson brothers involved, Berry could not ignore the possibility that there would be political implications arising from the activities of the Reprieve Committee that he might have to answer to.

And then suddenly a new and very real challenge to the council decision presented itself to the premier. A hastily printed pamphlet written by an author who only described herself as 'A Lady' was delivered to him. He was disturbed by the fact that it was not associated with the Gaunsons or the Kellys. It set out what was described as 'a woman's viewpoint' on the defences that might be raised to undermine the basis of Ned's guilt in relation to the death of Thomas Lonigan. The writer claimed that if Ned's views about the threats from the police against him and his family were to be believed (as 'she' herself believed) then Redmond Barry had been wrong at the trial in not admitting that the bushranger could be convicted of the lesser offence of manslaughter instead of murder.

The letter that accompanied the pamphlet contained an even more explosive argument. It informed him that there were people who were well aware of the official cover-up that had led to the suppression of public discussion on the nature of the bushranger's outlawry. They understood the effect of this in denying Ned the legal rights that should have been open to him at his trial. With evident knowledge of the law, the writer pointed out that during the period of Ned's outlawry the bushranger was 'simply like a kangaroo – liable to be shot at any moment', but Ned 'could not be legally accountable for anything said or done during that period'. Applying this to Ned's trial, as the letter concluded, any 'evidence in relation to this period was therefore wrongly admitted'. Berry could only hope the author did not intend to make 'her' accusations public.

In the days leading up to the execution, the government's position had been further strengthened by a wave of printed rhetoric against Ned and those who wanted to save his life. The supporters of the Reprieve Committee were damned as 'nondescript idlers' and members of the 'criminal and depraved classes'. The *Age* had singled out women as being the pro-Kelly campaign's principal adherents and described them as 'weak-minded'. Not much was said about the fact that a large proportion of Kelly supporters had entered the fray simply because they were deeply opposed to capital punishment. Many of them felt little or no sympathy at all for Ned Kelly the man. They were there to voice their moral objection to the taking of human life in the name of the government of the land. Others might very well have participated out of pure curiosity and a desire to witness the 'entertainment' that surrounded the fate of this notorious criminal figure.

The fact that so much press attention focused on the activities of the Reprieve Committee inadvertently became a kind of smoke-screen, diverting any serious public discussions about the legal issues – such as the outlawry act – that might have thrown doubts on the validity of the conviction. Journalists at the *Age* must have known they were printing a scurrilous untruth when they claimed once again that bringing Ned to trial in the ordinary way had been an act of 'generosity' when he could simply have been executed as an outlaw.

In late July, two days before the Kitchen Court hearing in Melbourne Gaol, a tiny inconspicuous item was printed under the heading 'Notices to Correspondents'. The writer, identified only as 'W.C.Z.', claimed to have been informed that 'Ned Kelly was not an outlaw at the time of is capture, the outlawry notice having expired through the failure of the Ministry to renew the expiring act before the dissolution'. Like Melbourne's other newspapers, it did not attempt any examination of this assertion and its possible ramifications, and ignored any other claims that might have raised doubts about the legal fairness relating to Ned's treatment at the hands of the courts.

Back on the front line, William Gaunson was still determined to have one more public demonstration to agitate for a reprieve, followed by a march on Parliament House. His brother David had formally withdrawn from all public protest. On Saturday 6 November he made his last appearance when, along with a small delegation, he went to Government House and appealed to the governor to accept the 'prayer' spoken at the previous evening's Hippodrome meeting which had asked that 'the life of the prisoner might be spared'. The governor's response was gentle but unequivocal: he could 'not hold out any hope of mitigating the sentence'.

The meeting then descended into farce when Archibald Hamilton stepped forward and, clasping Kate Kelly by the hand, urged Ned's sister to beg for mercy on her knees. The embarrassed governor swiftly brought the meeting to a close. Such was the hysterical nature of the protest, it's not surprising that David Gaunson wanted to exclude himself from the possibility of any further spectacle and so at this point he disassociated himself from the campaign once and for all.

The next day a second Executive Council meeting determined there would be no reversal of the decision. By Sunday night more than thirty thousand signatures had been recorded on petition forms that were rushed to the Robert Burns Hotel and then presented to the offices of the premier. After a cursory examination of the documents, Graham Berry announced to a deputation of Kelly supporters that 'whole pages of it were written in the same hand'. He also wryly observed that many signatures named all the members of a single family, including small children. (Hundreds of these petition forms are currently housed in the Public Records Office of Victoria, and Berry's accusations do indeed appear to be borne out.)

Finally bowing to what he now regarded as inevitable, William Gaunson approached Graham Berry in the hope that he could have one last meeting with Ned in private as he had no desire to witness the hanging in person. He was refused.

In the halls of government the pamphlet from 'A Lady' disappeared into an official file, along with the letter that had come with it. When they became available for public scrutiny at the end of the twentieth century, they were devoid of any official annotation. This was highly unusual in light of the fact that all other filed documents were meticulously identified and often summarised for posterity. It looks like the identity of 'A Lady' will forever remain a mystery.

Like the newspapers, it appears Graham Berry wanted no 'technicalities' to impede Ned's progress to the gallows. It was a sentiment that Ned seems to have understood too, as he dictated one more letter to the governor just before the third and final Executive Council meeting. 'I know now it is useless trespassing on your valuable time', he wrote, because in the end 'they will only be satisfied with my life'.

Maggie visited Ned for the last time on 9 November and, even then, still clung to a slim hope that the government might have a change of heart. Together with Kate Lloyd and Kate's mother, Maggie had been led to believe they would be allowed to make a final plea for Ned to the Executive Council. Then, to their dismay, they learned the council meeting had taken place hours before it was originally scheduled. The last decisive ruling had been handed down and the exact time of execution confirmed. Only then, it seems, did Maggie finally give up. On 10 November she announced to the gathering of family and friends that she was heading back to Greta. The following morning when Elijah Upjohn was due to place the rope around her brother's neck, she wanted to be at home with her children.

On the eve of Ned Kelly's execution, his eldest sister slipped away from the hotel to Spencer Street station and boarded a train bound for the northeast. Maggie Skillion was going home. She had fought courageously and with great dignity for the life of her brother, but in her mind the battle was over. The tremendous power and relentless tenacity of the opposition had triumphed. As Maggie's train began its journey northwards, the news of the Executive Council's decision was made public in the *Herald*. Now everyone knew it had been decided unanimously that 'the law should take its course'.

The atmosphere in Melbourne Gaol was tense as the count-down commenced. For the gaol governor and his colleagues it was, as always, a time of great anxiety. Executing a prisoner was the most onerous and difficult official function for the gaol staff to carry out. In Ned's case it was particularly so. For just over four months John Castieau had been one of the bushranger's chief confidants. The wardens guarding him had witnessed Ned's darkest moments of physical and mental anguish. Night after night they had listened to him mournfully singing to himself, returning again and again to his favourite song, 'In the Sweet Bye and Bye'. Several of them had dutifully written down many pages of dictation as the bushranger made his pleas for mercy. They took great pains to ensure the grammar, spelling and punctuation were as accurate as they could be. Now their roles were suddenly reversed as, with Castieau, they became the chief instruments of the state in organising the rituals and practicalities of hanging him.

Castieau himself was primarily responsible for ensuring that the machinations of execution would run as smoothly as possible. Fortunately, many of the barbarisms imposed by the British were now a thing of the past. There had not been an execution open to the general public in Australia for decades, though the last one in Britain had occurred only twelve years earlier. Condemned prisoners were no longer hanged in chains or urged to show remorse as they faced the gallows with the promise that their execution would be quicker and more efficient if they showed repentance. Although more humane methods of hanging had been developed, there was never a guarantee that the apparatus of death would perform satisfactorily. In Britain, some executioners had even resorted to surrounding the gallows with black draping so that witnesses would not see the often agonising death throes.

Castieau paid special attention to the length of the rope and the tying of the noose so that the bushranger might die as quickly and painlessly as possible. The strength of the stout Oregon beam that would take the full weight of the condemned man was checked and checked again. The trapdoor mechanism was also examined and tested to ensure it swung open swiftly and cleanly, allowing the body to drop unimpeded into the space below.

With the hanging less than twenty-four hours away, Castieau ensured that Elijah Upjohn fully understood his role as executioner. First thing in the morning Ned would be taken from the Condemned Cell to a second block where the gallows was located. He would ascend a flight of steps with the gallows in full view and enter another cell. With Upjohn standing by, official orders for his execution would be read to Ned and he would have him arms pinioned – a practice that was introduced as a direct response to horrific scenes in the past when condemned men had either struggled with their hangman or had reached up and grasped the rope as they swung, desperately clutching on to life for a few more tortured minutes. After the noose was placed around Ned's neck, a white

Cell door

hood would be draped over his head so that he would not know the precise moment when Upjohn pulled the trapdoor lever.

And so to the final goodbyes. On Wednesday 10 November, in an atmosphere with all the gloom and gravity of a deathbed scene, seventeen-year-old Kate met her brother for the last time. Later she told a newspaper reporter she wished she 'had not been born' after living through all of the agonies her family had suffered in recent years. By her side was her sister Grace, who had turned fifteen in August, and her brother James. They were allowed to converse with Ned through the iron grille in the Condemned Cell door and, though shaken, the family appears to have stood up remarkably well under the circumstances.

If the unofficial records of the time are correct, the most emotional meeting that took place in Ned's cell that same day occurred on the final visit of Kate Lloyd, who was accompanied by her cousin Tom Lloyd. Kate had remained devoted to Ned with an intensity equalled only by Maggie. If Ned had once 'taken a wife' as he claimed in the Jerilderie letter, even the best endeavours of the police had failed to track her down. Whatever their true marital status, Kate had always been described as 'Ned's girl' by Greta locals. Of course, there has been an enormous amount of speculation surrounding Kelly's love-life, fuelled in recent years by Peter Carey's vividly imagined but, as he freely admits, decidedly fictional account of Ned in his Booker prize-winning novel *The True History of the Kelly Gang*. Nevertheless, most surviving evidence points to Kate as the ultimate object of his affections.

Castieau also arranged for Ellen to see her son that afternoon. In the letter Ned dictated in the morning he implored for her release from prison, arguing it 'could not make any difference now', but his plea fell on deaf ears. The details of this last meeting between mother and son were not recorded. Certainly there is no evidence to support the claim by one Melbourne newspaper that Ellen told him: 'Mind you die like a Kelly, son'. Such a statement is highly

unlikely given that Ellen had no pressing loyalty to her first husband's family. The Kellys had hardly treated her well since her first
husband's untimely death. (In 1868, Red's brother James was driven
from Ellen's shanty after an evening's drunken antics became intol-
erable. In mean-spirited vengeance he set fire to the place and
Ellen, her two sisters and their children were lucky to escape with
their lives.)

Apart from family reunions, Castieau was also deeply concerned with Ned's spiritual requirements during his last days. The
prisoner had been giving strong indications of a belief in an afterlife. He was clinging to the idea that whatever earthly judgements
were made against him, it was the final judgement beyond life that
mattered. In one of the letters he had dictated for transmission to
the government he stated, 'My life is so short on earth that I have to
make the best of it to prepare myself for the other world'.

To this end, Castieau ensured that Dean Donaghy, the Roman
Catholic chaplain of Melbourne Gaol, was on hand to sit with Ned
at the completion of family visits. After the Protestant evangelist Dr
Singleton had been barred from any further contact with him, the
dean had become Ned's chief spiritual adviser, spending many
hours in religious discussions with him before and after his trip to
Beechworth. He was also the first civilian visitor to see him on the
morning after his conviction.

In addition, arrangements were being made for another
Roman Catholic clergyman, Dean Charles O'Hea, to speak to
Ned. His connection was a lifelong one for it is believed he bap-
tised the infant Ned. The two clergymen became vital members of
the small team helping to prepare the bushranger for death. Both
would play a major part in the final rituals. Ned Kelly would die in
communion with the church of his childhood, surrounded by
all the trappings of its believers. This is how he chose to prepare
himself for the other world where final judgement would be made
on his earthly life.

As the Town Hall clock struck ten on the morning of 11 November 1880, a woman crumpled to her knees on the footpath outside Melbourne Gaol. Reporting on the incident the next morning, the *Daily Telegraph* said the unidentified female had 'offered up an audible prayer for the repose of Ned Kelly's soul'.

As the chimes died away an expectant hush settled over the spectators gathered inside the gaol to witness the hanging. It was time for the final ceremony. Outside the cell where Ned waited, the sheriff of Melbourne, a pensioned-off British officer named Colonel Robert Rede, stood stiffly to attention formally attired in a frock coat and striped trousers. Brandishing Ned's death warrant signed by the governor, he demanded the body of the bushranger from John Castieau. Like his American counterpart, the sheriff held a range of the broad powers that had once been available to those exercising this antiquated office in England dating back to Anglo-Saxon times. On this day, the sheriff's legal responsibility was simply to ensure that the bushranger's execution was carried out on the hour.

This was final confirmation that all efforts to reprieve Ned had failed. The night before, a deputation that included one of Ned's uncles, John Quinn, had met with Graham Berry in the lobby of Parliament House to plead again for the bushranger's life. Quinn had remonstrated with the premier that the period between the time of Ned being condemned to death and the date for his execution was too short. To this Berry had replied sharply: 'Some of the victims did not have three seconds'.

As soon as Ned had entered the Condemned Cell he had resumed the religious observances ordained by the Roman Catholic church that would take up much of his last day on earth. Overnight he had sung hymns he remembered from his childhood, along with old favourites like 'In the Sweet Bye and Bye', before he was ordered to bed at half past one. At five o'clock he awoke, knelt down and prayed for twenty minutes before going back to bed for a couple of hours.

This return to his childhood faith had made little impact on those who represented Catholicism in the community. To them he was just another penitent sinner and they had taken no stand on his behalf. People seeking signatures for the Reprieve Committee's petition forms had been banned from the precincts of St Patrick's Cathedral and St Francis Church where his mother and father had been married. No prominent lay members or higher dignitaries of the church had supported the moves to reprieve him. Nor had the *Advocate*, the leading church newspaper in Victoria, voiced any kind of protest. In fact, the paper took the opportunity to remind its readers that there were members of the Catholic faith who were still suffering from the Kelly gang's raid on the police camp at Stringybark Creek.

In a special article dated 13 November, the paper reported that permission had unsuccessfully been sought on behalf of Sergeant Kennedy's widow for her to meet with Ned and question him about the death of her husband. Two years later she was still deep in mourning and would never marry again. Nevertheless, in accordance with the church's principles of tolerance and forgiveness, Ned was being granted the last rites of the Roman Catholic faith. Also in line with the church's principles, he had foregone any breakfast to ensure that after making his last confessions to Dean Donaghy, he could then join in a private communion service with him.

Castieau tapped on the cell door, opened it and, as newspapers recorded, told Ned that his 'last hour had arrived'. Before being taken from the Condemned Cell, the leg bracelets, chains and special belt attached to him after his conviction were finally removed. To hold up his pants he was provided with a large blue handkerchief to tie roughly around his waist.

Elijah Upjohn then entered the cell. Tall and burly, dressed only in the trousers and shirt of his prison uniform, the fifty-eight year old's most significant physical attribute was a carbuncle-like growth on his large nose. Despite Ned's protest that it wasn't necessary, Upjohn pinioned his arms behind him with a leather strap. A white hood was folded on the bushranger's head in readiness for the moment when it would be pulled down over his face.

Upjohn exited the cell and made his way towards the gallows and a procession formed behind him. Led by a novice priest holding a cross aloft (at least one artist also depicted the scene with an altar boy) Deans Donaghy and O'Hea paced slowly in front of the prisoner, who was flanked by two warders. The two priests murmured prayers for the repose of the soul dying and they would continue to do so right up until Upjohn pulled the lever.

As Ned was positioned at the gallows, a group of witnesses on the floor below, including representatives from all of Melbourne's daily newspapers, gaped up at him. An attending medico checked the positioning of the noose around the bushranger's neck and the hood was lowered.

What happened next has been one of the most famous and potent inaccuracies of the Kelly myth. The fact that the journalists were too far away to hear what was said did not stop some from providing their own special descriptive colour to mark the occasion, claiming they alone heard his last words. The *Herald* said: 'As he

stepped on the drop he remarked in a low tone "Such is Life"'. The
Argus said he exclaimed: 'Ah, I suppose it has come to this'. In fact
the most reliable surviving witness statement came from a police
officer, standing only feet away from the condemned man, who
recorded that the prisoner's remarks on the scaffold were inaudible.
Ned's last sentence, he said, was incomplete. Although it sounded
like he had begun to say something, the words were muffled when
the white hood was pulled down. A second later he was gone.

Outside the gaol the crowd waited tense with expectation. The
numbers were never accurately ascertained. One reporter for the
Herald claimed it was upward of six thousand people, although
another journalist in the same issue stated it was only half that
number. There was general agreement, however, that the gathering
was remarkably ordered despite predictions to the contrary. Clearly
some were deeply distressed by the imminent hanging, but many
more would have been merely curious spectators, part of the ever-
present anonymous rabble in search of diversion. Sydney's *Bulletin*
reported with a distinct note of distaste: 'Such is the morbid taste of
the ordinary sightseer that if they had their way, Kelly's suspension
would take place on the dome of the Exhibition'.

At the Robert Burns Hotel, members of the Kelly clan who
had remained in Melbourne came quietly together as the hour of
execution approached. When the appointed time had passed, James
Kelly was heard to say: 'Ah well, the poor devil is out of his misery
anyhow'.

Ned's body hung suspended beneath the gallows for thirty
minutes – a time-honoured rule to ensure that no breath of life
remained before the corpse was borne away. According to the
medical accounts, Elijah Upjohn carried out his gruesome task with
admirable efficiency. The bushranger died almost instantaneously
after the trapdoor's release. A number of witnesses representing
the community then solemnly attached their signatures to the
declaration affirming that Ned's execution had been carried out

successfully. The official document contained twenty-two names, including the gaol doctor Andrew Shields, Governor Castieau, Police Superintendent Winch and several journalists and warders.

Meanwhile, at the city coroner's office a jury was empanelled to declare that his death could be formally tabulated in the public records of the colony. In one last irony, the certification referred to Ned simply as a 'Labourer', leaving Joe Byrne with the exclusive distinction as the only person known in Victoria to have his occupation registered in death as 'Outlaw'.

And last came the disposal of the body. In England hundreds of years earlier it was possible for relatives to recover the remains of an executed prisoner for burial. Ned himself had requested this, and also asked that his body be buried in consecrated ground according to the rites of the Roman Catholic church. However, the bodies of executed prisoners in both England and Australia later came to be regarded as the property of the Crown. And with this had come official acceptance that it was permitted to subject human remains to a variety of ministrations that these days would be seen as somewhat barbaric.

For more than fifty years, the waxworks museums operating in Victoria had been allowed to take casts from dead bodies for their displays. As a result, one of the first to deal with Ned's remains was Max Kreitmayer. Swiftly he hacked off the full head of hair followed by the moustache and beard that the bushranger had tended so carefully until the very end. Then he made a cast of the naked head just as he had with Joe Byrne's at Benalla. This death mask would be mounted and ready to go on public display within a day or so.

For many years there had been a severe shortage of bodies for medical dissection. This led to the practice, pioneered in England, of allowing the remains of executed prisoners to be turned over for examination by medical students. Ned was no exception. Once Kreitmayer had finished, the body was taken to 'hospital' as recorded in the *Bendigo Independent*. Most probably the institution in question was the old Melbourne hospital located just down the road from the gaol next to the public library and museum complex on the corner of Swanston and La Trobe streets. There the head was severed from the body in the presence of students from Melbourne University so that its contents could be examined. This was of special interest as there was a strong theory circulating among doctors and scientists at the time that certain physical attributes of the brain could explain why some individuals had a predetermined propensity to commit serious crimes. Whether this theory was borne out by the examination of Ned Kelly's remains was never documented.

What happened to the corpse once they had finished is anyone's guess. A photograph exists of a tombstone in the gaol yard with the letters 'EK' stamped near the base, but its authenticity is dubious. According to the *Bendigo Independent,* a rumour maintained that certain body parts had been 'purloined as curiosities' and that the head was preserved in formalin for many years. The University of Melbourne's medical school magazine, *Speculum*, remains mute on the subject.

There is one more tale to be told about Ned's final hours. A warden named William Buck had the bleak duty of guarding the prisoner during the last night of his life. At some point before he retired to his bed, Ned confided to Buck that he would reappear in the Condemned Cell at two o'clock the following morning.

Afterwards the warden told Thomas McIntyre that the next night he secretly made his way to the cell at the appointed hour 'in strict accordance with the compact'. But he found no 'manifestation' there in the inky gloom. Search as he might, he could detect no definitive sign that the bushranger had reached the afterlife that he had so fervently hoped for – a state of grace that would allow him to freely wander the world which had tormented him so when he inhabited it.

In the Sweet Bye and Bye

There's a land that is fairer than day and
By faith we can see it afar
For the Father waits over the wave
To prepare us a dwelling place there

Chorus
In the sweet bye and bye
We shall meet on that beautiful shore
In the sweet bye and bye
We shall meet on that beautiful shore

Verse 2
We shall sing on that beautiful shore
The melodious songs of the blest
And our spirit shall sorrow no more
Not a sigh for the blessing of rest

Chorus

Verse 3
To our bountiful Father above
We will offer a tribute of praise
For the glorious gift of his love
And the blessing that hallow
Our days

Chorus

AFTERWORD
by Dr John Williams

Ned Kelly was a criminal. Or was he? The law in its majesty can create and alter what appears to be reality. The dead can live through testimonial instruments and the living can be declared to be civilly and criminally beyond the reach of the law. In a colony founded upon a resilient, though fictitious, premise that the land at colonisation belonged to no one, the legal status of Ned Kelly at the time of his capture would appear to be yet another quirk of the law's empire.

The war on terrorism is not a twenty-first century phenomenon. For late-1870s Victorians the emergence of bushrangers required a swift and fatal response. In the words of the preamble to the *Felons Apprehension Act* 1878, the fact that 'persons charged with murder and other capital felonies' were 'availing themselves unduly of the *protection* [emphasis added] afforded by law to accused persons before conviction' was to be rectified. The Kelly gang, under the Act, were 'deemed' to be outlaws. The result of the legislation was that it was lawful, after a series of perfunctory steps, for any of Her Majesty's subjects to use a deadly weapon to apprehend any member of the gang 'alive or dead'.

With the proclamation of Sir George Ferguson Bowen, the Governor of Victoria, on 15 November 1878, the gang were beyond the protection of the law – outlaws – and could be shot on sight without repercussions. The suspension of the rights of the accused should rankle with citizens of contemporary Australia – yet for the subjects of Victoria in the 1870s it was the action of a responsible government. A concession to civil liberties of sorts was offered through the sun-setting of the Act upon the ending of the session of the Victorian parliament. Despite an extension the Act expired, in accordance with the sun-setting clause, with the prorogation of the parliament on 26 June 1880.

So was Ned Kelly a criminal? His murderous actions were, with the assistance of the statutory guidance, perpetrated in a kind of legal vacuum. This arguably remains the legal paradox that his outlaw status had bestowed upon him and one of the fascinating aspects of the Kelly trial.

However, legal niceties are not the only element of the Kelly story. There can be little doubt that whatever shortcomings there were with Kelly's legal status they would have been quickly ratified by the Victorian parliament through retrospective criminal law. This would have been the case if Kelly had raised them at his various court appearances. The prosecution must have passed knowing glances when Kelly, unassisted, meekly submitted himself to the jurisdiction of the Supreme Court in Melbourne when he professed his innocence.

The politics of law and order is as old as the conquest of the continent. The choice of law, the preference of charges and the processes associated with the execution of those laws in colonial Australia often bridged the gap between the professed objectivity of law and the subjectivity of power. The trial of Ned Kelly was an object lesson in the conjunction of politics and law. The forces ranged against Kelly were determined that nothing would be left to chance. He was denied access to his family, his legal representation was generally inadequate and his trial was moved and truncated to ensure that it did not clash with great public events. Lastly, his trial judge could only be described as a safe pair of hands into which the government could deliver its prey.

The trial of Ned Kelly is not, however, a simple conspiracy story. The law is defining of, and is defined by, the community within which it operates. At every turn the motivations of those who made the law and the community who live by it are open for exploration. The newspapers of the time, even those which would have been expected to display a modicum of sympathy for his plight, were damning. As the first draft of history they remain the most immediate connection with the people and processes of the last days of Kelly. Ned Kelly was no saint. In the long term, the newspapers were unsuccessful in blackening the reputation of Kelly as he has escaped to advance through Australian culture in a more favourable light – perhaps even more so than he would have anticipated.

The Outlawry Act remains more than a curiosity in Australia's legal history. It stands as a marker as to how the law, and the protection of rights, has progressed in this country. The Victorian Act that was passed in response to the marauding of the Kelly gang was itself based on the New South Wales Act of 1865, a statute enacted to deal with the threat that other bushrangers, Ben Hall and his gang, posed to the people of New South Wales. A version of the 1865 Act was re-enacted in 1879 in New South Wales in response to the suspected cross-border activities of the Kelly gang. In 1899, the 1879 Act was repealed and replaced with more permanent outlaws legislation.

Curiously, the 1899 New South Wales Act did not easily fade from the statute books. Seventy-odd years later, in 1971, the New South Wales Law Reform Commission in its report on statute law revisions used as an example of Acts still in force that were 'obsolete because of social and industrial change and progress' the *Felons Apprehension Act* 1899. Other such Acts included the *Coal-lumpers Baskets Act* 1900, which set the size of the baskets to be used to move coal from coal ships, and the *Legal Practitioners (War Service) Amendment Act* 1940, which ceased to have operation with the ending of hostilities with Germany and her allies after the Second World War.

In response to the Law Reform Commission Report the New South Wales Parliament passed the *Statute Law Revision Act* 1976 which removed, amongst other Acts, the *Felons Apprehension Act* from the NSW statute books. This, however, was not to be the final gasp of the anti-bushranger legislation in Australia.

Due to the historical application of New South Wales laws to the Australian Capital Territory there remained, even after self-government was obtained in 1989, some doubts as to the continued operation of some 690 New South Wales Acts – one of which was the *Felons Apprehension Act* 1899. The nagging doubts, no matter how well founded, prompted the Legislative Assembly of the Australian Capital Territory to pass the *Law Reform (Miscellaneous Provisions) Act* 1999 which repealed the persistent *Felons Apprehension Act* 1899. So 134 years after its enactment in New South Wales to deal with the panic of bushrangers the last jurisdiction in Australia had formally rejected the use of such brutal policing methods.

But could such an Act be enacted today? Federation in 1901 was both the birth of the Commonwealth and the birthday of the Australian states. The colonies, through a combination of local participation and imperial blessing, were transformed into States of the Commonwealth of Australia. Politically their collective futures, and legally their constitutions, were now subject to the overarching power of the Commonwealth and its constitution.

One feature of the Australian constitution is that the judicial power of the Commonwealth, which is vested in the High Court and 'such other federal courts as the Parliament creates', can also be shared with the state Supreme Courts. In 1996 the High Court pronounced that the Supreme Courts of the states could not be pressed into service in ways that would not be compatible with the exercise of the Commonwealth's precious judicial power. Since that time it can be assumed that a law, such as the *Felons Apprehension Act,* which required state Supreme Court judges to declare bushrangers like Ned Kelly to be outlaws, would be constitutionally forbidden if they involved in similar ways the state Supreme Courts.

Such comforting constitutional guarantees are, of course, rare. Ned Kelly could still be declared guilty without trial by an Act of a state parliament when it did not involve the cooperation of the state judiciary. Similarly, a stateless non-citizen can be detained by the Commonwealth government for the term of their natural life while officials negotiate a country that will accept them. Kelly is not alone in experiencing the full, and at times, brutal weight of the law. He is, however, unique in that we know his name and his story.

Biography is the art of reduction. It is the craft of reducing the complex and contradictory into digestible portions. For most of us this process concludes with our names on masonry. Ned Kelly has succumbed, in one way, to this process of reduction. He has become iconic. He is representative of a number of tangled themes in Australian history. A rogue, a republican and a victim of the establishment and now a reliable prop in our popular culture. The brevity of his life has proved to be no handicap to the ability of his biographers to project yet another nuanced account of his history and relate it to our own.

Alex Castles – a Victorian of a 'certain age' – has added another chapter to the burgeoning 'life' of Ned Kelly. He has done so from the two perspectives for which he was uniquely qualified. Alex was a newspaperman. His professional calling as a lawyer – a career that would see him rise to be Australia's pioneering legal historian – only barely disguised his love for, and understanding of, journalism. His account of the last months of Ned Kelly's life and his encounter with the law is enveloped in coverage of the popular scribblers of the time. This is a legal history which is buttressed by newsprint. It is an account that places the reader in the cells and the courtrooms of Victoria in the late 1870s. Political and legal intrigues were to be found in the vaults of the archives and Alex had the temperament and perseverance to uncover them.

The myth and mystique of Ned Kelly is founded upon the

interaction of his community and its law. The killing of Ned was the culmination of a series of events. At these moments there appeared a chorus of players: his family, his foe, the state and its instrumentalities. Each had their part to play and their motivations, be they for good or ill. Their appearances remind us that a life is complex.

DR JOHN WILLIAMS *came to know Alex when he was on the staff at the University of Adelaide Law School in 1997. He has had visiting positions at the Universities of Cape Town and Melbourne, and in 2003 was the Menzies Foundation Fellow at King's College, London. In 2004 he joined the Law Faculty of the Australian National University.*

ELLEN KELLY

It seems Ellen was determined to break from the past and start afresh following the events that robbed her of two beloved sons. On the hot and sultry evening of 9 February 1881, a local constable was at the Glenrowan station meeting the night train from Melbourne when he observed the return of Ned's mother, newly released from gaol, accompanied by her daughter Kate. There was no one to greet them, he reported later, and they put up for the night at the nearby Railway Hotel.

After almost three years away, this homecoming was very much the way Ellen wanted it. The constable went on to say 'it was as quiet at Glenrowan and Greta as it can possibly be, and the Kelly sympathisers seem to be on friendly terms with the police stationed there'. And this was exactly as Ellen had planned it to continue. Despite her past ill-treatment, she seemed determined to meet with police officers stationed at Greta as friends rather than enemies. In one notable incident some years later, she took a member of the local constabulary in her buggy to a racing carnival, publicly demonstrating the spirit of reconciliation she now successfully sustained.

When Ned's mother died in 1923, no one was certain of her age. Government records stated she had been born in 1836, making her eighty-seven or thereabouts. Her death certificate under the surname of King recorded that she had died at ninety-five, while convincing evidence suggests that she was born in Ireland in 1832, making her about ninety-one. But on one matter the local newspapers agreed: Ellen Kelly had found her own special place in her community, living quietly and unobtrusively, much like other members of her extended family still residing nearby. The *Benalla Ensign*, which had once fulminated against her and her kin, remarked kindly that she died as a 'very old and highly esteemed resident of Greta West'. With circumspection still echoing down the years, the paper named her Ellen King and made no mention of the Kelly Outbreak or the deaths of her sons Ned and Dan.

MAGGIE SKILLION

Like her mother, Maggie Skillion merged back into the community, her daily life perpetually burdened with heavy family responsibilities until her death in 1896 at the age of thirty-eight. Already pregnant with a child by Tom Lloyd at the time of her brother's execution, she was ultimately to bear ten children in thirteen years with her cousin, in addition to the two she had borne as the wife of William Skillion. She never married Tom. A meeting in gaol with her husband appears to have confirmed a permanent separation between the Skillions, but their marriage was never formally dissolved.

TOM LLOYD

Often described as 'the fifth member of the gang', Tom Lloyd lived on for many years after the death of Maggie Skillion. The ten children born from their relationship were all registered under her married name. After her death Lloyd married and had six more children. He died in 1927, one of the last surviving depositories of direct knowledge about the Kelly Outbreak.

CATHERINE (KATE) KELLY

Within hours of his execution, Ned's sister appeared on the stage of the Apollo Hall in Melbourne. Hundreds of handbills had been hastily printed up announcing that Kate Kelly and her brother James would 'interview all comers', accompanied by Steve Hart's sister Ettie, for the extravagant entry fee of one shilling. The *Daily Telegraph* reported it as a display 'insensible to all the decencies and decorums of life', and William Gaunson himself was said to have been among those who managed to have the show immediately closed down. Soon after, James and his sister ventured to Sydney, again to feature in an entertainment about the Kelly gang. It was also shut down peremptorily.

Deeply troubled and increasingly dependent on alcohol, Kate Kelly wandered the country for several years until she married and settled in Forbes in New South Wales in 1888. She gave birth to six children in the next ten years and drowned tragically in 1898 at the age of thirty-five.

JAMES KELLY

In 1881 Ned's sole surviving brother moved away from Glenrowan. He soon found himself on the wrong side of the law and served five years penal servitude at Wagga Wagga in New South Wales for stealing two horses. In 1886 Ellen told a visiting police officer she was 'very anxious to keep him straight', a wish he fulfilled by carrying on a business as a bootmaker for a time.

His sister Kate's death proved to be a turning point for James Kelly. When the news reached him that it looked like her children would be abandoned, he set off alone in a horse-drawn buggy to find them. He brought them back to Greta where he and his mother raised them. A lifelong bachelor, he died in 1946, the last child of the union between Ellen and Red Kelly.

CATHERINE (KATE) LLOYD

Ned's closest relationships with the opposite sex appear to have been with women who came from families he knew well. Like the English aristocracy, marriage between first cousins was not unusual, especially when it served to protect family interests. Ned was linked with a number of young women, including his cousin Mary Miller and Steve Hart's sister Ettie, but in the last year of his life he had become especially attached to his cousin Kate Lloyd. Just how attached, we'll never know for certain.

After Ned's execution Kate returned to northeastern Victoria, taking no part in the attempts by Ned's sister Kate, brother Jim and Ettie Hart to cash in on their connection with the most infamous Kelly. She finally married William John Cleave in 1895, and died in the first decade of the twentieth century after giving birth to several children.

THOMAS McINTYRE

In September 1881, one of Thomas McIntyre's greatest fears overtook him when he was invalided out of the Victorian police service. In the two years between the Stringybark shoot-out and Ned's trial he had lost more than nine kilograms in weight and was spitting blood: one of the most ominous signs of tuberculosis, which had decimated the ranks of his family in Ireland.

Released from the police force in 1881 with a modest annual pension of ninety-three pounds, the amount was specially increased to reward him for his services in relation to the Kellys, though it was not drawn from the official reward money. Twenty years later he remarked that with this he 'returned to the ranges where the pure mountain air and change of employment re-established my health'. He retired to Ballarat with his bride of two years, Eliza Ann, and they went on to produce eight children.

Until his death in 1918, his involvement in the Kelly Outbreak continued to play an important part in his life, including one of his most treasured friendships with none other than Ned's lawyer, David Gaunson. In addition, McIntyre spent many years working on his unpublished memoirs, meticulously compiling information gleaned from long hours of research in various libraries. He also conducted several interviews, among them an extended conversation with his old colleague Senior Constable John Kelly, who recalled memories of the siege at Glenrowan and further encounters with the Kelly clan in the ensuing years. A condensed version of his memoirs eventually surfaced in an Australian journal in the unusual form of shorthand, printed specifically for the few who could read it.

He died unheralded and unsung despite the pivotal role he played in the events that finally led to Ned Kelly's execution. His remarkable achievement in struggling his way back to Mansfield in the twenty-four hours after Stringybark Creek to report the killings has never been officially acknowledged for what it was: one of the most courageous feats in the history of Australian policing.

ROBERT RAMSAY

The former chief secretary emerged unscathed from the events surrounding Ned Kelly's last days. Just before Ned's execution he again had occasion to address a meeting of old Scotch Collegians and clearly his attitude towards the condemned man had not altered in the slightest. But he was to enjoy the unofficial title as the man who had destroyed the Kelly gang for a short time only. He died in May 1882, much lamented by those who looked to him as a politician untainted by the increasing moral corruption running rampant in the colony's government. Upon his death the *Argus* said that he was someone who did what he regarded as 'right', that his 'word was the truth' and that he was 'honest to the State' – accolades that even his hardened political opponents did not dispute.

CHARLES STANDISH

Charles Standish found no solace in the proceedings of the Royal Commission that was finally established in March 1881 to investigate the working of the police service. As one of the principal witnesses who appeared before it he was faced with a barrage of criticisms. He defended himself as best he could, but often betrayed attitudes from his upper-class English upbringing, expecting they would be enough to justify his actions. Needless to say it did not satisfy the commission.

Ironically, as he lay dying in the militantly Protestant Melbourne Club in March 1883, he called for a priest to give him the last rites of the Roman Catholic church – a return to the religion of his youth. For more than twenty years he had been regarded as one of the pillars of anti-Catholic sentiment in the colony, not least as District Grand Master of the English Constitution of Freemasons in Victoria. Melbourne's newspapers announced that his funeral would be 'private' and, not surprisingly, there was no official representation by the Freemasons.

FRANCIS HARE

Superintendent Francis Hare's connection with the Victorian police ended in 1882. He received a sum of eight hundred pounds from the board set up specifically to distribute reward money for the destruction of the Kelly gang. His role in capturing the Kellys was examined very critically by the Royal Commission appointed in 1882 to investigate the police service. It ultimately recommended his immediate 'retirement' from the force. To save face he was appointed police magistrate, a position he still held when he died in July 1892 at the age of sixty-two.

An unusual legacy of his involvement with the Kelly Outbreak came to light only recently. It seems he took possession of a set of the armour used by the bushrangers at Glenrowan, although his legal entitlement to it can be seriously doubted. He gave the pieces to Sir William Clarke, to whom he was related by marriage, and it remained in Clarke's family for many years.

There was also evidence at Hare's funeral of longstanding relationships with others involved in the Kelly saga. One of his pall-bearers was Police Magistrate Frederick Call, who had ensured Ned was locked away for weeks without any legal or family assistance after his arrival in Melbourne. Another was leading barrister J.L. Purves, who had complicated efforts to obtain legal assistance for Ned by being one of several barristers (the most notable was

Hickman Molesworth) who refused a brief to defend the bushranger. A third pallbearer was Dr Charles Ryan, the physician who had been sent to take charge of Ned after his capture.

THOMAS CURNOW

The schoolteacher hero of Glenrowan was awarded five hundred and fifty pounds by the Kelly Reward Board as well as an award by the Victorian Humane Society. In 1880 he moved his family to Ballarat where he was employed as a teacher for the next thirty-five years and died in 1922. A portion of the red scarf Curnow used to flag down the police special train is in possession of the National Trust of Victoria.

JOHN SADLEIR

Superintendent John Sadleir did not emerge unscathed from the proceedings of the Royal Commission. It was recommended he be demoted to the lowest grade of superintendent after findings criticised his actions in the Kelly hunt and during the siege at Glenrowan. He did, however, survive this admonition.

Of all the senior police officers engaged in dealing with Ned and his compatriots, Sadleir's qualities of integrity, compassion and plain commonsense marked him off decisively from others like Police Commissioner Standish and Francis Hare.

In 1883 he was appointed to the metropolitan district of the Victorian police, became the highly ranked Inspecting Superintendent in 1892 and retired in 1896 after serving the force for forty-four years. The *Age* noted on his passing in September 1919 that he was 'an efficient and exemplary officer of police, with a high sense of duty'.

Not long before his death, Sadleir's *Recollections of a Police Officer* was published. It contains one of the two finest accounts of the Kelly Outbreak written by contemporaries, the other being Thomas McIntyre's unpublished manuscript.

REDMOND BARRY

Just twelve days after Ned's execution, a myth had already begun to take root concerning the death of his old nemesis Redmond Barry. As Thomas McIntyre recalled the scene, the bushranger had actually added the word 'soon' after telling Barry he would 'meet him again' where the final judgement would be made on him in a 'higher court'. Years later, many were still claiming that the judge's death could be directly linked to his harsh treatment of the bushranger. A letter attributed to James Kelly written in 1930 asserted: 'In the case of Barry, the challenge of my brother Ned to meet him [Barry] before a higher court seemed to have preyed on a guilty conscience, to such an extent that Barry died a few days after Ned Kelly'.

In reality, the judge appears to have died quite predictably from a long untreated case of diabetes that caused fatal complications when he developed a skin eruption on his head (said to be either a carbuncle or a boil).

DAVID GAUNSON

David Gaunson's subsequent career in the colonial legislature was a chequered one. In 1881 he finally achieved ministerial rank in a short-lived government, but only very briefly. In the aftermath of Ned's hanging he was roundly scorned by most of the colony's newspapers for his efforts to reprieve the bushranger. (One particularly outlandish excuse for his behaviour was that he had been born and partly educated in New South Wales!) Under the constitutional practice of the day, his ministerial appointment could not be finally confirmed until he faced a new election, and he was ignominiously ousted at the poll in the electorate of Ararat, which he had represented since 1875. Undeterred, he returned to parliament as the member for the city electorate of Emerald Hill in 1883, which he continued to represent until 1889. A political maverick to the end, in 1904 he was again elected to the Assembly to represent Labor's interests, though he was not a member of the newly emergent

Australian Labor Party. Following his election he quickly transferred his political allegiance elsewhere.

As a lawyer Gaunson attracted some notable clients in addition to Ned Kelly. He was the solicitor for Madame Brussels, keeper of the most select of Melbourne's many brothels, located strategically close to Parliament House and the Melbourne Club. Another of his more high-profile clients and a pallbearer at his funeral was John Wren, whose illegal betting organisation and involvement with other shady sporting activities marked him as a powerful and controversial figure in Victoria. A father of three, by the time Gaunson died in 1909 he had converted to Catholicism.

HENRY BINDON

Inexperienced and only recently returned to the country after qualifying for the bar in London, Kelly aptly summed up his barrister's position: 'Mr Bindon knows nothing of my case'. As a 'Berryite Liberal' attempting to make his way professionally in the club-like, ultra-conservative Victorian bar, he was readily attacked by his barristerial contemporaries for reasons that owed more to his liberal thinking than his performance at Ned's trial. Ultimately seen as a traitor to his class, he suffered the ostracism imposed by his powerful conservative peers in the legal profession, effectively stifling his career as a barrister. He continued to practise law but his unspectacular career was cut short when he died of a wasting illness at the age of fifty.

ROBERT McBEAN

Robert McBean was never called upon to give an official explanation of his actions along with Police Commissioner Standish in dealing with the body of Joe Byrne. He remained a highly influential figure in Benalla, president of the local shire council from 1879 to 1882 and again from 1885 to 1886, while continuing to sit on the bench of its Court of Petty Sessions for many years. He was the foundation chairman of the local gas company in 1886 and engaged in other successful business enterprises in a town where anti-Kelly sentiment remained strong well into the twentieth century.

HENRY GURNER
The death of Redmond Barry left Henry Gurner as one of the few surviving officials with direct links to the time when Victoria was still part of New South Wales. His experience with Kelly was one of his last opportunities to express the attitude drummed into him in childhood: that people of convict parentage were beyond redemption in the eyes of civilised society. Such opinions were rapidly dating as so many convict offspring had blended in, becoming inconspicuous, highly productive and law-abiding members of local communities right around Australia.

A pallbearer at the judge's funeral, their personal association had extended well beyond their long-time membership of the Melbourne Club. Gurner acted as Barry's personal solicitor for many years, lent him five hundred pounds when he purchased a house to accommodate his long-term mistress (Mrs Louisa Barrow) in 1855, and was his confidant in subsequent dealings concerning their children. As a testament to the intimacy of their relationship, Barry once wrote to Mrs Barrow that she was 'not to mention the contents of my letters to any person but Gurner'.

CHARLES SMYTH
By all accounts a skilled and proficient lawyer, Smyth acted as a Crown prosecutor for thirty-five years as well as maintaining a successful private practice. He died in 1908 at the age of eighty, having fathered twelve children.

[JC: One of several small mysteries that Alex was still trying to solve centred on a couple of pages of shorthand that accompanied the Crown brief in the Sir Thomas Ramsay Collection. Smyth had learned to write shorthand as a young man in Ireland. The system of shorthand known as

Pittman was widely used until the 1880s when an entirely new method was introduced. Alex approached a number of shorthand experts in an attempt to decipher Smyth's notes, but none of them were familiar with the old form. His next step was to try to find an expert in Ireland who specialised in outmoded styles of shorthand, but unfortunately, that's as far as he got.

Alex was intrigued by the idea that these notes might reveal something more than just the standard legal commentary. He wondered if they might contain some interesting observations or, even better, some personal opinions about the trial. Hopefully one day someone might take up the task of unlocking the code . . .]

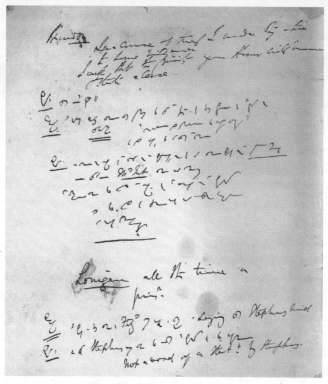

Sample of Smyth's shorthand

DR JOHN SINGLETON

After Ned's execution Dr John Singleton and his wife Isabella continued on with their efforts to aid those who were all but ignored by the more self-righteous elements in the Victorian community. Until the foundation of the Salvation Army in Victoria in the early 1880s, their activities stood out with a handful of others in bringing succour to the destitute and homeless, to unmarried mothers and to many in prison. One of Singleton's major achievements was to establish a free medical dispensary that served many thousands during his lifetime.

In the 1890s he penned his memoirs, finally confirming his belief that during Ned's last months in gaol, a religious reawakening had dramatically influenced his outlook on life and the things he had done. He said the bushranger had arranged to send his 'love' to him in the hours immediately before his execution and concluded '... from various things that I have known since, he looked to Christ alone for forgiveness and salvation. His blood can save even one so blood-stained and guilty as was the unfortunate Ned Kelly.'

JOHN CASTIEAU

During his time as prison governor, Castieau presided over a total of fifteen hangings (Ned's was the fourteenth). In 1881 he was appointed Inspector-General of Penal Establishments and held the position until 1884, when failing health forced him to retire. He died in 1885.

A measure of Ned's esteem for his gaoler is demonstrated in the story told about the occasion when Castieau took his thirteen-year-old son, Godfrey, to meet the condemned man. Apparently, Ned reached through the bars and placed his hands on the boy's head, saying, 'Son, I hope you grow up to be as fine a man as your father'.

Ned Kelly was not the only iconic historical figure who crossed paths with Castieau. While employed as the town gaoler in

Castlemaine in the late 1850s, Castieau became good friends with Robert O'Hara Burke, a local policeman. Burke would later lead the famously doomed Burke and Wills expedition.

ELIJAH UPJOHN

Ned Kelly's executioner was paid five pounds for his services. He continued to work as a hangman until 1884, when complaints about his raucous public behaviour (including indecent exposure) saw the appointment of a successor. Upjohn went to New South Wales and ended his days in 1885, wandering the desert near Bourke, penniless and alone.

SOURCES AND BIBLIOGRAPHY

JC: In November 2003 the manuscript for 'Ned Kelly's Last Days' was almost finished. The introduction was in draft form and a comprehensive list of notes and sources was next on the list of things to do.

Quality and thoroughness of research meant a great deal to Alex and properly accounting for the material was almost more important than the material itself (have a look at his 1994 publication Annotated Bibliography on Australian Law 1788–1900 *and you'll see what I mean!). He always endeavoured to use the original primary sources even though it was invariably more difficult to locate and access them.*

I know he would have gone to great pains to make this part of the book as detailed and complete as possible, so it's with great regret that I've been unable to even approach the kind of list that Alex would have presented. The jumbled pile of manila folders stuffed full of photocopies (often unlabelled); the random scribbles, names and numbers in dozens of notepads; and my own dim memory of his mentioning places he'd been and people he'd spoken to is all I have to go on. Alex kept so much information in his head, and when he died the information went with him.

What follows is the basic list of resources that I am aware figured largely in his research. I would welcome any corrections, additions or suggestions so they can be included in future reprints.

PRIMARY SOURCES

Burke Museum, Beechworth (mainly Beechworth Court of Petty Sessions case book).

Interview with Mrs Irma Hookey, grand-daughter of Constable Thomas McIntyre.

La Trobe Collection, State Library of Victoria (includes manuscript copy of Police Commissioner Standish's diary, correspondence and diary of Superintendent John Sadleir, and Sir Redmond Barry's papers).

Mitchell Library Manuscript Collection (includes four unsorted envelopes of newspaper clippings about the Kelly gang from the 1900s to the 1950s).

New South Wales Archives (includes correspondence between the colonial secretary of New South Wales and the chief secretary of Victoria 1878–1881).

Parliamentary papers – both New South Wales and Victoria – from approximately 1870 to 1883 (including *Parliamentary Debates, Government Gazette* and *Police Gazette*).

Sir Thomas Ramsay Collection, Scotch College Melbourne (includes prosecution briefs for the murders of Thomas Lonigan and Michael Scanlan as well as addenda containing evidence in the form of witness statements, and copies of 'Young Victorian' – an occasional school paper published between 1877 and 1895).

Victorian Government Statistics (specifically birth, death and marriage certificates).

Victorian Police Historical Unit Archives (includes correspondence to and from Police Commissioner Standish, detective reports, witness statements and a transcript of Constable Thomas McIntyre's memoirs: *A Narrative of My Experience with the Kelly Gang and a Short Account of Other Bushrangers*).

Victorian Public Records Office (includes Crown law files and correspondence, prosecution briefs, correspondence of Chief Secretary Robert Ramsay, pamphlet and letter from 'A Lady', Executive Council minutes, copies of the Cameron letter and Jerilderie letter, police department correspondence and Royal Commission on the Victorian Police Force 1881–1883).

NEWSPAPERS AND PERIODICALS

Age, Alexandra and Yea Standard, Alpine Gazette, Argus, Australasian, Australasian Sketcher, Australian Illustrated News, Australian Star, Ballarat Courier, Ballarat Star, Benalla Ensign, Benalla Standard, Bendigo Independent, Brisbane Courier, Bulletin, Daily Telegraph, Express and Telegraph, Geelong Advertiser, Herald, Illustrated Adelaide News, Mansfield Guardian, Melbourne Leader, Melbourne Punch, Melbourne Weekly Times, North-Eastern Ensign, Ovens and Murray Advertiser, Port Phillip Herald, Sam Slick in Victoria, Shepparton News, South Australian Advertiser, South Australian Register, Spectator, Sydney Evening News, Sydney Mail, Sydney Morning Herald.

SECONDARY SOURCES

JC: Alex had a formidable library of Kelly-related books. I am unable to determine those that directly related to the ideas and contents of this book, but the following list constitutes the titles and extracts of titles that he kept close to hand as he worked on the manuscript.

Australian Dictionary of Biography, 1851–1890 and 1891–1939

Blackmore, R. D., *Lorna Doone*, Collins, London, 1869

Castieau, John Buckley (edited and introduced by Mark Finnane), *The Difficulties of My Position: The diaries of Prison Governor John Buckley Castieau, 1855–1884*, National Library of Australia, 2004
[JC: Alex had access to Castieau's diaries which are now available in this volume published in 2004.]

Colligan, M., *Canvas Documentaries*, Melbourne University Press, Melbourne, 2002

Cowley Coles, J., *Life and Christian Experience of J. C. Coles*, London, 1893

Gurner, Henry Field, *The Practice of the Criminal Law of the Colony of Victoria*, Stillwell & Knight, Melbourne, 1871

Hare, F. A., *The Last of the Bushrangers: An account of the capture of the Kelly gang*, Hurst & Blackett, London, 1894

Jones, G., *Ned Kelly – The Larrikin Years*, Charquin Hill Publishing, Wangaratta, 1990

Jones, I., *The Friendship That Destroyed Ned Kelly – Joe Byrne and Aaron Sheritt*, Lothian, Melbourne, 1992

McDermott, A. (ed.), *The Jerilderie Letter, Ned Kelly*, Text Publishing, Melbourne, 2001

McMenomy, K., *Ned Kelly, The Authentic Illustrated History*, Hardie Grant, Melbourne, 2001

McQuilton, J., *The Kelly Outbreak 1878–1880: The Geographical Dimension of Social Banditry*, Melbourne University Press, Melbourne, 1979

Reece, B., *Exiles from Erin – Convict Lives in Ireland and Australia*, Macmillan Academic, London, 1991

Sadleir, J., *Recollections of a Victorian Police Officer*, Penguin, Melbourne, 1973

Seal, G., *Ned Kelly in Popular Tradition*, Hyland House, Melbourne, 1980

Seal, G., *The Outlaw Legend*, Cambridge University Press, Cambridge, 1996

Singleton, Dr J., *A Narrative of Incidents in the Eventful Life of a Physician*, M. L. Hutchinson, 1891

Wannan, B., *Tell 'em I Died Game*, Lansdowne Press, Melbourne, 1967

JC: Two articles that I have been able to identify among Alex's papers:

McDermott, A., 'Who Said the Kelly Letters?', *Australian Historical Studies*, 118, 2002

Pryor, L. J., 'The Diseased Stock Agent', *Victorian Historical Journal*, Vol. 61, No. 4, December 1990

JC: In the past year I have repeatedly used the following titles for my own research and cross checking as I prepared the manuscript for publication:

Corfield, J., *The Ned Kelly Encyclopedia*, Lothian, Melbourne, 2003

Jones, I., *Ned Kelly, A Short Life*, Lothian, Melbourne, 1995

McMenomy, K., *Ned Kelly, The Authentic Illustrated History*, Hardie Grant, Melbourne, 2001

Phillips, J.H., *The Trial of Ned Kelly*, Law Book Co., Sydney, 1987

NOTES ON AFTERWORD

'a resilient, though fictitious ... belonged to no one' *Mabo v Queensland (No. 2)* (1992) 175 CLR 1 and Alex C. Castles, *An Australian Legal History*, Law Book Company, Sydney, 1982, pp. 20–31.

'"persons charged with ... alive or dead"' *Felons Apprehension Act* 1878 (Vic), s 3. Emphasis added.

'With the proclamation ... on sight without repercussions' *Government Gazette*, 15 November 1878, No. 119, pp. 2927–8.

'the sun-setting ... the Victorian parliament' *Felons Apprehension Act* 1878 (Vic), s 10.

'Despite an extension' *Expiring Laws Continuance Act* 1879 (Vic), s 2.

'the New South Wales Act of 1865' *Felons Apprehension Act* 1865 (NSW).

'In 1899, the 1879 Act ... permanent outlaws legislation' *Felons Apprehension Act* 1899 (NSW), s 2.

'Other such Acts ... Second World War' Law Reform Commission (NSW), *Statute Law Revisions*, Report No. 10 (1971), pp. 5–6, 13.

'the *Statute Law Revision Act* 1976 ... NSW statute books' *Statute Law Revision Act* 1976 (NSW), s. 2.

'the Australian Capital Territory ... *Felons Apprehension Act* 1899' *Law Reform (Miscellaneous Provisions) Act* 1999 (ACT), s 4.

'Politically their collective ... and its constitution' Australian Constitution 1900, s 106.

'One feature of ... state Supreme Courts' Australian Constitution 1900, ss 71, 77(iii).

'In 1996 the High Court ... precious judicial power' *Kable v Director of Public Prosecutions (NSW)* (1996) 189 CLR 51.

'Ned Kelly could ... the state judiciary' *Kable v Director of Public Prosecutions (NSW)* (1996) 189 CLR 51, esp 73–74 (Dawson J). See also *Fardon v A-G* (Qld) [2004] HCA 46 (1 October 2004) [2] (Gleeson CJ).

'a stateless non-citizen ... will accept them' *Al-Kateb v Godwin* [2004] HCA 37.

'Biography is the ... into digestible portions' Inga Clendinnen, 'In Search of the "Actual Man Underneath": A. W. Martin and the Art of Biography', *The Inaugural Allan Martin Lecture,* Pandanus Books, Canberra, 2004, pp. 9–10.

ACKNOWLEDGEMENTS

Many, many people helped Alex over the years with this project, and I cannot begin to account for all of them. My apologies to all those librarians, historians, curators, legal scholars, friends, colleagues and fellow Kellyphiles that I don't know about who deserve thanks and haven't been mentioned here.

On behalf of Alex and myself I would like to express sincere gratitude to the following people:

Kay Gibson – a scrupulous researcher and a historical detective in her own right. She acted as a frequent sounding board for Alex's Ned theories, and was an enthusiastic assistant to him and very good friend. Her extraordinary memory and constant encouragement have been invaluable as I put the final pieces together.

Dick Briggs, curator of the Sir Thomas Ramsay Collection at Scotch College, Melbourne, and another exemplary historian whose commitment to exploring and preserving our heritage was an inspiration to Alex and a great help to me.

Bob Reece, Alex's much-respected colleague at Murdoch University, and Tony Moore, Alex's long-time colleague, footy companion and treasured mate, who put in literally years of Kelly discussion and conjecture with Dad over numerous bottles of bourbon. Also Kathleen McEvoy, Alex's brilliant student who became comrade-in-arms, intellectual sparring partner and, along with her husband, Jim MacDonald, a very dear friend.

Martin Powell at the Victoria Police Historical Unit; Scott Jessup at the Burke Museum, Beechworth; and Mrs Irma Hookey, who generously gave her time and fuelled Alex's interest in her grand-father's plight as the sole police survivor at Stringybark Creek.

John Williams has risen to the occasion with his characteristic eloquence, bringing considerable legal knowledge and understanding of the way Alex operated to his fine conclusion. Special thanks to him. And, of course, to the Honourable Gough Whitlam and the Honourable Justice Michael Kirby for the kind words that would have meant so much to Alex.

I am indebted to the team at Allen & Unwin that produced this handsome publication. Sue Hines, who met with Alex in 1998 to talk about a 'Ned Book' and kept the faith all these years; Andrea McNamara who's been there from the start, employing her great talent of knowing when to talk and when to listen; and editor Clare Emery whose clarity, patience and encouragement steered me on the straight and narrow. They are uniquely talented bookpeople, wonderfully supportive friends, and exceptional women all. Accolades to Jo Jarrah who edited the manuscript with the most astonishing precision, insight and sensitivity. Also miracle-worker Pauline Haas (so much more than a typesetter) and designer Phil Campbell who uses his formidable skills to prove once again that he truly 'gets' Ned.

I would personally like to thank Damien O'Shea for many Saturday mornings of lively discussion, Edward Highett of Steamrail Victoria for coming to the rescue with his encyclopaedic knowledge, and Keith McMenomy for his guidance and generosity with illustrative material. Also the blokes from NextByte – Sasha, Keith and above all, Theo – who did their best to ease the nightmare of a dud iBook.

Deepest gratitude to my sisters Margy and Kathryn, my brother Alan, my mother Florence, and to dear friends who supported me in the toughest of times: Anne-Marie and Jock Allan, Tricia Bowen, Adam Richard, Andrea McNamara, Troy Hunter, Emma Ashmere, Anna Read and Rose Ljubicic.

Finally, my love and thanks to Paul who got me through the dark days of December 2003, and to Marymaeve, who came into the world three months after her grandpa left it, and reminded me what this Life–Death thing is all about.

ILLUSTRATION CREDITS

Alex Castles portrait reproduced with permission from the *Good Weekend*/Fairfax Photos

Map of Kelly Country by Guy Holt Illustration and Design

Robert Ramsay, from *Australasian Sketcher*, 3 June 1882 (La Trobe Picture Collection, State Library of Victoria)

Charles Standish 'in camp' (Royal Historical Society of Victoria)

Proclamation by Governor Sir George Bowen on 15 November 1878 (Public Records Office Victoria, VPRS 1182/PO, Unit 54)

Thomas McIntyre (Victoria Police Historical Unit, courtesy of Keith McMenomy)

Kate Lloyd (by kind permission of Ian Jones and Myra Brolan, courtesy of Keith McMenomy)

Joe Byrne's corpse (close-up) by A. Burman (Victoria Police Historical Unit, courtesy of Keith McMenomy)

'Wake at Greta' from *Australasian Sketcher*, 17 July 1880 (La Trobe Picture Collection, State Library of Victoria)

'At the Waxworks' from *Australasian Sketcher*, 23 December 1876 (La Trobe Picture Collection, State Library of Victoria)

Maggie Skillion by D. Isley, 1881 (by kind permission of Elsie Pettifer and Leigh Olver, courtesy Keith McMenomy)

Detective report 6 July 1880 (Victoria Police Historical Unit)

John Castieau (Burke Memorial Museum Beechworth)

David Gaunson by J. W. Lindt (Mitchell Library, State Library of New South Wales)

'After an all-night sitting in the Legislative Assembly – the morning view' from *Australasian Sketcher,* 30 December 1886 (La Trobe Picture Collection, State Library of Victoria)

'Ned Kelly in the Dock' from *Melbourne Punch,* 19 August 1880 (La Trobe Picture Collection, State Library of Victoria)

Sir Redmond Barry by T. F. Chuck from *Explorers and Early Colonists of Victoria*, Mason, Firth and M'Cutchen, Melbourne,1872 (La Trobe Picture Collection, State Library of Victoria)

Portion of Crown brief (probably) used by Arthur Chomley (Public Records Office Victoria, VPRS 4966/PO, Unit 1 © State of Victoria 2005. Reproduced with permission)

Portion of Crown brief used by Charles Smyth (Sir Thomas Ramsay Collection, Scotch College Melbourne)

Cell door in Melbourne Gaol (Victoria Police Historical Unit)

Sample of shorthand on Crown brief used by Charles Smyth (Sir Thomas Ramsay Collection, Scotch College Melbourne)

SONG LYRICS

From 'Stringybark Creek', in Wannan, B., *Tell 'em I Died Game*, Lansdowne Press, Melbourne, 1967

'In the Sweet Bye and Bye' by Joseph P. Webster, 1868 <www. school. edu.nf/bounty/sweet_bye.htm>